WOMEN'S ROLES IN EIGHTEENTH-CENTURY EUROPE

**Recent Titles in
Women's Roles through History**

Women's Roles in the Renaissance
Meg Lota Brown and Kari Boyd McBride

Women's Roles in Nineteenth-Century America
Tiffany K. Wayne

Women's Roles in the Middle Ages
Sandy Bardsley

Women's Roles in the Middle East and North Africa
Ruth Margolies Beitler and Angelica R. Martinez

WOMEN'S ROLES IN EIGHTEENTH-CENTURY EUROPE

Jennine Hurl-Eamon

Women's Roles through History

 GREENWOOD

AN IMPRINT OF ABC-CLIO, LLC
Santa Barbara, California • Denver, Colorado • Oxford, England

Copyright 2010 by Jennine Hurl-Eamon

All rights reserved. No part of this publication may be reproduced, stored in a retrieval system, or transmitted, in any form or by any means, electronic, mechanical, photocopying, recording, or otherwise, except for the inclusion of brief quotations in a review, without prior permission in writing from the publisher.

Library of Congress Cataloging-in-Publication Data

Hurl-Eamon, Jennine.
  Women's roles in eighteenth-century Europe / Jennine Hurl-Eamon.
    p. cm. — (Women's roles through history)
  Includes bibliographical references and index.
  ISBN 978–0–313–37696–2 (hard copy : alk. paper) — 978–0–313–37697–9 (ebook)
1. Women—Europe—History—18th century. 2. Women—Europe—Social conditions—18th century. 3. Sex role—Europe—History—18th century. 4. Europe—Social conditions—18th century. I. Title.
HQ1587.H87   2010
305.4094′09033—dc22   2010000918

ISBN: 978–0–313–37696–2
EISBN: 978–0–313–37697–9

14 13 12 11 10   1 2 3 4 5

This book is also available on the World Wide Web as an eBook.
Visit www.abc-clio.com for details.

Greenwood
An Imprint of ABC-CLIO, LLC

ABC-CLIO, LLC
130 Cremona Drive, P.O. Box 1911
Santa Barbara, California 93116-1911

This book is printed on acid-free paper ∞

Manufactured in the United States of America

Contents

Series Foreword vii
Acknowledgments ix
Introduction xi
Chronology xix

1. Women and Family 1
2. Women and Work 25
3. Women and Politics 47
4. Women and Law 65
5. Women and Arts and Sciences 89
6. Women and Religion 111
7. Women and War 131

Selected Bibliography 149
Index 163

Series Foreword

Women's history is still being reclaimed. The geographical and chronological scope of the Women's Roles through History series contributes to our understanding of the many facets of women's lives. Indeed, with this series, a content-rich survey of women's lives through history and around the world is available for the first time for high school students to the general public.

The impetus for the series came from the success of Greenwood's 1999 reference *Women's Roles in Ancient Civilizations*, edited by Bella Vivante. Librarians noted the need for new treatments of women's history, and women's roles are an important part of the history curriculum in every era. Thus, this series intensely covers women's roles in Europe and the United States, with volumes by the century or by era, and one volume each is devoted to the major populated areas of the globe—Africa, the Middle East, Asia, and Latin America and the Caribbean.

Each volume provides essay chapters on major topics such as

- Family Life
- Marriage and Childbearing
- Religion
- Public Life
- Lives of Ordinary Women
- Women and the Economy
- Political Status

- Legal Status
- Arts

Country and regional differences are discussed as necessary. Other elements include

- Introduction, providing historical context
- chronology
- glossary
- bibliography
- period illustrations

The volumes, written by historians, offer sound scholarship in an accessible manner. A wealth of disparate material is conveniently synthesized in one source. As well, the insight provided into daily life, which readers find intriguing, further helps to bring knowledge of women's struggles, duties, contributions, pleasures, and more to a wide audience.

Acknowledgments

It seems particularly fitting that I began writing this book on women's roles when I was buried in the role of motherhood with a two-year-old and a four-month-old infant. I would not have even known of this opportunity if it were not for a fellow York Ph.D., Karen Macfarlane, who sent me the H-Net ad at a time when I was barely at my computer. I have enjoyed so many advantages denied my eighteenth-century sisters, and I found this project fit beautifully with my other work and family responsibilities. Typing away in my attic office, ordering sources online, and making brief forays onto campus to pick them up allowed me to enjoy my sons while they were awake and work during their naps. I feel so blessed to live in a world where this is possible.

Thanks are also due to my colleagues in the History Department at Trent University, for providing an atmosphere that fosters faculty research. I am especially fortunate to have colleagues like Kevin Siena, who provided me with his chapter on searchers for the dead before its publication. The university also has a very helpful library staff, all of whom were indispensable for this project. Sharon Bosnell and Kristy McKeown, in particular, dealt patiently and efficiently with at least a dozen interlibrary loan requests each month. Inge Lovell went above and beyond her duties to make material available to me at a particularly difficult time in her personal life, and I will not forget it.

The staff at Greenwood has been wonderful to deal with. The press has been very supportive and efficient throughout. Editor Wendi Schnaufer provided unstinting praise in response to each chapter's draft submission, which spurred me to finish the manuscript earlier than I expected.

I thank my two boys, Sam and Will, for unconsciously providing a welcome daily distraction, and I hope they will bear future book projects as patiently as they accepted this one. My parents, John and Sherelene Hurl, erected a special shelf in the living room after the publication of my first book and are the only people I know who have read every word I have ever published. To them I owe more than I can ever repay.

As usual, the largest burden was borne by my husband, Michael. Not only was he constantly sought for his knowledge and opinions as a fellow eighteenth-century historian, but he also has been a true partner in providing emotional support and childcare. Best of all, he has been working on his own book in the same attic office, and I know that I shall always look back on these days as some of the most precious of my life.

Introduction

A woman's experience in eighteenth-century Europe might have differed little from that of her counterparts in the previous or following century in the most basic sense. She was still subordinate to her husband and parents, still subject to the same agonies of childbirth, and burdened by the same domestic concerns that plagued her forbears. A woman who found herself among the exceptional few occupying a masculine role—as a writer or political leader, for example—continued to walk a very difficult tightrope and make the same apologies for her femininity made by her predecessors.

In other ways, however, subtle changes had occurred. Her work in the fields would now be more often interspersed with some sort of craftwork, such as straw hat-making or wool spinning, or she might even have left the fields entirely for work in the textile industry (see Chapter 2). Her urban counterparts who had previously worked as domestic servants or in artisan workshops continued to do so, only now their work was often more menial and less likely to involve as many male co-workers. If she were fortunate enough to have been born into a middling family, she now distinguished herself from those above and beneath her by her industry, piety, and chastity and enjoyed a wealth of consumer goods that had been unavailable to her seventeenth-century counterparts.

By mid-century, many European women noticed—or were themselves part of—a growing undercurrent of dissatisfaction with the social order. Demonstrations and riots erupted as people protested high grain prices or the abuse of feudal privileges. These protests often sought to reestablish the old paternal duties of the social hierarchy, rather than eradicate it altogether. The women directly involved or on the sidelines experienced a growing radicalization of such conflicts as the century progressed. The concept of "citizen" gained significant ground in some centers, and the vocabulary of "rights" and "freedoms" came to the lips of more people than ever before.

Within their homes, women held the same subservient position to the male patriarch, but mothers took a new pride in their role of raising the next generation of citizens. As Chapter 1 explains, new ideas about the biology of sexual difference made women appear to be much more distinct from men. This laid the foundation for a new perception of femininity as inherently pious, moral, and nurturing. These strengths provided added justification for women's presence in the home and helped to bring about a decline in corporal punishment of female servants and criminals. At the same time, however, the eighteenth-century understanding of femininity only further fueled existing arguments against women's involvement in political or economic life.

It is impossible to talk about women in eighteenth-century Europe as a homogeneous group. If she were rich or poor, married or single, urban or rural, a woman's world view, opportunities, and comfort varied accordingly. Virtually all of the women who gained notoriety in the arts and sciences (Chapter 5), and almost all women who got involved in European political life (Chapter 3) came from middling or aristocratic backgrounds. Poor women, by far the majority, experienced the age of Enlightenment only from the periphery.

The Enlightenment was a cultural and intellectual movement that swept across Europe in the eighteenth century. Its temporal boundaries are disputed, but its origins can be found in the scientific revolution of the previous century, and it has been linked to events well into the nineteenth century. The Enlightenment has been seen as many things. The privileging of reason, questioning of superstition, observation of nature, and the improvement of knowledge through experience are all distinct Enlightenment principles. These led to a host of social and political changes, including the calls for citizenship and the ideas of sexual difference.

Enlightenment existed in some form in virtually every country in Europe. Each language had a term for its intellectuals, such as *philosophes* in French, *ilustrados* in Spanish, and *aufklärers* in German, though the French term has had the widest use. From west to east, the European continent attempted dramatic change inspired by an Enlightenment agenda. The Portuguese, for example, had begun to curb the power of the Catholic church by mid-century; they also abolished slavery and placed Newtonianism on the curriculum of their universities. At the same time, on the other end of the continent, the first Russian university and the first permanent Russian theatre were founded. Generally, however, these reforms were cautious and limited. Leaders embraced only those Enlightenment principles that threatened their power the least, and they continued to pursue many policies that were antithetical to Enlightenment.

In 1789, the French Revolution sought to establish a new government that would pursue the ideals of the *philosophes* much more aggressively. This experiment shook the foundations of absolutism in the Western world. The revolutionaries began by attempting to reform the French government within many of its existing institutions but grew increasingly more radical and decapitated King Louis XVI in 1793, after finding him guilty of treason. The new French Republic was built on the ideas of France's famous *philosophes*, Voltaire and Rousseau in particular. Its most radical phase is characterized by "the Terror," the infamous campaign against counterrevolutionaries personified by Maximilien de Robespierre and the guillotine.

The Terror revealed the limits to Enlightenment ideals of equality and rights, but eighteenth-century women had already encountered its boundaries in the debates over sexual equality. The institution of slavery existed in various forms throughout European states and empires, and it fell under attack by the *philosophes* and their adherents in the eighteenth century. They expanded the definition of slavery to include "unfree labor, feudal dues and services..., arranged marriages, abuse of paternal power, artificial forms of deference, and more."[1] It was not long before the arguments against enslavement were connected with the rhetoric on female subordination. As early as 1706, England's Mary Astell asked pointedly, "If all men are born free, how is it that all women are born slaves?"[2] Though herself a conservative, Astell's words took on their own life and joined those of others throughout the century who pointed out the hypocrisy of treatises expounding rights to men but denying them to women.

Thus, the eighteenth century was also a time in which the status of women and the meaning of femininity were the subject of intense dispute. The *Encyclopédie*, first published in 1751 with the ambitious goal of recording all knowledge, exhibited within its own pages vastly contradictory images of women's inherent nature. An anthropology entry on women, for example, described them simultaneously as "a failed man and as man's equal."[3] As the century wore on, more *philosophes* wrestled with the question of how a society could have equality yet offer full political freedom only to a select group. Prussian professor Immanuel Kant argued that women—like servants—were dependants, and thus could be considered equal in their humanity, but "passive citizens" politically, with no voice outside of that of their husbands and fathers.[4] Ultimately, therefore, the situation of women changed little in this century, but the debates—once unleashed—never entirely subsided and, indeed, grew in force over the next hundred years.

The Enlightenment both inspired and was itself a product of significant alterations in eighteenth-century society. Improved technologies and economic imperatives drove colonial expansion. Imperialism was not a new phenomenon, but it took on a new significance as more European nations began to dream of their own empires around the globe. The Enlightenment condemned the excesses of the conquistadors (the Iberian conquerors of the last era) and embraced the idea of the "noble savage." Indigenous peoples embodied humanity in its "natural state," the theory went, unblemished by artificial political systems or distinctions of rank. The concept of the noble savage was somewhat patronizing, however, and coexisted with another Enlightenment discourse that held colonization to be a necessary civilizing process for a backward people.

Gender was deeply intertwined in the ideologies of empire. The *philosophes* judged all societies by their treatment of women and considered Europeans to be leaders in this regard, for valuing courtesy and decency towards the sex so highly. In the Orient, European writers held up the harem "as a trope of absolute female submission" and made the case for the necessity of white Christian rule.[5] A popular narrative of first contact between whites and Amerindians held that women saw male Europeans as their rescuers and protectors. Dutch canon Cornelius de Pauw—a man who had never set foot on American soil—regaled readers with tales of the first whites to meet American natives. "The Indian women were exceedingly pleased at the arrival of the Europeans," he wrote, "and the morning thereafter more than five thousand American women came to the Spaniards' camp and surrendered voluntarily."[6]

By the eighteenth century, a tradition was already established in Europe depicting Native American and African women as monstrous or ugly. In 1774, Edward Long published his *History of Jamaica*, which described African women as possessed of an unusual level of fecundity, equivalent to apes more than humans. Their lack of labor pains, he argued, left them "no more occasion for midwifes than the female oran-outang, or any other wild animall.... Thus they seem exempted from the course inflicted upon Eve and her daughters."[7] This image of African femininity set the race so far apart from Europeans as to justify the subordination of the former by the latter. Because African women birthed like animals, the reasoning went, it was acceptable to treat them like animals. Colonization and the slave trade were simultaneously made right and necessary.

To become reality, dreams of empire required strong armies. Russia was particularly ambitious in this regard, beginning the century by joining Denmark, Saxony, and Poland against Sweden in the Great Northern War (1700–1721). Russia, along with other European nations, also addressed the Ottoman Turk threat at various times in the century. Russia finally wrested control of a portion of the Black Sea coast from the Ottomans in 1774, but the latter had secured the Peloponnese (Morea) in the Greek peninsula from Venice in 1715, only to lose control of Belgrade when Austria stepped in to assist the Venetians in the Austro-Turkish War waged between 1716 and 1718. Poland underwent three partitions at the hands of Prussia, Russia, and the Austrian Habsburgs between 1772 and 1795, when it effectively disappeared from the map as an independent nation. The Seven Years' War (1756–1763) also stands out among the conflicts of the eighteenth century. It stretched across the globe, involving Britain, Prussia, and other German states against Austria, France, Russia, Sweden, and Saxony in battlefields as far-reaching as America and India.

Enlightenment theorists eagerly applied principles of knowledge through observation to military questions, citing past battles to understand and guide future strategies. Officers' identity changed; emphasis on education, national uniforms and honors, and greater professional rewards brought a new life to the military elite of eighteenth-century Europe. Frederick the Great of Prussia emerged as a leader in the new "science" of war. He wrote extensively of his experiences, boasting, "I have seen enough to offer general rules which are of special application in Prussia."[8] European leaders admired his military successes and remade their armies in the Prussian image. Another military leader emerged at the end of the century: Napoleon Bonaparte, who was to extend the boundaries of the French Empire dramatically before his fall from favor.

Europeans waged war and expanded their borders in part because of their own internal demographic pressures. The eighteenth century saw an unprecedented population explosion that had an enormous effect on the European economy and culture. Its cause still puzzles historical demographers. Earlier attempts to explain the steady rise of population in the first half of the eighteenth century and (its acceleration after 1750) as a result of the increasing availability of food due to more efficient agricultural techniques, or as a result of Enlightenment-driven improvements to public health and hygiene, are simply inadequate. Though the Netherlands did not experience quite the same level of growth, China and the Americas certainly did, and they did not undergo the same agricultural revolution or medical advancements as did Europe.[9] Finland, for example, experienced a falling death rate by the mid-eighteenth century, which "had nothing to do with industrialization" and can only partly be explained by the growing cultivation of the potato and the decrease in violent wars.[10]

Though the causes of the population explosion are unknown, its results are clearly visible. Higher levels of unemployment, increased poverty, and a greater number of landless peasants migrating from rural areas became increasingly apparent as the century progressed. These conditions further exacerbated the divisions between the rich and the poor. Old guild rules that had protected artisans were now drawn tighter to shield a much smaller and more exclusive group. The printing trade in France went through such a process, eliminating the smaller shops where apprentice and journeyman printers had more chance of working alongside master printers. Nicolas Contat, one such journeyman printer, wrote bitterly of his experiences in an account dated 1762. "Workers, apprentices, everyone works," he complained. "Only the masters and mistresses enjoy the sweetness of sleep." Contat dreamed of restoring the imagined past where masters and mistresses were "associates (*associés*)" of workers, performing their tasks at one another's side.[11]

Demographic change, expansionist wars, and Enlightenment ideals affected most European women only peripherally. The majority of middling and poor women in eighteenth-century Europe were concerned with much more immediate issues. Husbands' industry and sobriety, children's health and progress, the availability of work and food, and the oppressiveness of local authorities were generally far more pressing on women's minds, yet all of these things could be affected by distant events. The chapters that follow interweave these issues into the larger tapestry woven by state officials, military commanders, judges, and priests.

NOTES

1. Elizabeth Fox-Genovese, "Women and the Enlightenment," in *Becoming Visible: Women in European History*, 2nd ed., edited by Renate Bridenthal, Claudia Koonz, and Susan Stuard (Boston: Houghton Mifflin, 1987), 264.

2. Mary Astell, *Reflections upon Marriage*, preface to 3rd ed. (1706), quoted in Mark Goldie, "The English System of Liberty," in *The Cambridge History of Eighteenth-Century Political Thought*, edited by Mark Goldie and Robert Wokler (Cambridge: Cambridge University Press, 2006), 62.

3. Fox-Genovese, "Women and the Enlightenment," 262.

4. Iring Fetscher, "Republicanism and Popular Sovereignty," in *The Cambridge History of Eighteenth-Century Political Thought*, edited by Mark Goldie and Robert Wokler (Cambridge: Cambridge University Press, 2006), 591.

5. Betty Joesph, "Proxies of Power: Woman in the Colonial Archive," in *The Global Eighteenth Century*, edited by Felicity A. Nussbaum (Baltimore: Johns Hopkins University Press, 2003), 132.

6. Cornelius de Pauw, *Recherches Philosophiques sur les Américains*, vol. I (1768), quoted in Susanne Zantop, *Colonial Fantasies: Conquest, Family, and Nation in Precolonial Germany, 1770–1870* (Durham, NC: Duke University Press, 1997), 52–53.

7. Edward Long, *History of Jamaica, 2, with Notes and Corrections by the Author* (1774), quoted in Jennifer L. Morgan, "'Some Could Suckle over Their Shoulder': Male Travelers, Female Bodies, and the Gendering of Racial Ideology, 1500–1770," *The William and Mary Quarterly*, Third Series, vol. 54, no. 1 (January 1997), 189.

8. Frederick the Great, *Military Testament* (1768), quoted in Azar Gat, *The Origins of Military Thought: From the Enlightenment to Clausewitz* (Oxford: Clarendon Press, 1989), 58.

9. Antoinette Fauve-Chamoux, "Marriage, Widowhood, and Divorce," in *The History of the European Family, Volume One: Family Life in Early Modern Times 1500–1789*,

edited by David I. Kertzer and Marzio Barbagli (New Haven, CT: Yale University Press, 2001), 223.

10. Jarl Lindgren, *Towards Smaller Families in the Changing Society: Fertility Transition during the First Phase of Industrialization in Three Finnish Municipalities* (Helsinki, Finland: The Population Research Institute, 1984), 12.

11. Nicolas Contat, *Anecdotes typographiques oùl'on voit las description des coutumes, moeurs et usages singuliers des compagnons imprimeurs*, (1762), quoted in Robert Darnton, *The Great Cat Massacre and Other Episodes in French Cultural History* (New York: Vintage Books, 1985), 82.

SUGGESTED READING

Browne, Alice. *The Eighteenth-Century Feminist Mind*. Detroit: Wayne State University Press, 1987.

Fox-Genovese, Elizabeth. "Women and the Enlightenment." In *Becoming Visible: Women in European History*, edited by Renate Bridenthal, Claudia Koonz, and Susan Stuard, 2nd ed. Boston: Houghton Mifflin, 1987.

Gat, Azar. *The Origins of Military Thought: From the Enlightenment to Clausewitz*. Oxford: Clarendon Press, 1989.

Goldie, Mark, and Robert Wokler, eds. *The Cambridge History of Eighteenth-Century Political Thought*. Cambridge: Cambridge University Press, 2006.

Nussbaum, Felicity, ed. *The Global Eighteenth Century*. Baltimore: Johns Hopkins University Press, 2003.

Simonton, Deborah, ed. *The Routledge History of Women in Europe Since 1700*. London: Routledge, 2006.

Chronology

1700	Birth of Count Zinzendorf, a leader in the Moravian Pietist movement (d. 1760)
1700–1721	The Great Northern War, involving Sweden, Russia, Denmark-Norway, Poland-Lithuania, and Saxony
1702	Reign of Queen Anne of Britain begins (d. 1714)
1702	German Astronomer Maria Winkelmann discovers the Comet of 1702
1702–1714	War of Spanish Succession, involving the Holy Roman Empire, Britain, the Netherlands, Portugal, the Savoy, France, Spain, and Bavaria
1703	Birth of John Wesley, founder of English Methodism (d. 1791)
	Birth of Italian writer Luisa Bergalli Gozzi (d. 1779)
	British Admiralty issues order preventing women from serving as nurses onboard its hospital ships
1705	Publication of *Metamorphosis Insectorum Surinamensium* by Dutch naturalist Maria Sybylla Merian
1705	Death of Sophie Charlotte, Queen consort of Prussia (b. 1688)
1706	Birth of Emilie du Châtelet, French scientist and lover of Voltaire (d. 1749)

	Publication of third edition of *Reflections upon Marriage* by Mary Astell
	Forcible deportation of the Jansenist nuns of Port-Royal, France
1707	Silesia gains freedom of worship
1710	Birth of English author Sarah Fielding (d. 1768)
1710–1733	Anne-Thérèse de Marguenat de Courcelles (Mme de Lambert) hosts prominent salon in Paris
1710–1711	Russo-Turkish War, involving Russia and the Ottoman Empire
1711	Birth of Mikhail Lomonosov, Russian polymath and member of the Russian Academy of Sciences
	Birth of Laura Bassi, Italian scientist and professor (d. 1778)
1712	Birth of Jean-Jacques Rousseau, Swiss-born *philosophe* (d. 1778)
	Birth of Francesco Algarotti, Italian author of *Il Newtonianismo per le dame* (Newtonianism for Women) (d. 1764)
1713	Spanish Capuchin nun Mother Maria Rosa becomes prioress of a new convent in Lima, Peru
	Birth of Denis Diderot, French *philosophe* spearheading the publication of the *Encyclopédie* (d. 1784)
	Birth of German author Luise Adelgunde Gottsched (d. 1762)
1714	Birth of French novelist Marie-Jeanne Riccoboni (d. 1792)
	Birth of George Whitefield, leader in English Methodism (d. 1770)
1714–1718	Venetian-Turkish War, involving Venice and the Ottoman Empire
1715	Russia introduces legislation raising the penalty for rape from exile to execution
	Birth of Anna Nitschmann, a leader of Moravian Pietist movement (d. 1760)
1715–1760	Peak of campaign against magical healers in Portuguese inquisition
1716	Birth of Anna Morandi, Italian anatomical modeler (d. 1774)

1716–1718	Austro-Turkish War, involving the Austrian and Ottoman Empires
1717	Birth of Maria Theresa, head of Austrian Empire (d. 1780)
	Death of Maria Sybylla Merian, Dutch naturalist (b. 1647)
1718	Birth of Maria Gaetana Agnesi, Italian mathematician and charity worker (d. 1799)
1718–1720	War of the Quadruple Alliance, involving France, Spain, Britain, the Netherlands, and (later) the Savoy
1719	Birth of Leopold Mozart, Austrian father of musicians Nannerl and Wolfgang Mozart (d. 1787)
	Birth of Marie Marguerite Bihéron, French anatomical modeler (d. 1795)
	Austrian and Holy Roman Emperor Charles VI publicize the Pragmatic Sanction in an attempt to guarantee the throne of the Austrian Empire for his eldest daughter, Maria Theresa
1720	Birth of Anna Maria Mozart (née Pertl), Austrian mother of musicians Nannerl and Wolfgang Mozart (d. 1778)
	Birth of author and English bluestocking Elizabeth Montagu (d. 1800)
	Death of German astronomer Maria Winkelmann (b. 1670)
1721	Birth of Anna Dorothea Lisiewska-Therbusch, German painter (d. 1782)
	Birth of Jeanne-Antoinette Poisson, Marquise de Pompadour, mistress of French King Louis XV and patron of literature and the arts (d. 1764)
1723	Birth of Italian singer Anna Maria Teresa Imer (Teresa Cornelys) (d. 1797)
1724	Birth of Immanuel Kant, Prussian-born *philosphe*
	Birth of German composer Maria Antonia Walpurgis, Electress of Saxony (d. 1780)
1725	Death of Emperor Peter I (Peter the Great) of Russia (b. 1672)
	Reign of Empress Catherine I of Russia begins (d. 1727)
1727	Reign of Emperor Peter II of Russia begins (d. 1730)
1729	Birth of Empress Catherine II (Catherine the Great) of Russia (d. 1796)

	Englishwoman Mary Toft's pregnancy with and delivery of seventeen rabbits become notorious in British press
	Birth of Sarah Crosby, English Methodist preacher (d. 1804)
1730	Reign of Empress Anna of Russia begins (d. 1740)
1731	Birth of Sophie von La Roche (née Gutermann), first German woman to publish a novel (d. 1807)
	Laura Bassi is offered a professorship at the University of Bologna, making her the first female professor in Europe
1732	Birth of French painter Jean-Honoré Fragonard, whose works capture Enlightenment femininity (d. 1836)
1733	Death of French author and salonnière Anne-Thérèse de Marguenat de Courcelles (Mme de Lambert) (b. 1647)
	Death of Salzburg miner and Protestant leader Joseph Schaitberger (b. 1658)
1733–1738	War of the Polish Succession, involving Austria, Russia, France, Spain, Sardinia-Savoy, Tuscany, Naples, and Sicily.
1733–1749	Claudine-Alexandrine Guérin de Tencin (Mme de Tencin) hosts prominent salon in Paris
1734	General Code requires official church weddings to formalize marriage in Sweden
	Birth of Portuguese queen Maria I, first queen regnant in 1777 (d. 1816)
1735	Birth of Italian salonnière Maria Pizzelli Cuccovilla (d. 1807)
	Birth of Hamburg salonnière Elise Reimarus (d. 1805)
1735–1739	Austro-Russian-Turkish War, involving the Austrian, Russian, and Ottoman Empires
1736	Birth of Ann Lee (Mother Ann), radical English Protestant and founder of New Lebanon Society in New York (d. 1784)
	Black Caribbean former slave Rebecca Protten meets Moravian missionaries and converts to Pietism
1739	Birth of Swiss author and Parisian salonnière Suzanne Curchod (Mme Necker) (d. 1794)
	Publication of *Die Pietisterey im Fischbein-Rocke* (*Pietism in a Whale-Bone Corset*) by German Luise Adelgunde Gottsched
1740	Reign of infant Emperor Ivan VI of Russia begins (d. 1764)

	Reign of Maria Theresa as head of Austrian Empire begins (d. 1780)
	Reign of Frederick II (Frederick the Great) of Prussia begins (d. 1786)
	Birth of Swiss novelist Isabelle-Agnès-Élizabeth de Charrière (d. 1805)
	Approximate end of musician Anna Maria della Pietà's term as director of the Venetian Pietà music school orchestra
1740–1742	First Silesian Wars, involving Austria, Silesia, and Prussia
1740–1748	War of the Austrian Succession, involving France, Bavaria, Saxony, Spain, Austria, Silesia, Prussia, Britain, and Bohemia
1740–1758	Term of Pope Benedict XIV (Prospero Lambertini), patron of female scholars
1741	Emperor Ivan VI of Russia is deposed and reign of Empress Elizabeth begins (d. 1762)
	Birth of Joseph II of Austria and Holy Roman Emperor, son of Empress Maria Theresa of Austria (d. 1790)
	Death of Italian composer and violinist Antonio Vivaldi (b. 1678)
	Birth of Swiss artist Angelica Kauffmann (d. 1807)
1742	Birth of German author Charlotte von Stein (d. 1827)
1744–1745	Second Silesian Wars, involving Austria and Prussia
1745	Birth of Venetian composer and violinist Maddalena Laura Lombardini-Sirmen (d. 1818)
	Expulsion of Jews from Bohemia by Austrian Empress Maria Theresa
1746	Birth of Madame de Genlis, French governess and author on education (d. 1830)
	Dutch woman Maria van Antwerpen enlists as soldier Jan van Ant (she is discovered and reenlists in new disguise in 1762)
1747	Publication of *Letters d'une Péruvienne* by French novelist Françoise d'Issembourg d'Happencourt (Mme de Graffigny)
	Birth of Russian poet Princess Ekaterina Sergeevna Urusova (d. ca. 1817)
1748	Publication of *Instituzioni Analitiche*, a book on calculus by Italian mathematician and philosopher Maria Gaetana Agnesi
1749	Death of French author and salonnière Claudine-Alexandrine Guérin de Tencin (Mme de Tencin) (b. 1682)

1749–1777	Marie-Thérèse Rodet Geoffrin (Mme Geoffrin) hosts prominent salon in Paris
1749–1751	Marquise of Sarría's *tertulia* (salon) promotes literature and poetry in Spain
1750	Legislation requiring formal obstetrics training for midwives is issued in Spain
	Death of Dutch painter Rachel Ruysch (b. 1664)
	Birth of Joanna Southcott, radical English religious leader (d. 1814)
1751	First publication of the *Encyclopédie*
	Birth of Maria Anna (Nannerl) Mozart, Austrian musician and sister of Wolfgang Mozart (d. 1829)
1752	Birth of English novelist and letter writer Fanny Burney
	Death of Madam Sidney Griffith, traveling companion to Welsh Methodist leader Howell Harris
	Real Academia de Bellas Artes de San Fernando is founded in Spain on the model of the Accademia di San Luca in Rome (founded in 1593) and the Académie Royal de Peinture et de Sculpture of France (1648)
1753	Hardwicke's Marriage Act requires official church weddings to formalize marriage in England
	Birth of Portuguese singer Luisa Rosa Todi (d. 1833)
1754	Birth of Jeanne-Marie Pilipon (Jeanne-Marie Roland), author and moderate French revolutionary (d. 1793)
1755	Austrian Empress Maria Theresa gives birth to Marie Antoinette, later Queen Consort of France (d. 1793)
	Birth of French painter Elisabeth-Louise Vigée-Lebrun (d. 1842)
1756	Death of English writer Eliza Haywood (b. ca. 1693)
1756–1763	Seven Years' War involving Britain, France, Austria, Russia, Sweden, Saxony, Prussia, and Hanover
1757	Publication of *Lettres de Mistress Fanny Butler*, first novel of Marie-Jeanne Riccoboni of France
	Death of Venetian portraitist Rosalba Carriera (b. 1675)
1757–1775	English women gather in Bluestocking circle, a series of salon-like conversation evenings in London
1758	Death of French novelist Mme de Graffigny (b. 1695)

	Birth of Maximilien de Robspierre, a chief architect of the Terror (d. 1794)
	Publication of Lizzy Bates' *Female Rights Vindicated, or the Equality of the Sexes Morally and Physically Proved*
1759	Birth of Mary Wollstonecraft, English governess, author, feminist, and advocate of the French Revolution (d. 1797)
1760	Spanish King Charles III issues new marriage statutes reinforcing the 1632 legislation requiring military men to secure royal assent to marry
	Publication of *Poleznoe Uveselenie* (*Useful Entertainment*), the first poem by Russian author Elizaveta Keraskova
	Birth of German soprano Aloysia Weber (d. 1839)
	Portugal expels Jesuits from all of its territories and withdraws Portuguese subjects from Rome
	Spanish government begins to offer pensions to officers' wives and children
1761	Englishwoman Sarah Crosby begins preaching at a Derby Methodist society meeting
1762	Birth of Helen Williams, English author and advocate of the French Revolution (d. 1827)
	Parisian *Parlement* abolishes the Jesuit order
	Reign of Emperor Peter III of Russia begins (d. 1762)
	Reign of Empress Catherine II (Catherine the Great) of Russia begins after overthrowing her husband, Emperor Peter III (d. 1796)
	Birth of Anne-Josèphe Théroigne de Méricourt, French revolutionary (d. 1817)
	Death of Lady Mary Wortley Montagu, English writer and wife of the ambassador to Turkey
1764	Birth of Berlin salonnière Henriette Herz (d. 1847)
	Birth of Dorothea Mendelssohn (Dorothea Schlegel), a German Jew who converts to Lutheranism and then Catholicism (d. 1839)
	Meeting of General Synod of Moravian Pietists where women's official activities are severely limited
1766	Rising of the Esquilache, a protest against high grain prices by Spanish women in Madrid

	Swiss-born Parisian salonnière Mme Necker gives birth to daughter who becomes the famous author and salonnière Germaine de Staël (d. 1817)
1768	Birth of Charlotte Corday, moderate French revolutionary and assassin of the more radical Jean-Paul Marat (d. 1793)
	Royal Academy of Arts is founded in London
	Birth of English singer Elizabeth Weichsel (Elizabeth Billington) (d. 1818)
1768–1774	Russo-Turkish War, involving the Russian and Ottoman Empires
1770	Marie Antoinette, Austrian daughter of Empress Maria Theresa, weds King Louis XVI of France
	Spinning jenny, a machine for spinning wool or cotton, is patented in England
	English radical religious leader Mother Ann Lee receives vision that she is the new female messiah
1771	Publication of *Geschichte des Fräuleins von Sternheim* (*History of Lady Sophia Sternheim*) by German author Sophie Von La Roche
1772	First partition of Poland by Russia, Prussia, and Austria
1773	Publication of *The History of the Female Shipwright . . . Written by Herself*, an autobiography by Englishwoman Mary Lacy, who served in the Navy disguised as a man
	Spanish artist María Luisa Carranque is invited to join the Academia de Bellas Artes
1773–1775	Yemelyan Ivanovich Pugachev leads serf uprising in eastern territories of Russia
1774	Reign of Louis XVI begins (ends with abolition of monarchy in 1792)
1775	The Austrian Empire places a total ban on wives traveling with the army
1776	Publication of *Rino*, first play by German author Charlotte von Stein
1776–1783	War of American Independence, involving Britain, France, Spain, the Netherlands, and the thirteen British North American colonies
1777	Death of French author and salonnière Marie-Thérèse Rodet Geoffrin (Mme Geoffrin) (b. 1699)

	Death of Italian salonnière Clelia Borromeo (b. 1684)
1777–1794	Suzanne Curchod (Mme Necker) hosts prominent salon in Paris
1777–1816	Reign of Queen Maria I, first queen regnant of Portugal
1778	Publication of *Evelina* by English novelist Fanny Burney
	Death of renowned French *philosophe* Voltaire (b. 1694)
	Sweden introduces legislation allowing unmarried mothers to give birth without harassment or enquiries
1778–1779	War of the Bavarian Succession, involving Austria, Prussia, Bavaria, Bohemia, and Saxony
1780	Austrian Emperor Joseph II passes laws to protect unmarried mothers
	Royal Academy of Sciences of Lisbon is established by Queen Maria I
1780–1784	Anglo Dutch war involving England and the Dutch Republic
1781	Austrian Emperor Joseph II issues edict advocating religious toleration
1782	Swiss courts executed Anna Göldi, the last witch in Europe
	English Judege Buller issues the infamous "rule of thumb" assertion that a man could beat his wife if the rod was no thicker than his thumb
1784	Georgiana, English Duchess of Devonshire, reputedly kisses a butcher while canvassing for a political candidate and creates a scandal
	Publication of *Dei delitte e delle pene* (later published in English as *Crimes and Punishment*) by Italian legal theorist Cesare Beccaria
	Publication of *Lettres de Mistriss Henley publiées par son amie*, Swiss novelist Isabelle de Charrière's first epistolary novel
1786	Birth of Agustina Zaragoza, who resisted French occupation of Spain at the siege of Zaragoza in 1808 (d. 1857)
1787	Publication of *Thoughts on the Education of Daughters* by Mary Wollstonecraft
1789–1791	National Assembly governs France, marking the start of the French Revolution
1789	Spinning school for the poor of Hamburg opens

1789	October March of Parisian women to palace at Versailles
1790	Publication of English composer Ann Young's book of harpsichord lessons
1791	Dutchwoman Etta Palm D'Aelders writes "Adresse des citoyennes françoises à l'Assemblée Nationale"
	Publication of *Declaration des droits de la femme et de la citoyenne* by Olympe de Gouges
	Jews of France receive full civil rights
1791–1792	Legislative Assembly governs France, marking a more radical phase of the French Revolution
1792	French Legislative Assembly passes the first nationwide divorce law, the most liberal of its kind in Europe
	Publication of *A Vindication of the Rights of Woman* by Mary Wollstonecraft
	Joanna Southcott, radical English religious leader, has a vision of the Second Coming of Christ
1792–1795	National Convention governs France and establishes the Terror, a campaign against counterrevolutionaries that oversaw at least 16,000 executions in nine months.
1792–1797	War of the First Coalition, involving Austria, Prussia, Spain, the United Provinces, and Great Britain against the French Republic
1793	Execution of King Louis XVI of France
	Establishment of Revolutionary Tribunals for the trial of political offenders in France that become one of the main engines of the Terror
	Execution of Queen Marie Antoinette of France
	Second partition of Poland by Russia, Prussia, and Austria, provoking a national uprising led by Thaddeus Kosciuszko
	Society of Revolutionary Republican Women is formed, the first all-female political interest group in the West
	Charlotte Corday assassinates radical French revolutionary Jean-Paul Marat and is found guilty and executed a few days later
	Execution of Jeanne-Marie Roland, moderate revolutionary, in France

1794	Passage of the 22 Prairial Year II Law in France, whereby counterrevolutionary suspects could be condemned without the opportunity to defend themselves
	Polish resistance leader Thaddeus Kosciuszko is taken prisoner by the Russians after his defeat in battle and is given aid by his former love, Ludvika Sosnowska, now Polish Princess Lubomirska
	Maximilien de Robespierre, the newly elected president of the National Convention government, leads the festival of the *Être Suprême* (Supreme Being) in Paris, with similar celebrations across France
	Execution of Maximilien de Robespierre marks an end of the Terror
1795	Prairial uprising of Parisian women whose failure signifies one of the final defeats of the original revolutionary goals
	Third partition of Poland by Russia, Prussia, and Austria, by which the state of Poland ceased to exist
1795–1799	The Directory governs France in the final and more moderate phase of the French Revolution
1796	Spain introduces legislation to protect those leaving infants at foundling hospitals
1798–1801	War of the Second Coalition, involving Britain, Russia, the Ottoman Empire, Naples, Portugal, and Austria against Napoleon and the French Republic
1799	Napoleon Bonaparte, an officer in the French Army, forms a new Republic in France after a coup d'état
	Italian laborer's daughter Maria Dalle Donne receives a medical degree

1

Women and Family

Women's roles within the family had long been central to femininity in early modern Europe, and the eighteenth century was no exception. In some ways, the family grew in its importance to female identity in the Enlightenment age. An exploration of women's familial roles in this era unearths many paradoxes. Education for girls was promoted more than ever before, but mainly on the basis of their eventual role as mothers. Women increasingly became sexualized as objects of the male gaze, while simultaneously being considered to have no libido themselves.

Women's reproductive function was becoming their sole claim to significance. Mothers and wives were elevated as men's partners in preparing a new generation of Enlightenment thinkers and workers in the colonial enterprise. Of course, this only further marginalized widows and spinsters, despite their burgeoning ranks in many European populations. In order to fulfill the Enlightenment ideal of femininity, an eighteenth-century girl needed the social position and beauty to attract a husband, the fertility to produce children, and the resources of the middle class to permit her to focus all of her attentions upon nursing and educating them.

GIRLS

Many historians have seen the eighteenth century as one of growing consumerism in Europe, and children were among the beneficiaries of the increasing availability of consumer goods. Commercially produced toys began to flood the marketplace in the Enlightenment age. Modern museums contain fascinating remnants of the toys that were produced for sale in the eighteenth century: artefacts such as dolls with elaborate wardrobes or lead-cast mechanical toys with intricate detail. Though these extreme examples would be within reach of only girls of the wealthiest families, their existence attests to the fact that childhood and children's play was becoming increasingly celebrated in Enlightenment culture. The Enlightenment focus upon literacy and learning was visible in the growing availability of children's literature, which was so prevalent that a Dutch author acknowledged, in 1779, that "this is the first century in which books are explicitly written for children."[1] Indeed, the celebration of childhood was consciously linked to the Enlightenment enterprise. As an eighteenth-century Swiss physician wrote, "one has to be a child in childhood to be reasonable in the age of reason."[2]

Certainly, the daughters of the "middling sort"—the socio-economic group whose burgeoning ranks helped to drive commercial consumption—would have possessed a variety of toys. Significantly, these playthings often would have been housed in a nursery. In contrast to earlier architecture, where the communal prevailed over the private even in the homes of the more well-to-do, Enlightenment-era houses were designed to separate children from adults to protect their innocence. Where seventeenth-century girls were bound to be aware of parental copulations—not to mention those of other adults who may have slept nearby, eighteenth-century daughters growing up in the shelter of the nursery probably retained throughout their maidenhood an ignorance of the mysteries of sex. Whether a girl's mother was a frequent presence in the nursery depended mainly upon her social class. Victorine de Chastenay, daughter of French nobility, professed herself "subjugated" and awed by her mother, and spent the vast majority of her time with her nurse, as did many of her aristocratic contemporaries.[3] After the Revolution broke out in 1789, aristocratic mothers underwent a significant transformation to become more maternal, and they increasingly oversaw personally their daughters' upbringing and education.

Recent studies of the history of childhood have revised earlier views that medieval and early modern parents did not love or cherish their children as much as their modern counterparts. The current interpretation is that parental devotion has remained relatively consistent throughout history, though there was a slight shift by the eighteenth century to seeing childhood as a more separate age of innocence. Prior to the Enlightenment, children's misbehavior might have been understood to have been caused by original sin, but eighteenth-century philosophers, especially Rousseau, offered an image of children as innocent creatures whose misbehavior could be corrected by proper upbringing and education. Witness the care and attention lavished on the baby sketched by François Boucher in mid-century France,

Mother or nurse with child in play chair under title Du porte-feuille de Mr. Néra, crayon of original drawing by François Boucher (ca. 1740–1770) Paris: chés Demarteau Graveur et Pensionnaire du Roi . . . (Courtesy of Library of Congress)

or "The good Mother" painted by Fragonard a decade or more later. By the end of the 1700s, parents and citizens in many parts of Europe had embarked upon new pedagogical experiments to implement Rousseau's views.[4]

To understand eighteenth-century girls, it is also important to understand what made them different from boys. Contemporary notions of sexual difference underwent dramatic transformation in the Enlightenment age. Modern thinking accepts as a basic truth that males and females are fundamentally different at a biological level. This was not a standard belief before the eighteenth century. A look at sixteenth-century medical drawings

La bonne Mere [The good Mother], hand-colored stipple engraving of painting by Jean-Honoré Fragonard (ca. 1780–1800). (Courtesy of Library of Congress)

quickly reveals the medieval and early modern physiology that characterized human sex organs as more similar than different. The theory embraced what one historian has called a "single sex model," which regarded female sex organs as imperfect versions of male genitalia. Because women had an imbalance of humors, the theory—which went back at least as far as Hippocrates—went, they were possessed of what were essentially inverted penises. The shaft was equated with the "neck" of the womb. The ovaries were likened to testes. In pre-Enlightenment theory, all had remained inside women's bodies instead of dropping out, as they would on a man.[5]

This went hand-in-hand with other "flawed" elements of female anatomy that made women leaky vessels. They menstruated, cried, and ejaculated "seed" more than their male counterparts. This ideology helped to form the basis for medieval and early modern views of feminine inferiority. If the female was simply a botched male, it made sense that she should hold a lower position in European society. Also, if women were deficient in important elements of the four humors, it naturally followed that they would thirst for that which they were lacking. Early modern women were thus seen as sexually voracious, obsessed with obtaining the hot, dry semen of men. Hence, medical treatises like that of 1658, with advice to men in choosing a wife:

> men must make a good choice and not presently take what comes next to hand rashly. For he that hath got a lean slender woman of declining years, hath such a one as is always itching [desiring], and will never bee satisfied; Let him know that he hath got a perpetuall torment, that is continually lusting, and is daily more and more exasperated: She will stick to her Husband like a Horseleach, and she will never let him rest, though he be tired out quite, nor give him so much respite as to recover his strength.[6]

By the eighteenth century, this image of libidinous femininity was in decline, and new understandings of sexual biology more familiar to our modern understanding had emerged.

By seeing the feminine generative organs as completely distinct and functionally different from the penis and testes, eighteenth- and nineteenth-century medicine underpinned a quite different notion of femininity. Girls were now seen as biologically destined for motherhood, as divinely created to serve as nurturers and moral compasses to the rest of their family. Rather than the sexual voracity imputed to their forbears, eighteenth-century girls and women were seen as naturally asexual. Literally, within the span of one lifetime, women's "desexualization" was complete.

This is clear in an English novelist's biography describing his great-aunt asking to read a seventeenth-century story she recalled enjoying in her youth. She was so offended by the salacious content of the book that she told him to burn it. Her observation nicely illustrates the total transformation of eighteenth-century morality: "Is it not a very odd thing that I, an old woman of eighty and upwards, sitting alone, feel myself ashamed to read a book which, sixty years ago, I have heard read aloud for the amusement of large circles, consisting of the first and most creditable society in London?"[7] Similarly, the Count d'Haussonville's sisters were always sent out of hearing when their grandmother spoke of lewd stories from her youth in the *ancien régime*.[8] Elder generations were conscious of a new moral purity among their daughters and sought to protect it.

With motherhood elevated as a special strength of femininity in Enlightenment thought, the education of girls took on a new significance. John Locke's theory that every new life should be regarded as a *tabula rasa*, or blank slate, became popular among Enlightenment philosophers. Each blank slate could—and deserved to—be written on with a sound education. This was justified for girls not in language of sexual equality but because, as mothers, they would be responsible for educating the next generation in its earliest years. According to Rousseau, "the earliest education... undoubtedly is woman's work. If the author of nature had meant to assign it to men he would have given them milk to feed the child."[9] Though far from a language of sexual equality, this is nonetheless the first time that female education was strongly promoted across Europe.

Of course, the sort of instruction required to make early childhood educators of future mothers was not necessarily well rounded. Nannerl Mozart was one of the rare European women to receive a thorough education as a girl. Elder sister of the famous Austrian composer, Nannerl was taught by her father at home.[10] Germany's Sophie von La Roche (née Gutermann) is another unusually well-educated eighteenth-century girl. She is reputed to have been able to read at the age of three, and by twelve years of age was capable of acting as her father's "librarian." She had formal training in a variety of disciplines and was later courted by men who continued instructing her, first in mathematics and Italian and later in an ever-burgeoning array of subjects.[11] This contrasts starkly with the advice of the author of *Letters on the Improvement of the Mind, addressed to a Young Lady*. Her 1773 treatise counseled the girl to avoid "the learned languages" and focus upon things like "dancing and the knowledge of the French tongue," which she deemed "both... useful as well as ornamental."[12]

Nannerl Mozart was from the middle class, but she was exceptional even within this slightly more privileged group. Marie and Marianne Lamothe, daughters of a Bordeaux lawyer, clearly received a far inferior education to their brothers. Though literate, they labored over their letter writing, professing it very hard work.[13] Most girls of the period could expect a very rudimentary education. Indeed, the vast legions of impoverished women of the eighteenth century had little chance of even a basic level of literacy. One French example from late in the century shows that only one girl in fifty might expect to receive schooling, in contrast to two-thirds of boys.[14] This does not negate the benefits of the Enlightenment's elevation of femininity, but the ideal tended to differ quite starkly from the reality.

Many of the distinctly eighteenth-century changes to girlhood existed largely for upper and middling girls. Opportunities for education or play with commercial toys were denied most poorer girls. Depending upon their circumstances, young girls could have been drawn into a variety of tasks to help their families survive. Some girls worked at small-scale manufacturing in the family home, part of the so-called cottage industries discussed in the next chapter, but they had to be "strongly disciplined" and "carefully controlled" to ensure that they produced a quality product.[15] Other girls worked in the fields alongside their parents or at household jobs. In rural Spain, one's sons and daughters were welcomed as a source of cheaper labor, a way for the household to save the expense of hiring an external person for the same task. In the words of one Cuenca peasant, "It was always better to have children. No matter how cheap shepherds might be, they were always more expensive than children."[16] For many, then, the day-to-day experience of girlhood probably remained quite similar to what it had been centuries before. Nonetheless, the changing ideology of children as innocents and new notions of sexual difference would make a gradual impact on the generations of European girls to follow.

MOTHERHOOD

The Enlightenment redefinition of femininity clearly had serious ramifications for mothers. To them went the responsibility for the education, health, and well-being of the next generation in its earliest years. Seeing women as biologically destined for motherhood had a sinister side. Elevating the female for her "natural" nurturing abilities could also end up subjugating her further. The growth of imperialism in eighteenth-century Europe led to a corresponding desire to create more healthy new citizens and soldiers to expand the empire and colonize new lands. It was this obsession with population growth that prompted Peter the Great's legislation to encourage more fraternization among Russian youth and (it was hoped) happier marriages. In the words of England's Jonas Hanway in 1756: "Increase alone can make our *natural* Strength in *Men* correspond with our *artificial* Power in *Riches*, and both with the Grandeur and Extent of the *British Empire*."[17] Even Swiss physician Jean-André Venel considered it important for women to keep in mind their primary role in bearing the next generation of Europeans. At the end of his medical text on reproductive health, he reminded both men and women to stop themselves from reproducing and even from marrying if they had any "diseases or malformations" that could be passed on to their children.[18] Each eighteenth-century state concerned itself with the business of reproduction, and women were at the heart of this shift.

Unwanted children—those who were illegitimate, or were born to parents too poor to care for them—became the new focus of Enlightenment concerns over sustaining high population levels. Historians of the eighteenth century have remarked upon a perceptible rise in bastardy in Europe in this period. France was particularly visible in this trend, and it may be that Enlightenment culture fostered a more permissive attitude towards penetrative sex between unmarried men and women. In eighteenth-century Burgundy, most unmarried women who found themselves pregnant were able to go before the courts and obtain an order forcing the father to provide for his child. Significant means of persuasion, such as imprisonment, could be employed to force his compliance.[19] This century also saw the opening of many foundling hospitals across Europe, where mothers could anonymously abandon burdensome infants. One proponent of such hospitals in Spain imagined "how many strong arms ... how many workers, how many respectable farmers and grazers" would be produced by caring for the abandoned children (*expósitos*) of Spain.[20]

At first glance, this would seem to promise only advantages to the mothers of the Enlightenment. Protection and relief from the economic burden of an unwanted pregnancy would certainly seem beneficial. However, these developments emerged as part of the eighteenth-century desire for population growth. Thus, they must be regarded as another way that Enlightenment culture encouraged women to value themselves solely upon the basis of their reproductive function. The existence of legal protections for single mothers and foundling hospitals for bastards should also not overshadow the fact that illegitimacy maintained its scandalous taint in many parts of Europe. In 1780, a young Hungarian cook who found herself pregnant was pelted with stones whenever she ventured out of doors. Only intervention by manorial authorities prevented her family's expulsion from the village.[21]

Women who gave their children to foundling hospitals tended to exist on the margins of European society. Most mothers of the Enlightenment fell under cultural control in more subtle ways, especially through the debate over maternal breastfeeding. It had long been common practice, among those who could afford it, to send infants to peasant women to be breastfed in their earliest years. This allowed aristocratic mothers to focus upon courtly life and duties—not to mention allowing them to get pregnant again more quickly than if they were breastfeeding—and it offered working-class women an important source of income. By the latter half of the eighteenth century, this practice was redefined as very unhealthy for the infant and a selfish indulgence on the part of mothers. Wealthy women hiring wet nurses were seen as vain and—worst of all by Enlightenment standards—not maternal. The wet-nursing profession, vital to the income of some peasant women, was now regarded with contempt. As one historian put it, "this bodily service came to be constructed as part of all women's unpaid reproductive labour."[22]

The antipathy towards wet-nursing had the greatest impact in England, but it was felt all across eighteenth-century Europe. The campaigns against wet nurses were also launched in France, for example. Though the practice remained common among aristocratic mothers, they now made a more concerted effort to visit their babies while they were in care, and they brought them back home immediately upon weaning. Swiss doctor Venel advocated the beneficial effects of maternal breastfeeding and stated that a mother who considered herself too weak to breastfeed should not have had children in the first place.[23] One German newspaper reported that "there is no better or more natural food for an infant than [his mother's milk] which already nourished him before his birth."[24] By 1800, many middle-class women had been successfully indoctrinated with the ideology of appropriate maternity and dutifully breastfed their babies.

Not all theories around reproduction and infant health bore similarities to those of today, however. Indeed, a surprising number of traditional ideas of pregnancy and infant care prevailed in the eighteenth century. These, too, placed their own burden of constraint and responsibility upon European mothers. In eastern Europe, folk practices survived well into the nineteenth and twentieth centuries, despite Enlightenment assaults. Romanian babies, for example, were tightly swaddled, but also bound in chains, to make them "strong as iron." Some infants' eyes were also covered for months on end to protect them from "the evil eye."[25]

Johann Storch was a German doctor whose medical notes for 1720 through 1740 have survived. Like many of his contemporaries, Storch believed that a mother's emotions during gestation had a direct impact upon the developing fetus. One nineteen-year-old woman was six months pregnant,

> when she was suddenly overcome by a violent anger; whereupon on the next day ... a strong haemorrhagia uteri followed [and later a miscarriage, caused, according to Storch, because] ... the fruit had been so affected by the anger that it became deathly ill in utero, and died toward the seventh or eighth day. Afterward nature, in order to expel the fruit [fetus], produced the regular menses, namely the labor pains attendant on a birth.[26]

In other words, the woman's anger was the culprit for the death of her baby.

Another expectant mother, whom Storch described as "of a quarrelsome and angry temperament" to begin with, lost her baby because of this character flaw. The doctor's account blamed her anger for "divert[ing] more nourishment to the secundinae maliformi [afterbirth] than to the fruit."[27] Babies' health and general physical appearance were considered by physicians and popular lore alike to be enormously influenced by their mothers' thoughts and emotions while in utero. If a woman were unduly given to a strong thought or emotion at conception, the resultant infant would bear matching traits. Frightened women might have babies who were troubled with tremors in their limbs. Excessive body hair, black skin color, a hare lip: all could be attributed to the mother's obsessing about furry animals, Africans, and hares, respectively.

Perhaps the most fascinating example of these ideas in practice is the infamous story of Mary Toft. Toft was an Englishwoman who claimed, in 1726, to have given birth to seventeen rabbits. Word of the first births spread so quickly that King George I himself sent several experts to attend her and witness personally this "praeternatural" event.[28] After much publicity and heated debates between the medical experts sent to observe Toft, it was discovered that she had inserted rabbit parts into her vagina at opportune intervals and then faked labor in order to "deliver" them.[29] A barrage of ballads, pamphlets, and other print emerged from the incident, such as *The Doctors in Labour; or a New Whim Wham from Guildford*, printed in 1726. The verses make clear that many still believed it plausible for a woman to give birth to a rabbit if she was thinking of a rabbit during coitus:

> When I (says Moll [Mary Toft]) five weeks was gone with Child
> And hard at Work was weeding in the field,
> Up starts a Rabbet—To my grief I view'd it,
> And vainly tho with eagerness pursued it,
> The Effect was strange....
> The Rabbit all day long ran in my Head.
> At night I dreamt I had him in my Bed;
> Methought he there a Burrough try'd to make
> His Head I patted and I stroak'd his Back.
> My Husband wak'd me and Cry'd Moll for shame
> Lett go—What 'twas he meant I need not Name....[30]

A German story from 1715 has certain remarkable similarities to Toft's and attests to the persistence of traditional theories of conception. Christina Schauth of Württemberg purportedly gave birth to eight frogs, but she was later uncovered as a fraud. In her case, too, reputable men of medicine attested to the authenticity of the birth. A Doctor Rauchendorff theorized that "in springtime Christina had bathed in or swallowed water with frogspawn in it."[31] Credulity over such bizarre or "monstrous" births only gradually declined over the course of the century.

WIVES

By the eighteenth century, courtship and marriage practices were undergoing significant changes in most European countries. These changes are rife with paradox. While Enlightenment femininity was increasingly desexualized, young women were simultaneously becoming more objectified. At the same time that traditional religious rules governing weddings were relaxing, the role of the church was increasing in certain parts of Europe. The resulting marriages—especially those of the middle class—were both more affectionate on the outside and possibly more secretly violent within. Despite their many contradictions, eighteenth-century wives navigated betrothal and married life with many remarkable similarities to modern wives.

The objectification of women became more pronounced in the Enlightenment era. Europe saw a transformation in female sexual objectification, most visible in the era's fashions. Where earlier masculine fashion was at least as ostentatious as its feminine counterpart, Enlightenment men recoiled from gaudy display, leaving women much more exclusively in this role. Masculine attire—particularly that of middle class men—took on duller hues, while women's clothing remained colorful and became more diversified. Even salaried women and female servants tended to own multiple pairs of chemises, petticoats, stockings, and sleeves. This is a marked contrast to earlier eras, when only elite women would have been likely to possess more than a single change of linen. The growing complexity of undergarments was matched by an expansion in the variety of hats and outer garments for women.

These changes were not only because of the rise in the fundamental notions of a distinct female body (one of the components of which was a notion of vanity and self-adornment as more feminine traits), but also because the items of dress became more accessible. Even servant girls had ample opportunity to sport opulent fashions. Fashionable clothing could be purchased second hand, in a thriving marketplace that was fueled by theft as well as legitimate supply networks. With the decline of the tight breeches and suggestive codpieces that characterized Western male fashions of earlier centuries, young women now remained more exclusively on the stage of sexual display. Nowhere was this more dramatic than in Russia, where the reforms of Peter the Great included laws forcing the adoption of Western dress. For women in particular, this meant wearing "European dress, with its low-cut bodices," rather than the head-to-toe draping of traditional Russian attire.[32] Across Europe, courtship more frequently took the form of the passive asexual female parading before the libidinous male gaze. This is readily apparent in French painter Jean-Honoré Fragonard's *The Swing*. This 1767 painting depicts a young woman swinging in a lush garden setting. Lying on the ground beneath is a young gentleman whose eyes are directed beneath her billowing petticoats. This and many other eighteenth-century images depict courtship as a relatively passive female objectifying herself before the male gaze.

As a passive object, the eighteenth-century maiden was increasingly expected to maintain her chastity on her own. In previous centuries, youth of both sexes had been allowed a fairly wide range of premarital sexual experimentation in much of Europe. If an Italian girl found herself pregnant by her betrothed before the actual marriage had taken place, for example, she could expect her family and peer group to force him to fulfil his promise and marry her to protect her honor. There was little shock that she had indulged in premarital intercourse. By the eighteenth century, however, that same community believed that it was the young woman's duty to resist male advances and protect her own virginity. Now, private betrothals and whispered promises lost weight in official circles; formalities which included a church ceremony in the presence of witnesses, the exchange of gifts, and parental consent were required before the initiation of legitimate sexual relations. Rather than the entire community safeguarding her honor and holding her lover equally responsible for premarital pregnancies, eighteenth-century girls now had to guard their chastity alone, in scenes similar to that depicted in the mid-century French painting *Un baiser, ou ta Rose*.[33]

This is due, at least in part, to the Enlightenment notion of sexual difference. By redefining womanhood as more "naturally" maternal and asexual, eighteenth-century norms held that unmarried girls would have no desire for intercourse until marriage and the possibility of children allowed them to overcome their inherent repugnance for sex. Even Russian noblewomen, who were allowed—for the first time in centuries—to interact "indiscriminately" with young noblemen at elaborate balls after 1725, were now navigating the murky waters of courtship much more independently. In this case, however, it was generally a move to a more beneficial situation for wives. Russian women's preferences were taken into account more than ever before.[34] Whether for good or ill, the Enlightenment age saw a withdrawal of community involvement in youth romances across Europe.

Though the courtship had become more private and less subject to community scrutiny, the resulting weddings often became more public and formalized in the eighteenth century. Eighteenth-century concerns over maintaining and increasing the population prompted legislation to protect the institution of marriage, such as Sweden's General Code of 1734. This law made church weddings a must for a couple to have official status as husband and wife.[35] In England, Hardwicke's Marriage Act of 1753, which forbade marriages by minors without parental consent, also stipulated that bride and groom marry before witnesses in the Anglican Church after the publication of the banns. The renewed focus upon parental veto was an attempt to address the growing concern over heirs and heiresses being lured into marrying below their station.[36] Whether real or imagined, such worries existed throughout Europe. A French royal ordinance in 1730 made any servant punishable by death if he or she attempted to marry one of the household sons or daughters.[37] Episodes of kidnapping were visible throughout the 1700s in the Polish-Lithuanian state, where willing brides conspired with their chosen grooms in an abduction that allowed them to escape a repugnant suitor or a convent.[38] All over eighteenth-century

Un baiser, ou ta Rose, [A kiss, or your Rose] (ca. 1740–1777), engraving of painting by Louis Watteau. (Courtesy of Library of Congress)

Europe, statutes tightened marriage laws and made official church weddings a necessary prerequisite of marital status.

At the same time, however, the church ceremonies were less subject to the spiritual traditions of former times. Part of this is because the Enlightenment brought with it a move towards secularization. Russians could marry outside of their religion for the first time, as long as their children were raised in the Orthodox faith.[39] In some Scandinavian jurisdictions, a promise to marry had the essential legal weight of a marriage, and it might be many years before a cohabitating couple would bother with the church ceremony to bless the union.[40] May marriages, which had long been considered unlucky (especially in Switzerland), gradually grew in popularity over the course of the Enlightenment age. There was a perceptible shift in Europe from winter to spring nuptial ceremonies.[41] Though the earlier antipathy to May weddings had little canonical basis, it was a long-honored church tradition, and its abandonment illustrates the diminishing authority of the church in eighteenth-century culture.

First-time brides were marrying later than in the past in northwest Europe. This can be at least partially explained by the dramatic population rise over the latter half of the century and the urbanization and industrialization that resulted (discussed in more detail in Chapter 2). With unemployment driving higher proportions of young men and women to cities than ever before, marriage began to be postponed longer. In the French city of Rheims, for example, young women were brides at a mean age of 26.7 in the period 1775–1791, where the mean age a century before had been 24.3. Men, too, were marrying older.[42] For the nobility, of course, the same economic concerns that caused their poorer counterparts to wait were not an issue, and they continued to marry much younger in order to increase the chances of producing an heir. In Eastern Europe, even poorer women tended to marry as early as 14 and certainly by the age of 18, and this does not seem to have changed dramatically with industrialization.[43] In Spain, too, women generally always married slightly younger, usually around the age of 21–23.[44]

Once married, the experience of wifehood may have been discernibly different from previous centuries. Some historians believe that eighteenth-century wives had a better chance at achieving marital bliss than their earlier counterparts. Some have argued that greater affection emerged in the households of Enlightenment Europe.[45] Though this remains a subject of debate, much more archival evidence has survived of warm emotional bonds between husbands and wives than exists for the pre-Enlightenment era.

Mozart's parents provide an example of a middle-class couple in Austria. His father, writing to his wife in 1772, betrayed a rare glimpse of conjugal tenderness: "Today is the anniversary of our wedding day. It was twenty-five years ago, I think, that we had the sensible idea of getting married, one we had cherished, it is true, for many years. All good things take time!"[46] Statistics for late eighteenth-century Geneva show that men and women were now far more likely to commit suicide over unhappy marriages or unrequited love, indicating that their expectations of romance and marital felicity were much higher than in the seventeenth century.[47] A Polish wife finished her letter, "I kiss you, the only heart of mine ... on your dearest eyes, lovely mouth, hands, feet, on each toe and finger and each nail on your dearest feet and hands, not once, but a million times."[48] Regardless of their class, wives from across Europe provided evidence that eighteenth-century marriages could be quite romantic and affectionate.

Love often prevailed over parental vetoes, which, in many jurisdictions, held no legal weight. For many of the poorest in early modern Europe, parental control was not the only constraint upon their choice of marriage partner, and this changed only minimally after 1700. The serfs of Eastern Europe had to consider their landlord's wishes, though this had diminished in many jurisdictions after the reforms of Maria Theresa and Joseph II in the latter half of the century.[49] A servant girl in mid-century Finland was brought to court by her former master because she married before her contract with him was up.[50] She was fined in punishment. Hungarian Gypsies were forbidden to marry until they had provided proof that they could survive financially as a couple.[51]

As with modern-day relationships, not all Enlightenment marriages were harmonious. Magdalena Czapska married "a cruel psychopathic character."[52] His threatening letters have survived and indicate his desire for complete mastery over Magdalena:

> ... as a good wife ... you have to be obedient, for all those quarrels between us were caused just by the bad wives' persuasions. ... I wish not to suffer, since this is my idea of a real husband, someone who knows he is a head and not a tail. ... Obey me, please, so that I would not have to give proof that I want to be obeyed and will be ... [H]usbands by submitting to their wives change themselves into four letter things.[53]

By 1750, Magdalena could take no more and fled to a Warsaw convent. There are countless other examples of marital violence in the eighteenth century, but the historiography tends to focus upon whether there was an overall shift in attitudes in Enlightenment Europe. One study of Norwegian husbands shows a decline in wife abuse, attributing it to "the influence of the growing humanitarianism or rationalism" of the age.[54] The majority of Europeanists have a similar interpretation.

Public disapproval of violent husbands should not be equated with an overall benefit for battered wives. If the middle class, especially, regarded violence with more repugnance in the Enlightenment age, they may simply have become more discrete in administering it. Thus, middle-class husbands who beat their wives did so less publicly than in earlier centuries, and the wives themselves felt more ashamed of going to neighbors or police. More recent studies have added greater complexity to this issue, arguing that the real impact of this change was not experienced until the nineteenth century, and that "space, class and gender" had a significant influence over an individual's experience of domestic violence.[55] Certainly, many studies attest to the ongoing involvement of neighbors, servants, and extended kin in helping battered wives throughout the 1700s.

Adultery had long been a common practice among aristocratic families in most of Europe and—despite a possible shift to more affectionate marriages after 1700—the practice persisted into the Enlightenment. Prince Nicholaus of Hungary was reported to keep a mistress, but he went to great lengths to keep her a secret from his wife and father.[56] The Enlightenment age may actually have fostered a more tolerant attitude towards adultery in some circles. Madame du Châtelet, the celebrated Enlightenment scholar who translated Sir Isaac Newton's *Principia Mathematica* into French, was known to have several lovers. Her adultery was sufficiently commonplace that she had a child from her current lover, the Marquis de Saint-Lambert, while cohabitating with Voltaire, her former lover. In Poland, too, wealthy women openly indulged in affairs as part of their political intrigues, behavior that would have been abhorrent in previous centuries.

The unhappy wives of Enlightenment Europe had more opportunities to extricate themselves through separation or divorce, depending upon their nationality. In Geneva, for example, divorces rose dramatically in the second half of the eighteenth century.[57] Magdalena Czapska of Poland sued for a divorce in 1750, though most "moderately wealthy and poor gentry" or burgher Poles could not afford the legal costs.[58] The divorce laws of revolutionary France offered women an unprecedented level of freedom, allowing them divorces even on the grounds of simple incompatibility. In practice, eighteenth-century wives were still limited by a culture and economy that privileged married status. This must have been felt by Frenchwoman Catherine Joret, who sought a divorce in 1795. Her husband generously left her "the cow-shed in his field until the next St. Jean-Baptiste day, for her to live and keep her effects there, she being at present unable to procure any other lodgings."[59] For women like Joret, divorce only opened up a different set of problems.

The poorest women of Europe may actually have been the most free to end bad marriages. Russian peasants could go before the commune, or *mir*, and ask for a divorce in the simplest terms: "I do not wish to live with my husband Ivan because I hate him."[60] In England, eighteenth-century working men might "sell" their wives. It was a barbarous practice on the surface, but one that has been convincingly proven to be a plebeian form of divorce.[61] Generally, all parties were complicit in the exchange, and often the "purchaser" was the wife's lover and the sale a ritual signifying the end of one relationship and the start of another. The poorest city dwellers of Poland seem to have indulged in a similar casual attitude to nuptials, since social controls were more relaxed away from village authorities.[62]

Discussions of the growing availability of divorce, or of increasing affection in marriage, cannot obscure the fact that eighteenth-century wives were still part of a strongly patriarchal society. Their freedoms were limited by a culture and legal system that granted the lion's share of power and rights to husbands. Though there may seem to be more similarities to modern wives than existed in previous centuries, a bride in the Enlightenment age still had vastly different expectations from her twenty-first century counterpart.

WOMEN OUTSIDE MARRIAGE

Early modern European women were identified by their relationship to a man, and the eighteenth century was no exception. Spinsters and widows were so much more than women without husbands, however, and—in Western Europe, at least—they made up about half of the population.[63]

Their very status as single women made them gravitate towards cities. Studies in France, Italy, and Spain showed elder spinsters (those over age 50) to be concentrated in urban areas rather than rural. It seems likely that the women who were unable to find husbands in their villages migrated to towns to earn a living. At first glance, widows and spinsters who left the close confines of village culture—the informal and constant surveillance of the local clergy, magistrates, or even one's own family—may seem more fortunate and liberated. In many ways, however, this migration meant even more poverty. A study of Milan showed that female-headed households were concentrated among the upper floors and attics—much cheaper locations because of the many stairs tenants had to traverse to get to them and the dark, stale air that pervaded them.[64]

By contrast, the spinsters who remained at home may have exalted in their unmarried state. This seems to have been the case with the Lamothe sisters of Bordeaux, France. Though part of their "choice" was probably influenced by family pressure to remain at home, both women took great pride and joy in caring for their family estate and for their father and brothers. Their letters express their interest in maintaining a balanced household budget, performing a wide variety of household tasks with the help of servants, and involving themselves with various philanthropic projects among the poor in their community.[65]

Widows, too, were not always impoverished. When their husbands left them a decent inheritance, they could exercise a fair amount of power over their children and their children's spouses, many of whom resented the wealthy widow for hoarding her property and depriving them of its bounty. Such a fortunate widow had the freedom of choice to remarry, as she was very valuable on the marriage market. A master craftsman's widow could run his workshop in her own right after his death, though in Poland, for example, she was usually limited to two or three years in this capacity before having to close down production or remarry and continue the shop under the new husband's leadership.[66] The latter option again made such widows attractive to suitors.

Of course, single status was not always a choice for the spinsters and widows of eighteenth-century Europe, nor was it frequently liberating. Poorer women, not favored with the beauty, kinship connections, or earning skills that would have made them more valuable in the early modern marriage market, generally faced bleak futures where their mere survival was in the balance. For a widow with more than four living children, "remarriage [was] a necessity if one was to be able to cope with everyday life."[67] Emotional as well as material comforts hung in the balance when one had lost patriarchal protection. Some widows risked losing their children to their late husband's family. Countries like Italy, where the patrilineal system elevated the importance of the male bloodline, allowed widows' former in-laws guardianship of their children.[68]

Young maidens of Eastern Europe who failed to capture a husband were expected to enter a convent or take up a permanent post in domestic service. Even middle-class spinsters who lived in relative comfort with their parents and household servants may have preferred marriage and a home of their own. Nannerl Mozart, for example, still living in her parents' Salzburg apartments in her twenties, "'cried over the merest trifle', shouted at servants, succumbed to illness when crises occurred, . . . and probably imagined that she was destined to be at [her father's] irascible side for the rest of his life."[69] Widowhood or spinsterhood posed at least as many constraints as freedoms for women who found themselves in such a state, and for most impoverished women there were no advantages at all.

Eighteenth-century widows faced considerable difficulties in finding new husbands, despite the fact that their male counterparts—widowers—were *more* likely to remarry than in previous centuries. The demographic changes seen in the Enlightenment age certainly had an impact. People could expect to live longer than ever before, and there was already an imbalanced sex ratio in favor of women. According to one study of eighteenth-century Geneva, there were three times more widows than widowers.[70] Historians of Spain and France have also remarked upon widows' disadvantageous position in the eighteenth-century marriage market.[71]

An examination of the women outside of the institution of marriage cannot be limited to spinsters and widows. Prostitutes and nuns fall into this category as well, and are mentioned elsewhere in the book. Women who cohabited with men outside the institution of marriage also warrant a mention. In Sweden, cohabitation among working-class couples grew with industrialization and urbanization after 1800, but a certain amount of common law couples had always been visible in this part of Europe.[72]

These women occupied an uncertain space in eighteenth-century Europe, their identities oscillating between those of wife and harlot. Even more interesting, perhaps, are the new middle-class women who lived "in sin" with men. English feminist and novelist Mary Wollstonecraft is a prominent example. As one of her characters in *Maria* states:

> matrimony . . . was "the most unsufferable [sic] bondage." Ties of this nature could not bind minds governed by superior principles; and such beings were privileged to act above the dictates of laws they had no voice in framing, if they had sufficient strength of mind to endure the natural consequence.[73]

The eighteenth century saw the opening of more nonmarital unions for women from all walks of life, though they remained a minority.

NOTES

1. Betje Wolff (1779), quoted in Airanne Baggerman and Rudolf Dekker, "The Social World of a Dutch Boy: The Diary of Otto van Eck," in *Emotions in the Household, 1200–1900*, ed. Susan Broomhall (New York: Palgrave Macmillan, 2008), 256.

2. Jean-André Venel, quoted in Antoinette Emch-Dériaz, "Health and Gender Oriented Education: An Eighteenth-Century Case-Study," *Women's Studies* 24, no. 6 (1995), 528.

3. Margaret H. Darrow, "French Noblewomen and the New Domesticity, 1750–1850," *Feminist Studies* 5, no. 1 (Spring 1979), 44.

4. Baggerman and Dekker, 255, 256.

5. Thomas Laqueur, *Making Sex: The Body and Gender from the Greeks to Freud* (Cambridge: Cambridge UP, 1990).

6. L. Lemnius, *The Secret Miracles of Nature . . .* (1658), 19.

7. J. G. Lockhart, *Life of Sir Walter Scott*, (1848), quoted in Ruth Perry, "Colonizing the Breast: Sexuality and Maternity in Eighteenth-Century England," in *Forbidden History: The State, Society, and the Regulation of Sexuality in Modern Europe*, ed. J. Fout (Chicago: U of Chicago P, 1992), 114.

8. Darrow, 56.

9. Rousseau, *Emile*, quoted in John Darling and Maaike van de Pijpekamp, "Rousseau on the Education, Domination and Violation of Women," *British Journal of Educational Studies* 42, no. 2 (1994), 119.

10. Jane Glover, *Mozart's Women: His Family, His Friends, His Music* (London: Macmillan, 2006), 16.

11. Elisabeth Krimmer, "A Garden of Her Own? Noble Savages and Superior Europeans in Sophie von La Roche's *Ercsheinungen am See Oneida* (1798)," in *Harmony in Discord: German Women Writers in the Eighteenth and Nineteenth Centuries*, ed. Laura Martin (Bern: Peter Lang, 2001), 26–27.

12. Hester Chapone, from *Letters on the Improvement of the Mind, Addressed to a Young Lady*, 1773 in *Women in the Eighteenth Century: Constructions of Femininity*, ed. Vivien Jones (London: Routledge, 1990), 104–6

13. Christine Adams, "A Choice Not to Wed? Unmarried Women in Eighteenth-Century France," *Journal of Social History* 29, no. 4 (1996), 889.

14. Linda Pollock, "Parent-Child Relations," in *The History of the European Family, Volume One: Family Life in Early Modern Times 1500–1789*, ed. David I. Kertzer and Marzio Barbagli (New Haven, CT: Yale UP, 2001), 204.

15. Antoinette Fauve-Chamoux, "Continuity and Change among the Rhemish Proletariat: Preindustrial Textile Work in Family Perspective," *History of the Family* 6, no. 2 (2001), 172.

16. Quoted in David S. Reher, *Perspectives on the Family in Spain, Past and Present* (Oxford: Clarendon Press, 1997), 227.

17. Jonas Hanway, *Serious Considerations on the Salutary Design* . . . (1762), quoted in Perry, 110. Emphasis in original.

18. Jean-André Venel, quoted in Emch-Dériaz, 528. For Germany, see Mary Lindemann, "Love for Hire: the Regulation of the Wet-Nursing Business in Eighteenth-Century Hamburg," *Journal of Family History* 6 (1981), 379–80.

19. Jeremy Hayhoe, "Illegitimacy, Inter-generational Conflict and Legal Practice in Eighteenth-Century Northern Burgundy," *Journal of Social History* 38, no. 3 (2005), 673–84.

20. Bilbao y Durán, *Destrucción y conservación de los expósitos*, quoted in Joan Sherwood, *Poverty in Eighteenth-Century Spain: The Women and Children of the Inclusa* (Toronto: U of Toronto P, 1988), 182.

21. Rebecca Gates-Coon, *The Landed Estates of the Esterházy Princes: Hungary during the Reforms of Maria Theresa and Joseph II* (Baltimore, MD: Johns Hopkins UP, 1994), 102.

22. Perry, 123.

23. Emch-Dériaz, 526–27.

24. *Der Patriot*, Hamburger (January 27, 1724), quoted in Lindemann, 381.

25. Dan Dervin, "Childrearing in Central and Eastern Europe," *Journal of Psychohistory* 35, no. 3 (Winter 2008), 220.

26. 4/2:159, case 37, quoted in Barbara Duden, *The Woman beneath the Skin: A Doctor's Patients in Eighteenth-Century Germany*, trans. Thomas Dunlap (Cambridge, MA: Harvard UP, 1991), 169.

27. 4/2:125, case 26, quoted in Duden, 168.

28. Dennis Todd, "Three Characters in Hogarth's *Cunicularii*—and Some Implications," *Eighteenth-Century Studies*, 16, no. 1 (Autumn 1982), 27.

29. Glenda Leslie, "Cheat and Impostor: Debate Following the Case of the Rabbit Breeder," *The Eighteenth Century* 27, no. 3 (1986), 272–73.

30. *The Doctors in Labour; or a New Whim Wham from Guildford*, London, 1726, reprinted in Lisa Cody, "The Doctor's in Labour; or a New Whim Wham from Guildford," *Gender & History* 4, no. 2 (Summer 1992), 178.

31. Ulinka Rublack, "The Public Body: Policing Abortion in Early Modern Germany," in *Gender Relations in German History: Power, Agency and Experience from the Sixteenth to the Twentieth Century*, ed. Lynn Abrams and Elizabeth Harvey (London: UCL Press, 1996), 70–74.

32. Natalia Pushkareva, *Women in Russian History from the Tenth to the Twentieth Century*, ed. and trans. Eve Levin (New York: M.E. Sharpe, 1997), 125.

33. Sandra Cavallo and Simona Cerutti, "Female Honour and the Social Control of Reproduction in Piedmont between 1600 and 1800," in *Sex and Gender in Historical Perspective*, ed. Edward Muir and Guido Ruggiero, trans. Mary M. Gallucci (Baltimore, MD:

Johns Hopkins UP, 1990), 98, and Lloyd Bonfield, "Developments in European Family Law," in *The History of the European Family*, 105.

34. Pushkareva, 155–57.

35. D. Bradley, "Unmarried Cohabitation in Sweden: A Renewed Social Institution?" *Journal of Legal History* 11, no. 2 (1990), 301.

36. David Lemmings, "Marriage and the Law in the Eighteenth Century: Hardwicke's Marriage Act of 1753," *The Historical Journal* 39, no. 2 (1996), 345–47.

37. Cissie Fairchilds, *Domestic Enemies: Servants and Their Masters in Old Regime France* (Baltimore, MD: Johns Hopkins UP, 1984), 175. Note that this applied only to those sons or daughters who had not yet reached their twenty-fifth birthday (i.e., minors).

38. Maria Bogucka, *Women in Early Modern Polish Society, against the European Background* (Aldershot, Hampshire: Ashgate, 2004), 9.

39. Pushkareva, 159.

40. Kirsi Ojala, "Servants' Social Networks and Relationships in Eighteenth-Century Turku and Odense," in *Emotions in the Household, 1200–1900*, 214.

41. Fauve-Chamoux, "Marriage, Widowhood, and Divorce," 225, 228. See also Tamás Faragó, "The Seasonality of Marriages in Hungary from the Eighteenth to the Twentieth Century," *Journal of Family History* 19, no. 4 (1994), 333–50.

42. Fauve-Chamoux, "Marriage, Widowhood, and Divorce," 241.

43. Bogucka, 4. See also Jarl Lindgren, *Towards Smaller Families in the Changing Society: Fertility Transition during the First Phase of Industrialization in Three Finnish Municipalities* (Helsinki: The Population Research Institute, 1984), 97.

44. Reher, 152, 169–70.

45. Lawrence Stone, *The Family, Sex and Marriage in England, 1500–1800*, abridged edn. (London: Penguin, 1990); Philippe Ariès, *Centuries of Childhood: A Social History of Family Life*, trans. Robert Baldick (New York: Vintage Books, 1962); and Edward Shorter, *The Making of the Modern Family* (New York: Basic Books, 1975).

46. Leopold Mozart, quoted in Glover, 45.

47. Jeffrey R. Watt, "The Family, Love and Suicide in Early Modern Geneva," *Journal of Family History* 21, no. 1 (1996), 69–73.

48. Letter of Konstanja Czapska to her husband, 1735, quoted in Bogucka, 22. See also Gates-Coon, 14.

49. Gates-Coon, 97.

50. Ojala, 206.

51. Gates-Coon, 154.

52. Bogucka, 18.

53. Hieronim Florian Radziwiłł, quoted in Bogucka, 19.

54. Ferdinand Linthoe Naeshagen, "Private Law Enforcement in Norwegian History: The Husband's Right to Chastise His Wife," *Scandinavian Journal of History* 27, no. 1 (2002), 27.

55. E. Foyster, *Marital Violence: An English Family History, 1660–1857* (Cambridge: Cambridge UP, 2005), 233 and Joanne Bailey, " 'I Dye by Inches': Locating Wife Beating in the Concept of a Privatization of Marriage and Violence in Eighteenth-Century," *Social History* 31, no. 3 (2006), 22.

56. Gates-Coon, 14, 17. For Russia, see Pushkareva, 165.

57. Watt, 73.

58. Bogucka, 20.

59. Quoted in Roderick Phillips, "Women's Emancipation, the Family, and Social Change in Eighteenth-Century France," *Journal of Social History* 12, no. 4 (Summer 1979), 561.
60. Quoted in Pushkareva, 169.
61. E. P. Thompson, *Customs in Common* (New York: The New Press, 1991), 404–66.
62. Bogucka, 20.
63. In Eastern Europe, only 30 percent of the women aged 15–50 lived as widows or nuns (spinsters), which Fauve-Chamoux parallels with non-European marriage patterns. Fauve-Chamoux, "Marriage, Widowhood, and Divorce," 224–25. Susan Cotts Watkins also attributes the prevalence of single women to the late age of marriage in Western Europe, which meant that there were always lots of women on the landscape who had not yet married and needed employment as servants or agricultural workers, and thus "the example of single, self-supporting adult woman was set." Susan Cotts Watkins, "Spinsters," *Journal of Family History* 9, no. 4 (1984), 317.
64. Maura Palazzi, "Female Solitude and Patrilineage: Unmarried Women and Widows during the Eighteenth and Nineteenth Centuries," *Journal of Family History* 15, no. 4 (1990), 454–55.
65. Adams, "A Choice Not to Wed?" 883–94.
66. Bogucka, 28, 50–51.
67. Fauve-Chamoux, "Marriage, Widowhood, and Divorce," 242. Gates-Coon, 137, placed such widows in the category of "extreme poverty," and Reher offers a similar assessment of Spanish widows' lot.
68. Palazzi, 448.
69. Glover, 97.
70. Watt, 67.
71. Reher, 212, Fauve-Chamoux, "Marriage, Widowhood, and Divorce," 242–43.
72. Bradley, 303.
73. *Posthumous Works of the Author of a Vindication of the Rights of Women* (London, 1798), quoted in Emily Sunstein, *A Different Face: The Life of Mary Wollstonecraft* (New York: Harper & Row, 1975), 241.

SUGGESTED READING

Adams, Christine. *A Taste for Comfort and Status: A Bourgeois Family in Eighteenth-Century France*. University Park: Pennsylvania State UP, 2000.
Ariès, Philippe. *Centuries of Childhood: A Social History of Family Life*. Robert Baldick, trans. New York: Vintage Books, 1962.
Bailey, Joanne. *Unquiet Lives: Marriage and Marriage Breakdown in England, 1660–1800*. Cambridge: Cambridge UP, 2003.
Bogucka, Maria. *Women in Early Modern Polish Society, against the European Background*. Aldershot, Hampshire: Ashgate, 2004.
Broomhall, Susan, ed. *Emotions in the Household, 1200–1900*. New York: Palgrave Macmillan, 2008.
Kertzer, David I., and Marzio Barbagli, eds. *The History of the European Family, Volume One: Family Life in Early Modern Times 1500–1789*. New Haven, CT: Yale UP, 2001.
Laqueur, Thomas. *Making Sex: The Body and Gender from the Greeks to Freud*. Cambridge: Cambridge UP, 1990.

Perry, Ruth. "Colonizing the Breast: Sexuality and Maternity in Eighteenth-Century England." In *Forbidden History: The State, Society, and the Regulation of Sexuality in Modern Europe*, edited by J. Fout. Chicago: U of Chicago P, 1992.

Phillips, Roderick. *Untying the Knot: A Short History of Divorce*. Cambridge: Cambridge UP, 1991.

Pollock, Linda. *Forgotten Children: Parent-Child Relations from 1500–1900*. Cambridge: Cambridge UP, 1983.

Reher, David S. *Perspectives on the Family in Spain, Past and Present*. Oxford: Clarendon P, 1997.

Stone, Lawrence. *The Family, Sex and Marriage in England, 1500–1800*. Abridged ed. London: Penguin, 1990.

2

Women and Work

Though European women's work experienced significant change in the eighteenth century, many of its fundamental features remained the same. While it became harder and harder for women to find regular work in the fields, they still sat at their spinning wheels, only for longer hours and piecework rates of pay. Female laborers still received lower wages for similar tasks and worked in subordinate positions. The Enlightenment era brought with it a population explosion, which helped to trigger wars, famine, and agricultural reforms that placed significant hardship on Europe's workers. When new industrial opportunities opened to them, they were often swallowed up by the increasingly protectionist, male-dominated guilds. They coped with these difficulties as they always had, finding new niches in sectors such as domestic service and seamstressing. When times became extremely tough, they turned to the parish for aid, or indulged in a variety of subsistence trades. As with their forbears, the story of women's work in the Enlightenment age is one of survival despite overwhelming odds.

DOMESTIC WORKERS

Almost all of the workers discussed here could reasonably be called domestic workers, because almost all of women's work in early modern Europe—and men's, for that matter—took place in and around the household. Farmers' wives and daughters combined cooking and childcare with other domestic tasks; artisans' wives and daughters performed a similar juggling act in the workshops that doubled as living space. At the same time, however, historians argue that a concept of separation between domestic and public spheres was emerging in the late eighteenth century, particularly among the middle classes.

Wives and daughters of the lawyers, doctors, and other professional men of eighteenth-century Europe would have been unable to work by their side in the same way as an artisan or farmer's wife. Thus, as the ranks of this professional class grew in the eighteenth century, so, too, did the visibility of the more domestically focused work of its female members. The detailed study of the family of Bordeaux lawyer Daniel Lamothe provides ample evidence of a gender divided system of labor. Though they had servants to do the most menial tasks, the Lamothe women were always very busy at a variety of household projects. They knitted, mended, cooked, and baked. They shopped and maintained a very careful household budget. In 1758, Marie Lamothe wrote her brother an extensive report that shows her control over the domestic economy, which included selling "six and a half tonneaux" of wines they had produced from the grapes grown on their estate.[1] Her pride in her knowledge of these "tedious details" is as evident as her complacency in their lack of importance to her brother.

The same was true for the rest of Europe. In Poland, for example, the mistress of the manor bred cattle and raised chickens. The proceeds from the milk, butter, cheese, eggs, and meat they produced made a substantial contribution to household coffers.[2] Women were also often the purchasers of domestic goods. The rise of consumer goods in the eighteenth century meant that middle class women's role in this regard was enhanced as well. Though recent research emphasizes that men, too, played a key role in the consumption that drove the eighteenth-century marketplace, it is nonetheless clear that certain purchases were more feminine. Late eighteenth-century Hamburg boasted new manufactures of "wallpaper, playing cards, enamels, powder, starch, straw hats, twine, precision instruments, umbrellas, bedding, and corks"—most of which would have been purchased by feminine consumers.[3] John Gay's 1725 poem "To a Lady on her Passion for old China" only moderately exaggerates the attraction of tea services for the female sex:

> China's the passion of her soul;
> A cup, a plate, a dish, a bowl
> Can kindle wishes in her breast,
> Inflame with joy, or break her rest....
> Husbands more covetous than sage
> Condemn this China-buying rage;
> They count that woman's prudence little;
> Who sets her heart on things so brittle.
> But are those wise-men's inclinations
> Fixt on more strong, more sure foundations?[4]

Women are seen (lower-left foreground) in the eighteenth-century marketplace of A view of ye great clock in St. Mark's place at Venice, engraving of painting by Canaletto (ca. 1715–1738). (Courtesy of Library of Congress)

While they may not have been the sole driving force of eighteenth-century consumerism, the middle-class women of the Enlightenment age saw consumption as part of their domestic responsibilities.

The rise in consumer goods triggered a corresponding growth in the number of shops, many of which staffed female assistants. Across Europe, those who ran retail establishments—both male and female—often employed servants who would either run errands for them while they presided over the shop, or would tend the counter in order to free their master or mistress to venture out-of-doors. This role could also be undertaken by apprentices. One such apprentice was depicted in an English play in 1778. "Miss Jenny" presided over a millinery shop while her mistress went out, later reporting that "nobody to Signify" had been in to buy a hat during the proprietress' absence.[5] As the largest city in Europe by the end of the century, London had the most sophisticated shops and would have had the most call for female shop assistants.

Women's presence as purveyors of food and drink in inns and taverns was a logical extension of their domestic role. Records exist throughout Europe testifying to female prominence in these trades. Stockholm authorities passed a law in 1747 that reserved innkeeping licences for "poor widows and married women who were disabled because of an accident, and could not support themselves or be supported by their husbands."[6] Many European women had been involved in such trades—including food and beverage sales and lodging-housekeeping—for several centuries leading up to the Enlightenment age, and the nature of the work had changed little. It did grow in volume, however, as the eighteenth-century demographic explosion caused more people to move to cities. As early as 1571 in the French municipality of Nantes, more than one-third of all of the tavern keepers and innkeepers were female.[7]

Women's domestic role is also visible among the poorer classes who faced the economic difficulties of the eighteenth century. War, famine, and agricultural reforms posed significant hardships for plebeian women across Europe. The century saw numerous riots and protests where women were highly visible participants, and their involvement was often justified by the same imagery that glorified middle class women's domestic work. As the buyers or bakers of bread, women were prominent participants in riots over high grain prices.[8]

Until the eighteenth century, local corporations and governments had closely scrutinized and controlled the marketplace, with a long history of rules governing wages, prices, and a host of other aspects of economic life. In England, this has been dubbed the "moral economy."[9] As Enlightenment thinking began to replace the traditional moral economy with a more laissez-faire "political economy" that appeared to benefit only the rich, plebeian women took action (on their own, or with men) to try to restore traditional economic practices.

This was visible in a variety of ways. A group of women descended upon a French farm in the village of Louvres, "carrying out wheat for which they had not paid" when it had been put up for sale at too high a price in 1775.[10] High grain prices also provoked Madrid's working-class women to rebel in March of 1766. The Rising of the Esquilache, as it was called, involved groups of women singing songs of defiance all over Madrid—even going so far as to congregate beneath the windows of the local nobility. Such feminine protests evoked enough fear among the authorities to cause them to pass a law prohibiting women from congregating in numbers of five or greater in Madrid's poorest neighborhoods.[11] Hungarian women "armed with rocks and sticks" joined the men of their village to protect their pasture rights against other villages, or participated in other resistance movements against local lords.[12] The pressures wrought by rapid demographic growth and shifts in agricultural practice placed severe burdens upon the poor that erupted in outbreaks of riot and protest throughout Europe by the second half of the century. In these actions, women were often as visible as men.

RURAL LABORERS

Agricultural reforms had a significant impact upon women's work in the countryside. By the end of the eighteenth century, the population increases and the adoption of new cultivation techniques hurt rural workers more than those in other economic sectors. The enclosure movement, whereby large landowners consolidated smaller farms into larger ones, accelerated after the mid-century, causing a flood of migrant workers to the cities. Ireland, Germany, and Italy saw large portions of marshlands drained and brought into cultivation. In the Trans-Danubian region, Hungarian landlords expropriated peasants' lands and pastured their livestock in meadows where villagers' animals had traditionally grazed. The new agricultural experiments had little to do with mechanization, but were instead trials of different crops that would restore nitrogen to the soil and therefore eliminate the need for a fallow-field rotation. Thus, the same plot of soil could yield more crops with less workers.

The brunt of the change was borne by female agricultural laborers, who were the first to be turned away from jobs. The late-century English caricature depicting a happy (and fat) female laborer hand-in-hand with a lascivious farmer captured a disappearing breed. Employers, who also paid the poor relief rates, were more likely to hire men, in the hopes that it would

Happy farmer and shepherdess holding hands, with caption "Together let us range the Fields," watercolor and ink drawing by G. M. Woodward (ca. 1790–1809). (Courtesy of Library of Congress)

keep their families off the relief rolls. In places like Sweden, the female rural laborer had begun to disappear from the landscape by 1800.[13] The same was true of Spain. In the Castillian countryside, *labradores* or *vecinos* (small independent farmers) constituted 64 percent of rural workers in 1750, but only 36 percent fifty years later, meaning that a whopping 64 percent of the workforce by then consisted of landless day laborers.[14]

When they could find it, women's agricultural work was essentially the same across Europe. It followed the rhythm of the harvests, and in order to stretch their periods of employment as much as possible, both women and men traveled significant distances for work. English women picked hops, fruit, and vegetables in various locations, and then might have taken up craftwork in nearby towns in the interim.[15] Accounts exist in Germany of all-female or mixed-sex gangs that would travel about the countryside to find work at various harvesting tasks.[16] Spanish women in Cuenca helped harvest grapes in La Mancha and olives in Andalusia.[17]

Very few agricultural tasks were considered too heavy for women to perform. Europe's feudal societies took their pound of flesh from female agricultural workers as well as from male workers. One German farmer's widow in Ebhausen had to cart bricks to the village church—no light task—as part of the community corvée in 1757.[18] Polish peasant women worked at least half of each week along with the men in their lord's fields to meet their feudal obligations. Their Russian counterparts could also be found performing a wide range of activities, ranging from stacking hay to pounding flax and hemp. Alternatively, when men such as those of Oldenburg and Friezland in Germany were ordered to "leave [their] work and go" to do twenty days of repairs and maintenance to roads within the region, their wives were then responsible for all aspects of the farm work in their absence.[19] Femininity did little to mitigate the agricultural burdens of serfdom.

Those in free labor markets fared little better. As with other types of labor, harvest work paid women considerably less than men for similar tasks. In the period from 1768–1785, the mean average wage of Englishwomen hired at Lincolnshire hiring fairs was "well below half" that of men.[20] The use of sickles and scythes further illustrates this point. The scythe—a tool that had been gendered male because of the height and strength required to use it—became the favored harvesting instrument for a variety of crops by the eighteenth century. Because women were limited to using a sickle, their work as reapers became increasingly devalued, earning them as little as 44 percent of male wages for the same job in 1725.[21]

Agricultural work was not the only gainful employment for rural women, though it tended to be the most popular. By the eighteenth century, cottage industries were well developed across Europe. Also known as the "putting-out system" or "proto-industrialization," the small-scale manufacturing work of farming families is now considered to have laid the groundwork for the factories of the nineteenth and twentieth centuries. Workers in cottage industries engaged in manufacturing goods that could be broken down into piecework, with different families employed at various stages of production. The entire process could be controlled by a so-called middle man, who provided workers with the materials and paid them piece rates—usually very low—for their work. These middle men tended to deal with the household head, but it was the entire family—especially its female members—who engaged in the required labors.

A variety of goods fit well into this proto-industrial production. In England, lace, button, and glove making, as well as straw plaiting, occupied many eighteenth-century farm wives and children. In Switzerland, linen, fustians, cotton, silk, and wool production took place in cottage industries. The textile trades made up the lion's share of proto-industrial activity, with different regions often specializing in a particular product. The southern parts of Germany and France were known, respectively, for producing linen and silk, for example.

Women participated in proto-industry at every level. The Canton of Zurich in Switzerland has an account of at least one eighteenth-century woman who acted as a middle man. She bought spun cotton and distributed it among a group of surrounding cottages. She paid her workers with bread she had baked.[22] In one seventeenth-century German example, a wife is clearly recorded as dealing directly with woollen weavers to whom her husband had given raw wool, and was much more assertive than he in the collection of the woven cloth.[23] More often, wives and daughters were left to run the household in the head's absence, or depart themselves on various trade-related errands. Swiss records show one daughter claiming that she had been sent on a task in 1699 to a village ten kilometers away, where her family had placed cotton with several weavers and spinners.[24] Women were engaged in the cottage system in a wide variety of ways.

Most often, however, they were the silent workers in the putting-out system. Thousands of women worked as spinners of wool, flax, and cotton across Western Europe. One German study found 60 percent of all of the widows in the community made their living by spinning.[25] Three-quarters of all of the French women in the Caux region and 80 percent of the Scots women in the linen-producing regions worked as spinners.[26] English research shows that seven to ten spinners were needed to equip a single weaver with sufficient yarn, so the undervalued feminine half of the agricultural work force was a natural fit to act as subordinate spinners to a single male weaver.[27]

The exploitation of Europe's spinners stands as yet another example of the extent of patriarchal control in early modern society. Württemburg's spinners were required by law to sell their wool to German weavers' guilds, despite the existence of foreign buyers offering better prices. The same was true of Swiss cotton production, where women performed the spinning, spooling, and warping tasks, leaving more profitable weaving to men.[28]

The eighteenth century also saw innovation in technologies that would eventually bring about the decline of hand-spinning, knitting, and weaving. Though some women gained employment in the new factories that began to sprout up, the majority of manual workers continued producing textiles for ever-decreasing wages. In Ireland, for example, a County Armagh factory owner observed that the "low price of labor" made hand-spun yarn "much cheaper than the same article manufactured by machinery in England."[29] The French experience of mechanization was mixed. In Rheims, linen weavers lost their market and failed to adopt the new mechanical techniques that might have ensured their survival. The same occurred in Champagne. Troyes was unique in experiencing overall positive efforts, its hosiery industry expanding with the help of new framework knitting machines.[30] Even here, however, the stocking frame often had to be rented from the middle man, resulting in further loss of control for cottage hosiers over the tools of production.

DOMESTIC SERVANTS

The growth in waged labor and the redefinition of the family lie at the root of fundamental shifts in domestic employment in the eighteenth century. Rather than earlier patriarchal arrangements, where a maid would have lived alongside her employers as part of the family, by this period she was separated from them. She slept far above their chambers in a bed under the eaves, prepared their meals in a cellar well below them, and went about her other household tasks in a back staircase so as to intrude as little as possible into the domestic privacy of her bourgeois master. As just another waged worker, the servant experienced a decline in status, which in turn made this occupation increasingly associated with women. Female servants were cheaper, so many jobs that had formerly been performed by men, such as cooking, became feminized. This was visible across northwestern Europe. In Aix, France, women made up 70 percent of domestic service labor in the 1700s and 90 percent by the 1790s.[31] In southeastern Europe, by contrast, where domestic service was a lifetime occupation—rather than an interim stage between the departure from the parental home and marriage, women had always outnumbered male servants.

There was often enormous disparity between the wages of female and male domestics. In the English Earl of Ilchester's household, for example, the house steward was paid an annual wage of £100 in the 1780s, while his female equivalent, the head housekeeper, received only £20.[32] One Italian maidservant was recorded as earning a salary equal to only one-fifth of that earned by a man.[33] It makes sense that employers who were now forced to offer wages rather than just bed and board would begin to prefer to hire female servants. This, teamed with the fact that female agricultural jobs were being snapped up by boys, drove women into the cities to find work as servants. A Swedish observer in 1741 noted that, "among rural migrants to the cities, females predominate, because they are less needed in agriculture than men, and they can easily find work as servants in the cities."[34] This was not true of everywhere across Europe. In eighteenth-century Spain, domestic servants seem to have been in less demand. Maids tended to be hired only when the household had little or no women of its own to perform typically feminine tasks like cooking, cleaning, and child-rearing.

Lest this image of single women flocking to cities be interpreted as liberation, there were many constraints imposed upon housemaids. In England, the courts allowed local officials to force any girl over the age of twelve into service, and the same law could be used by employers to compel her to remain with them. It effectively crippled female servants' bargaining abilities for improvements in salary and working conditions. The same did not apply to male servants; the law was informed by a patriarchal fear of bastardy or other ill effects that could result from having women run rampant in society without a clear master. German girls, too, could be ordered into service by the courts for a variety of reasons, including, but not confined to, the threat they posed as masterless girls. The Wildberg archives contain a case from 1777 in which a young woman was forced to work as a maidservant because she was too "idle" in her parents' home.[35]

At the same time, eighteenth-century maids may have been less subject than their predecessors to physical and sexual assault. Europeans' growing distaste for violence extended to female servants, especially. A Finnish town court intervened several times against one local artisan who was known to mistreat his servant girls. The surgeon who treated their injuries voiced his concerns to the authorities, for which the craftsman was given stern reprimands.[36] Quantitative studies show an overall decrease in evidence of master-servant sexual relations during the eighteenth century as well. In Aix and Nantes, for example, the number of maids charging their masters with impregnating them was a visibly smaller proportion of all bastardy claims in the second half of the eighteenth century compared to the first half.[37] This is generally deemed the product of the new desire for privacy in middle-class and elite households. The spatial separation of servants and their employers, teamed with a new sensibility that retreated from many of the bodily intimacies that characterized earlier domestic duties—such as bathing and dressing—lessened the opportunities for seduction.

The eighteenth-century housemaid also enjoyed better earning potential than many of her working-class contemporaries in other industries. On the surface, her wages were not especially good, but the bed and board that augmented her pay made this line of work among the most lucrative for lower-class women. Servants in traditional aristocratic posts, such as the Esterházy princes in Hungary, were given extravagant gifts and perquisites for loyal service. These might have been dispensed at New Year's celebrations, or after a successful visit of a royal personage such as Maria Theresa.[38] In Finland, the most devoted head housemaids were awarded a silver locket or chain.[39] The late eighteenth century saw an inflation in the costs of food and shelter. While those in other trades had to compensate with a decline in their real wages, domestic servants continued to enjoy these things at their employers' provision. Also, the salaries of domestic workers rose at a much higher rate than other sectors during this century.

MIDWIVES

The time-honored tradition of female midwifery began to decline in the Enlightenment age. The second half of the eighteenth century, in particular, saw the encroachment of male medical practitioners into obstetrics across Europe. The process was complex, not exclusively driven by the men themselves or by the state, or by the choices of birthing mothers, but rather by a combination of the three. In Italy, unlike the north and west of Europe, neither the childbearing women nor the church wanted a male surgeon presiding over deliveries, so many women continued to practice as midwives throughout the century.[40] Most pregnant middle-class women in the rest of Europe, with their growing concerns for respectability, rejected traditional lying-in rituals, where neighborhood women crowded the birthing chamber. This image did not fit as nicely with the companionate marriage and domestic privacy of the Enlightenment bourgeoisie.

Enlightenment concerns also caused a shift away from the guild style self-regulation of many early modern midwives to more state oversight. Spanish King Fernando issued a warrant in 1750, explicitly addressing "the lack of skill of midwives and some men, who to earn a living, have taken up the practice of midwifery."[41] The new policy encouraged formal education in obstetrics for midwives, physicians, and surgeons. In practice, this resulted in a clear hierarchy of medical practitioners that relegated midwives to the bottom, and made them entirely dependant upon male surgical professors for their education. Women's training gained a reputation for being markedly less rigorous and wide-ranging than that accorded male students. Similar training programs were launched throughout Europe.

As workers, midwives' experience was mixed. The church courts of Germany that licensed midwives paid them very little.[42] In Spain, too, women engaged in the trade earned paltry sums, though more than barbers.[43] Those who assisted midwives fared even worse. German midwife Antoinette Elisabeth Becker despaired of procuring a warming-woman to assist her in her work "because they can expect to earn nothing, and they are scared away by the fact that they must pay Professor Wagler thirty thaler pro informatione [for their instruction in midwifery]."[44] In rare cases, the reforms of the eighteenth century actually served to protect the profession. This was certainly the case in Holland, where *stadsvroedvrouwen*—municipal midwives with formal training and licensing—were increasingly employed to attend pregnant women among the urban poor.[45]

Those who practiced at the margins—the unlicensed village "cunning women" and "quacks"—formed a silent majority of women presiding over births in eighteenth-century Europe. There were too few licensed midwives to deal with all the births in most jurisdictions. Sometimes these local experienced women were preferred even when the official midwife was available. Such practices prompted Wildberg officials to threaten expectant couples with fines if they did not hire the licensed midwife in 1773.[46] Hungarian estate records refer to a "so-called Tyrolese doctor" who traveled around the countryside administering to various ills. Her abilities garnered her testimonials of more than ten people whom she had "cured . . . for a few groschen, when other assistance would have been far more expensive."[47] There is much in the surviving records to indicate that the women who worked as midwives and healers in eighteenth-century Europe took pride in their own abilities and felt a sense of professionalism that was independent of state sanction.

GOVERNESSES

A new vocation was emerging for women in the age of Enlightenment, which would reach its true zenith in the following century. Though the eighteenth century was not the first in which governesses were known to exist, it was the first to stress the importance of education for boys and girls of all classes. The *philosophes'* emphasis on this point meant that the most progressive parents were eager to find appropriate instruction for their children. The result was the opening of many more opportunities in the governess field and a rise in its occupational status. Throughout most of the eighteenth century, only aristocratic couples could afford to fully indulge and hire a governess, but by 1800, the *nouveau-riches* among the emerging middle classes were able to invite such women into their households. There are more accounts of the former because those households' papers were more likely to be preserved, but Eliza Bishop serves as an example of a governess for the latter. Her employer, a Mr. Tasker who had made his money in the East India Company, was one of the new upwardly mobile "self-made" men who wanted to educate his heirs in the new Enlightenment fashion.[48]

The new intellectual climate promoted teaching through play and experience rather than by rote repetition. In the words of Richard and Maria Edgeworth, authors of the 1798 publication *Practical Education*: "the danger of doing too much in education is greater even than the danger of doing too little."[49] Mme de Genlis, *governante* to the children of the Duc d'Orléans in France, violated many traditions with a truly enlightenment-inspired curriculum. Both girls and boys learned together in her classroom and were exposed to a variety of unconventional lessons, from rope climbing to the workings of local factories. She, like the Edgeworths, wrote pedagogical treatises and is proof of the rising status and respect that was awarded to a governess in Enlightenment culture. Agnes Porter, governess to the children of Britain's Earl of Ilchester from 1785–1797, keenly implemented the educational theories of Genlis and the Edgeworths. Her pride in the success of these new techniques is evident in her diary where she noted that, in the eyes of her eager young charges, "the grand punishment for misconduct is not to allow them to do their studies."[50]

Governesses were usually middle-class women themselves, whose families had fallen upon hard times. Women of this social background faced limited options for survival if they had no parents or husband to provide for them. Unlike those lower on the social scale, gentry women could not remain respectable and earn a living by trade of any sort. Governessing allowed them to maintain themselves and keep the few shreds of dignity that remained to them. After 1775, the government of Austria offered education to orphaned daughters of military officers to give them future livelihoods as governesses.[51] Aristocratic daughters fleeing revolutionary France took up governessing posts among the Russian nobility and helped to fuel a trend that resulted in the adoption of French as the language of the Russian aristocrat.[52]

The governess occupied a difficult position in her employer's household. With breeding and manners that set her apart from fellow servants, but clearly lacking the means to be identified with her master's status, the governess straddled both camps in great discomfort. One of the most famous of the eighteenth-century governesses, English author Mary Wollstonecraft, wrote:

> It is impossible to enumerate the many hours of anguish such a person must spend. Above the servants yet considered by them as a spy, and ever reminded of her inferiority when in conversation with the superiors. If she cannot condescend to mean flattery, she has not a chance of being a favourite; and should any of the visitors take notice of her, and she for a moment forget her subordinate state, she is sure to be reminded of it.[53]

Long hours and mediocre pay compounded the miseries of the job. It is not surprising that even the apparently happy Agnes Porter longed for the relative freedoms and status of wifehood and was "desperately angling for a husband" throughout most of her service as governess for the Earl of Ilchester.[54]

Mary Wollstonecraft, engraving of painting by John Opie (1797). (Courtesy of Library of Congress)

URBAN CRAFTSWOMEN

Guilds had long been protective of their monopoly in manufacturing, which generally had the effect of limiting women's freedoms to partake fully in the profits of any craft. Germany, for example, strictly enforced guild regulations to exclude women from the majority of craftwork, unlike France, where, by the last quarter of the century, women could manufacture a variety of products in so-called grey markets that escaped guild or state censure.[55] Poland, too, almost universally denied women guild memberships in their own right, though a special concession was often allowed to masters' widows. Occasionally though, certain guilds—like the butchers and basket-makers of Danzig, an especially prosperous industrial town—allowed female membership.[56] Even when they were permitted to engage in their husband's craft, European masters' widows were generally prohibited from many of the cost-saving measures allowed male guild members, such as employing cheap apprentices or enlisting their daughters' help.

The putting-out style of production familiar to rural workers existed in urban environments as well. Britain's silk-weaving industry, based mainly in London, had long hired women, but they tended to perform support work for a male weaver. Female tasks were considered menial and were much lower paid; they included winding the silk, setting up the warp to be woven (or "warping"), and twisting the silk fibers to make the threads (known as "twisting"). These women tended to be weavers' wives and daughters who worked in their homes.[57] Indeed, guilds across Europe responded to the putting-out system by excluding women from holding independent artisan status.

Many European women found new opportunities in the sewing trades because of the increased consumerism of the eighteenth century. With more middle-class women sporting a variety of hats, gloves, stays, and bodices—all elaborately decorated with lace and embroidery, a large body of seamstresses and other skilled needlewomen was required to produce them. Though male tailors tenaciously maintained their monopoly of commerce in male coats, jackets, and riding habits, they ceded some of the trade in feminine fineries to their female counterparts. Lest this appear to be too much of a coup for this sector of women's work, the dressmaking and millinery trades were very hard and uncertain, "with long hours, strained eyes and bad pay."[58] Würtemburg seamstresses, for example, earned less than even the young boys apprenticed to tailors.[59]

Like bakers and linen guilds, seamstresses were considered lesser because their work was not easily separated from tasks performed in any rural household. While it was comparatively straightforward to understand a trade like silversmithing as a commercial enterprise, it was not so easy to distinguish between making bread or sewing for profit and making the same goods for one's family. This made it difficult for these guilds to monitor and control production, and they became devalued as a result. Their loss of status, in turn, made it more likely that women would be allowed to participate in these particular craft guilds.

Needlework might have been the only skill a woman possessed, and it would have become her only source of survival in hard times. Often, such work could be as nomadic as that of day laborers following the harvest. A German seamstress was described by her brother-in-law in 1752 as having "only . . . her sleeping-place with him, and spend[ing] her entire time as a seamstress in other houses."[60] The earning potential was often very meager. One middle-class English girl who found herself in dire straits attempted to survive on the proceeds of needlework. Even with two women working together, she lamented, "it is utterly impossible" to earn more than "would just pay for furnished lodgings," leaving food and other necessaries unobtainable. This, she added, was "supposing they had constant employment, which is of all things the most uncertain."[61] The record of a thirty-eight-year-old widowed seamstress applying to Turin's poor relief officials in 1754 attests to the desperate plight of many needlewomen. When her application for aid for herself and her three children was granted only on the condition that she give up her eldest daughter to the workhouse, she refused, and has since disappeared from history.[62] Indeed, it is difficult to clearly distinguish the craftswomen in eighteenth-century Europe from those just scraping by in so-called hand-to-mouth trades.

SUPPLICANTS FOR AID AND WOMEN IN HAND-TO-MOUTH TRADES

It is not surprising that women, burdened as they were with pregnancies and childbirth, and already disadvantaged by economic systems that left them subordinate, were prominent among the poor of eighteenth-century Europe. Only one-third of the 866 inmates listed for an Italian poorhouse in 1713 were male; the rest were all girls and women who found themselves with nowhere else to turn.[63] The poorhouse, almsgiving, and various forms of parish relief were the point of last resort for many women in early modern Europe. The response to pauperism was culturally dependant and varied across the continent. In Switzerland, for example, relief for the poor was considered the responsibility of the wealthy. Thus, it was customary to see wills like that of Etienne de Rivaz, asking in 1750 that a portion of his estate be used for such things as "dress[ing] six poor people from head to feet."[64]

European attitudes towards the poor had undergone a long-term transition since the Middle Ages. The medieval Christian notion of "the poor of Christ" as constant and deserving of indiscriminate benevolence had eroded with the Renaissance and the Reformation in the fifteenth and sixteenth centuries. By the eighteenth century, the responsibility for dispensing charity had largely moved from church to municipality. Relief was also to be applied in a way that separated those who "deserved" it because their poverty came from a genuine inability to work and those who had fallen on hard times through idleness or vice. Almsgiving in its traditional forms was made illegal in many jurisdictions. Supplicants to relief systems generally had to meet certain criteria to qualify for aid. This meant establishing proof of residence in the municipality, among other things. As the ranks of the impoverished grew, so, too, did the strictness of the criteria for granting relief.

Many eighteenth-century reformers wrote about the poor as a growing problem in Europe during this period. This century's demographic growth, combined with the effects of failed harvests and military campaigns, enhanced their perception that the ranks of the poor were increasing and were posing a danger to the health and safety of rate-paying citizens. Enlightenment rationality was applied to the problem of poverty with the same idealism with which it was applied to other social and political issues. If mendicants could be retrained in useful occupations, they could transform from a source of fear and criminality into useful contributors to the state and economy.

One such plan in late eighteenth-century Hamburg saw the municipality create its own cottage industry, acting as the middle man while able paupers provided the labor. It opened a spinning school, and everyone applying for relief who lacked these skills was required to attend, "whether he desires it or not."[65] Graduates were provided with flax and loaned wheels or spindles. The earliest reports on the experiment were deceptively glowing: some 500 women, it claimed, "creatures once dependent on charity," were now getting at least a pittance from their own labor.[66] Other European cities, such as Turin, Italy, chose instead to offer training through workhouses. Upon admission, women were segregated from men and were forbidden to talk except for the singing of hymns or the recitation of the rosary, or for brief periods of recreation in the evening. They spent six days each week working, mainly at tasks related to the textile trades, similar to the Hamburg experiment.[67]

The early idealism of Enlightenment reformers was soon beset with failures—not the least of which being the attitudes of the pauper women themselves. Charitable institutions across Europe continued to experience the age-old resistance and defiance of mendicants protesting the conditions of their relief. Hungarian beggar Magdalena Glässlin caused so many problems for her benefactors in 1779 that she was ejected from the building and housed in the animals' stall, after which she was eventually sent to the "St. Marx hospital for the mentally ill" in Vienna.[68] Isabella Cornaglia of Turin was cut off from her weekly bread allowance in 1755 because of her bad attitude (*irritabilita*).[69]

Aid was not always forthcoming. Women who applied to parishes might be turned away for a variety of reasons, or admitted but given conditions—such as that of having to enter a workhouse—that they were not willing to accept. These women had to find other sources of survival. As mentioned earlier, the hand-to-mouth trades were many and varied, including seamstressing and spinning. Virtually any type of work could fall into this category for those at the bottom of the labor pyramid. Domestic servants without a permanent position might get a day's work during spring cleaning or a funeral, for example.

Women were also to be found peddling a wide variety of goods that garnered them a bare subsistence. The Ebhausen archives in Germany contain an account of a thirty-two-year-old unmarried woman supporting herself selling "nuts and other items" some distance from her home.[70] Their very femininity may have suited them to this type of work in particular. The Spanish maidens who sold oranges, chestnuts, or flowers certainly used their beauty to increase custom. Their reputation for being "flamboyant and temperamental" was also related to the stereotype of the feminine street vendor.[71] Laundry work was another resort of impoverished women but it, too, was sporadic and unreliable. One washerwoman in 1740 left a rare description of the drudgery of such a life:

> When Ev'ning does approach, we homeward hie,
> And our domestic Toils incessant ply:
> Against your coming Home prepare to get
> Our Work all done, our House in order set; . . .
> Early next Morning we on you attend,
> Our children dress and feed, their cloaths we mend;
> And in the Field our daily Task renew,
> Soon as the rising Sun had dry'd the dew.[72]

Such descriptions belie the common myth that the "domestic," household-based trades of early modern Europe allowed women to easily fit in their own housework with wage-earning activities.

Prostitution is perhaps the most infamous refuge for women desperate to live another day. Seventeenth-century moralist Johann Balthasar Schupp saw prostitution as the logical end of the feminine descent into poverty. Offering a hypothetical example of a maid forced out of her domestic service post, the short journey to prostitution seemed to him self-evident: "the maidservant goes away, rents a room of her own, becomes a laundress or seamstress, the seamstress becomes a whore. . . ."[73] At least one historian has theorized that the business opportunities for prostitutes were heightened in this period because elite men were no longer looking to their maidservants to satisfy their lust. The new lack of bodily intimacy between servants and their employers meant that masters were now going out to brothels rather than preying upon their household staff.[74] Poor or middle-class women who found themselves down on their luck in Enlightenment Europe might have turned to prostitution in the struggle to make ends meet.

NOTES

1. Letter from Marie Lamothe to Victor Lamothe, dated February 18, 1758, quoted in Christine Adams, *A Taste for Comfort and Status: A Bourgeois Family in Eighteenth-Century France* (University Park: Pennsylvania State UP, 2000), 45.

2. Maria Bogucka, *Women in Early Modern Polish Society, against the European Background* (Aldershot, Hampshire: Ashgate, 2004), 33.

3. Mary Lindemann, *Patriots and Paupers: Hamburg, 1712–1830* (New York: Oxford UP, 1990), 50.

4. John Gay, "To a Lady on Her Passion for Old China," (1725), quoted in Maxine Berg, *Luxury and Pleasure in Eighteenth-Century Britain* (Oxford: Oxford UP, 2005), 234.

5. Fanny Burney, *The Witlings*, Act One, Scene One (1778), reprinted in Fanny Burney, *The Witlings; and, the Woman-Hater*, ed. Peter Sabor and Geoffrey Sill (Peterborough, Ont: Broadview Press, 2002), 47.

6. Tom Ericsson, "Women, Family and Small Businesses in Late Nineteenth-Century Sweden," *History of the Family* 6 (2001), 230.

7. Gayle K. Brunell, "Policing the Monopolizing Women of Early Modern Nantes," *Journal of Women's History* 19, no. 2 (2007), 17.

8. For a slightly more complex picture, see John Bohstedt, "Gender, Household and Community Politics: Women in English Riots 1790–1810," *Past and Present*, no. 120 (August 1988), 97, and R. M. Dekker, "Women in Revolt: Popular Protest and Its Social Basis in Holland in the Seventeenth and Eighteenth Centuries," *Theory and Society* xvi (1987), 341.

9. E. P. Thompson, "The Moral Economy of the English Crowd in the Eighteenth Century," *Past and Present*, no. 50 (1971), 76–136. See also Sandro Guzzi-Heeb, "Close Relatives and Useful Relatives: Welfare, Inheritance, and the Use of Kinship in an Alpine Dynasty, 1650–1800" in *Family Welfare: Gender, Property, and Inheritance since the Seventeenth Century*, ed. David R. Green and Alastair Owens (Westport, CT: Praeger, 2004), 100.

10. Interrogation of Louis Marais, May 6, 1775, quoted in Merry E. Wiesner, Julius R. Ruff and William Bruce Wheeler, *Discovering the Western Past: A Look at the Evidence, Volume II: since 1500*, 5th ed. (New York: Houghton Mifflin, 2004), 35.

11. Joan Sherwood, *Poverty in Eighteenth-Century Spain: The Women and Children of the Inclusa* (Toronto: U of Toronto P, 1988), 88–89.

12. Rebecca Gates-Coon, *The Landed Estates of the Esterházy Princes: Hungary during the Reforms of Maria Theresia and Joseph II* (Baltimore, MD: Johns Hopkins UP, 1994), 102, 103.

13. Ankarloo Bengt, "Agriculture and Women's Work: Directions of Change in the West, 1700–1900," *Journal of Family History* 4, no. 2 (1979), 114–15.

14. Sherwood, 54.

15. Bridget Hill, *Women Alone: Spinsters in England, 1660–1850* (New Haven, CT: Yale UP, 2001), 27.

16. Sheilagh Ogilvie, *A Bitter Living: Women, Markets and Social Capital in Early Modern Germany* (Oxford: Oxford UP, 2003), 283.

17. David S. Reher, *Perspectives on the Family in Spain, Past and Present* (Oxford: Clarendon P, 1997), 230.

18. Ogilvie, 228. Corvées were the feudal duties that peasants householders owed their lords in early modern Europe.

19. T. Hodgskin, Travels in North Germany, (1820), quoted in W. R. Lee, "Women's Work and the Family: Some Demographic Implications of Gender-Specific Rural Work Patterns in Nineteenth-Century Germany," in *Women's Work and the Family Economy in Historical Perspective*, ed. Pat Hudson and W. R. Lee (Manchester: Manchester UP, 1990), Hudson and Lee, 52.

20. Hill, 18.

21. Michael Roberts, "Sickles and Scythes: Women's Work and Men's Work at Harvest Time," *History Workshop Journal* 7 (1979), 18.

22. Ulrich Pfister, "Women's Bread—Men's Capital: The Domestic Economy of Small Textile Entrepreneurs in Rural Zurich in the 17th and 18th Centuries," *History of the Family* 6, no. 2 (2001), 157–58.

23. Ogilvie, 164.
24. Pfister, 156.
25. Ogilvie, 240.
26. Mary Jo Maynes, "Gender, Labor and Globalization in Historical Perspective," *Journal of Women's History* 15, no. 4 (Winter 2004), 51.
27. Hill, 28.
28. Pfister, 158.
29. Andrew Gray, *A Treatise on Spinning Machinery* ... (1819), 18–19, quoted in Maynes, 49.
30. Antoinette Fauve-Chamoux, "Continuity and Change among the Rhemish Proletariat: Preindustrial Textile Work in Family Perspective," *History of the Family* 6 (2001), 183.
31. Sarah C. Maza, *Servants and Masters in Eighteenth-Century France: The Uses of Loyalty* (Princeton, NJ: Princeton UP, 1983), 277–78.
32. Ruth Brandon, *Governess: The Lives and Times of the Real Jane Eyres* (New York: Walker & Company, 2008), 31.
33. Angiolina Arru, "The Distinguishing Features of Domestic Service in Italy," *Journal of Family History* 15, no. 4 (1990), 555.
34. Johann Süssmilch, 1741, quoted in Deborah Simonton, "Women Workers; Working Women," in *The Routledge History of Women in Europe since 1700*, ed. Deborah Simonton (London: Routledge, 2006), 141–42.
35. Ogilvie, 135.
36. Kirsi Ojala, "Servants' Social Networks and Relationships in Eighteenth-Century Turku and Odense," in *Emotions in the Household, 1200–1900*, ed. Susan Broomhall (New York: Palgrave Macmillan, 2008), 207.
37. Maza, 255–56. See also Cissie Fairchilds, *Domestic Enemies: Servants and Their Masters in Old Regime France* (Baltimore, MD: Johns Hopkins UP, 1984), 189–90, for similar findings in Provence.
38. Gates-Coon, 26–27.
39. Marjatta Rahikainen, "Ageing Men and Women in the Labour Market: Continuity and Change," *Scandinavian Journal of History* 26, no. 4 (2001), 300.
40. Nadia Maria Filippini, "The Church, the State and Childbirth: The Midwife in Italy during the Eighteenth Century," in *The Art of Midwifery: Early Modern Midwives in Europe*, ed. Hilary Marland (London: Routledge, 1993), 168.
41. *Novísima Recopilación*, libro VIII, tit. X, ley X., quoted in Teresa Oritz, "From Hegemony to Subordination: Midwives in Early Modern Spain," in Marland, *Art of Midwifery*, 99.
42. Ogilvie, 236.
43. Oritz, 103.
44. Quoted in Mary Lindemann, "Professionals? Sisters? Rivals? Midwives in Braunschweig, 1750–1800," in Marland, *Art of Midwifery*, 182.
45. Hilary Marland, "The '*Burgerlijke*' Midwife: The *stadsvroedvrouw* of Eighteenth-Century Holland," in Marland, *Art of Midwifery*, 192.
46. Ogilvie, 158.
47. Gates-Coon, 142.
48. Brandon, 78–79.
49. Maria Edgeworth, *Practical Education; by Maria Edgeworth, ... and by Richard Lovell Edgeworth, ...* Vol. 1 (London, 1798), 35.

50. Agnes Porter, journal entry, July 1791, quoted in Brandon, 26.

51. Michael Hochedlinger, "Mars Ennobled: The Ascent of the Military and the Creation of a Military Nobility in Mid-Eighteenth-Century Austria," *German History* 17, no. 2 (1999), 175.

52. Natal'ia L. Pushkareva, "Russian Noblewomen's Education in the Home as Revealed in Late 18th and Early 19th-Century Memoirs," in *Women and Gender in 18th-Century Russia*, ed. Wendy Rosslyn (Aldershot, Hants.: Ashgate, 2003), 114.

53. Mary Wollstonecraft, *Thoughts on the Education of Daughters*, (1798), quoted in Brandon, 48.

54. Brandon, 23. On wages of eighteenth-century governesses, see pages 29–30.

55. Ogilvie, 306.

56. Bogucka, 50–51.

57. Hill, 37.

58. Brandon, 43.

59. Ogilvie, 307.

60. Wildburg Community Council record (December 14, 1752), quoted in Ogilvie, 284.

61. Fanny Blood to Everina Wollstonecraft, undated letter, quoted in Brandon, 51.

62. Margaret J. Moody, *The Royal Poorhouse in Eighteenth-Century Turin, Italy: The King and the Paupers* (Lewiston, NY: Edwin Mellen Press, 2001), 67.

63. Moody, 56.

64. The will of Etienne de Rivaz, St. Gingolph, Switzerland (1750), quoted in Guzzi-Heeb, 99.

65. Quoted in Mary Lindemann, *Patriots and Paupers*, 159.

66. 5te Nachricht (March 1790), quoted in Lindemann, *Patriots and Paupers*, 159.

67. Moody, 52–55.

68. Gates-Coon, 138–39.

69. Moody, 68.

70. Ogilvie, 285.

71. Sherwood, 89.

72. Mary Collier, *The Woman's Labour* (London: J. Roberts, 1740), quoted in Deborah Simonton, *A History of European Women's Work: 1740 to the Present* (New York: Routledge, 1998), 71.

73. Johann Balthasar Schupp, *Sieben böse Geister* (1659), quoted in Ogilvie, 313.

74. Fairchilds, 191.

SUGGESTED READING

Brandon, Ruth. *Governess: The Lives and Times of the Real Jane Eyres*. New York: Walker & Company, 2008.

Fairchilds, Cissie. *Domestic Enemies: Servants and Their Masters in Old Regime France*. Baltimore, MD: Johns Hopkins UP, 1984.

Grigg, David. *The Transformation of Agriculture in the West*. Cambridge, MA: Basil Blackwell, 1992.

Hill, Bridget, *Women, Work and Sexual Politics in Eighteenth-Century England*. Oxford: Basil Blackwell, 1989.

Hudson, Pat and W. R. Lee, eds. *Women's Work and the Family Economy in Historical Perspective*. Manchester: Manchester UP, 1990.

Marland, Hilary, ed. *The Art of Midwifery: Early Modern Midwives in Europe*. London: Routledge, 1993.

Maza, Sarah C. *Servants and Masters in Eighteenth-Century France: The Uses of Loyalty*. Princeton, NJ: Princeton UP, 1983.

Meldrum, Tim. *Domestic Service and Gender, 1660–1750: Life and Work in the London Household*. London: Pearson Education, 2000.

Moody, Margaret J. *The Royal Poorhouse in Eighteenth-Century Turin, Italy: The King and the Paupers*. Lewiston, NY: Edwin Mellen Press, 2001.

Ogilvie, Sheilagh. *A Bitter Living: Women, Markets and Social Capital in Early Modern Germany*. Oxford: Oxford University Press, 2003.

Sherwood, Joan. *Poverty in Eighteenth-Century Spain: The Women and Children of the Inclusa*. Toronto: U of Toronto P, 1988.

Simonton, Deborah. *A History of European Women's Work: 1740 to the Present*. New York: Routledge, 1998.

3

Women and Politics

There is much to celebrate, and much to lament, about women's political activity in the eighteenth century. The Enlightenment bequeathed a raised political consciousness for some women, and in the heady atmosphere of the early phase of the French Revolution, voices were raised in support of equal rights. A revolutionary fervor pervaded much of Europe, sweeping up women as much as men. Feminine marchers demonstrated against famine conditions, threw stones at imperial occupiers, or engaged in peaceful actions in support of equal citizenship. The initial enthusiasm waned in the face of reprisals from the state, but also from society as a whole. The political activity of eighteenth-century plebeian women was not to be replicated by their nineteenth-century counterparts.

In Eastern Europe, a variety of unusual circumstances combined in the 1700s to place several women in the highest seat of political power. The Austrian Empire and the Russian Empire fell under feminine rule for a significant part of the century. All of these women attempted reforms that reflected their consciousness of Enlightenment ideals. Noble birth and absolute authority did not protect empresses, queens, and duchesses from slurs on their sexuality, however. In many ways, their gender was far more central to their political identity than it was for men in similar posts in eighteenth-century political life.

REVOLUTIONARY WOMEN

The late eighteenth century was a time in which European women engaged in open political agitation to a degree not seen in the preceding or following century. In Belgium, for example, women marched at the head of political demonstrations in 1789, threw stones at Austrian armies, and drew up political treatises in support of a revolution against their Austrian occupiers.[1] Though most of the women of Spain attempted a more pacifist style of reform, becoming active in various aspects of public life, implicitly demanding recognition as patriotic citizens, they too, had a revolutionary heroine.[2]

Twenty-two-year-old Agustina Zaragoza emerged as a direct result of the French revolutionary wars. She and many other Spanish women joined soldiers in resisting French occupation in the late eighteenth and early nineteenth centuries. In the siege of the city of Zaragoza in 1808, Augustina fired a cannon into a group of French soldiers attempting to enter a breach in the wall and turned the tide of the siege in Spain's favor. Her valor was awarded with two medals and formal recognition as an artillery woman. Historians have dubbed her "a Spanish Lady Liberty of flesh and blood" who helped to overthrow the social and gender order in Old Regime Spain.[3]

Women's revolutionary activities did not always have to be overtly violent. Princess Lubomirska, the former love of Polish resistance leader Thaddeus Kosciuszko, used her influence at court to convince King Stanislas to engage him as a major general in the fight against Russian occupation in the 1790s. When Kosciuszko was defeated and taken prisoner by the Russians, she managed to get clothes and books to him and his fellow exiles to comfort them on their journey to Russia.[4]

German women responded to the events in France with a spate of literature calling for "liberty, equality, better marital laws and a different concept of marriage, [and] better education for women."[5] Even before the revolution, the women of Hamburg were active in transmitting republican values to their children and making their homes a "political space in civic-mindedness and patriotism." By the time the Bastille in Paris fell in 1789, the middling women of Hamburg had established a tradition of active political involvement, and it was not surprising to see them openly celebrating Bastille Day at the home of Georg Heinrich Sieveking in Harvestehude in 1791. Christine Westphalen published (albeit anonymously) so sympathetic an account of moderate French reformer Charlotte Corday's assassination of Jean-Paul Marat, a prominent member of the Convention government that orchestrated the Terror, that Westphalen established a prominent cult following for Corday in Hamburg.[6]

Other revolutionary women packed their bags and moved to Paris to experience these ideals first hand. English novelist and feminist Mary

Wollstonecraft was one of them. Another, Helen Williams (also an English author), wrote of the opposition she faced on her return to England:

> Must I be told that my mind is perverted . . . because I do not weep with those who have lost a part of their superfluities, rather than rejoice that the oppressed are protected, that the wronged are redressed, that the captive is set at liberty, and that the poor have bread? . . . It is not my intention to shiver lances, in every society I enter, in the cause of the National Assembly. Yet I cannot help remarking that, since the Assembly does not presume to set itself up as an example to this country, we seem to have very little right to be furiously angry, because they think proper to try another system of government themselves.[7]

Williams's exasperation makes it clear that she was frequently engaged in debates where she argued passionately in favor of the events in France. Those too poor to travel to France could show their support for the revolutionary ideals in other ways, such as guillotining one's chickens, which was the rumored practice of one Scotswoman.[8]

The most prominent revolutionary women were, without a doubt, the Parisian women in the French Revolution. The revolution, which began in 1789, caused massive cultural and political change in the decade that followed. However, by the time Napoleon Bonaparte seized power in 1799, many had tired of radicalism and accepted—or even celebrated—the restoration of a society quite similar to the *ancien régime* that had preceded the revolt. During the period of upheaval, the French legislature went through a number of incarnations, from the moderate National Assembly in June of 1789—which became the Legislative Assembly after a constitution and elections gave it a clear republican basis in 1791—to the increasingly radical National Convention, led most notably by Maximilien de Robespierre.

This latter phase of government is responsible for much of the infamy of the French Revolution. During this time, a committee of public safety was formed, which targeted those opposed to the radicalizing of the revolution: those sympathetic to monarchy, the Catholic Church, or the privileges of nobility. These enemies of the government were brought before a tribunal (discussed more in Chapter 4) and generally found guilty and sentenced to execution. A number of cultural changes were enacted, including a rejection of traditional Christianity in favor of a more nebulous "cult of the supreme being," where "reason" was worshiped above all else. The period that followed has become known as the Terror, when thousands were decapitated by the guillotine. Public antipathy grew against the Terror to the point that Maximilien himself was guillotined in 1794, followed soon after by the repeal of the laws of the Terror. France was then governed rather shakily by the Directory until Napoleon took power in 1799. Though women did not sit in the legislature during any of its phases, they participated in the revolution and its governments in a variety of ways.

Women joined men in writing political treatises, demonstrating, and rioting throughout the decade, but the October march and the Prairial rebellion, two events that bookend the most aggressive phase of reform, serve as illustrative examples. In October of 1789, thousands of women walked the long miles from Paris to the royal palace at Versailles to demand bread and political reforms from the king. They occupied the Assembly room, hanging their rain-soaked clothing about the hall to dry, and sat defiantly in the president's chair to mock the politicians. Louis XVI finally capitulated in the face of the women's passion and determination. Their triumphal march back to Paris brought not only wagonloads of flour and bread, but also the royals themselves, who then became virtual prisoners in Tuileries Palace for the next phase of the revolution.

The so-called Prairial uprising (named for its occurrence at the start of the Prairial month on the revolutionary calendar: May 20) occurred after an especially difficult winter in Paris in 1795. Starving and desperate, a group of women approached the Convention government to demand action to end the famine. The group became violent, and the fighting lasted several days, but ultimately the women's supporters succumbed to the National Guard. One historian has designated the Prairial uprising as the last to evoke popular sovereignty, and its failure as the final relinquishing of the original revolutionary goals.[9]

This differs greatly from the heady atmosphere of 1793, when Parisian political activists Pauline Léon and Claire Lacombe had formed the Society of Revolutionary Republican Women, the "first exclusively female interest group in western politics."[10] The government's move to bar women from organizing in political clubs by the end of the year attests to their incredible rise to prominence during this brief period. The consciousness of having accomplished unprecedented change left many contemporaries eager to explore new possibilities.

One of these possibilities was the extension of the rights of citizenship to women. Marquis de Condorcet, a member of the revolutionary government in its early (and more moderate) phase, was one of the first to demand in print that the women of the new republic have equal citizenship. The proponents of reform referred to women's revolutionary activism as justification. In the words of one of de Condorcet's circle, Etta Palm d'Aelders, in 1791:

> The chains of Frenchmen have fallen with a clatter; the noise of their falling turned despots pale and shook their thrones.... August legislators, would you weigh down with chains the hands that helped you raise the altar of the

fatherland with so much ardour? Would you enslave those who contributed so zealously to make you free?[11]

Olympe de Gouges, a butcher's daughter who became a playwright, penned a famous treatise in the style of the celebrated *Declaration of the Rights of Man* (the document that formed the basis for the republican government in 1789), whose first article succinctly observed that "woman is born free and remains equal in rights to man."[12]

Revolutionary women did not escape without blood on their hands. Charlotte Corday justified her assassination of Marat by saying that the loss of one life would save thousands, but she herself fell victim to the guillotine for her crime. Though most organized feminine political action, such as the October march, had the reputation for nonviolence because of the very sex of its participants, female demonstrators could become aggressive. The women of the Prairial crowd, for example, were certainly violent and have been implicated in at least one death.[13] There were also many female supporters of the Terror—arguably the bloodiest aspect of the French Revolution. European opponents of the revolution frequently made use of the image of Parisian women knitting as they witnessed the assembly debates and the executions. Dubbed *tricoteuses* (knitters), or "furies of the guillotine," these women became a symbol of the shocking events that were occurring in France.

Lest it appear that all women espoused the cause of equal rights and the French Revolution itself, most women were either quietly or vociferously opposed to even the mildest forms of eighteenth-century radicalism. Like their male counterparts, they had a variety of reasons for their opposition. Some felt alienated from the concerns that united only those in Paris at the expense of the needs of the countryside; others struggled with a government that had criminalized the Catholic faith. Noblewomen understandably hated and feared those who controlled the guillotine. Not all revolutionary women were unequivocal supporters of women in general. Louise de Keralio, a radical who penned a lengthy treatise against absolutism, was hardest on the queens, condemning Marie Antoinette as vituperatively as did any of her male critics. The essence of her polemic was that female despots were even worse than male despots.[14]

MARIA THERESA

Maria Theresa was a prominent figure on the eighteenth-century political stage, not least because her very accession to the throne of the Austrian Empire sparked a war. The empress was the eldest daughter of Charles VI, the man serving simultaneously as ruler of the Holy Roman Empire and the Austrian Empire from 1711–1740. Even in his earliest years on the throne, her father exhibited concern over the transfer of power upon his death. As early as 1713, before he had any children, he issued the Pragmatic Sanction. Later revised and publicized in 1719, the document stated that, should Charles die without a male heir, his eldest daughter would be the recipient over all other claimants.

Maria Theresa's gender clearly complicated the succession issue. Her sex barred her from gaining her father's title as Holy Roman Emperor. The Emperor, although in practice essentially powerless, was the symbolic head of a huge expanse of central Europe, and the throne had been in Maria Theresa's Habsburg family for three hundred years. Charles VI's position as the imperial leader of the Austrian territories had also never been held by a woman, and he worried about some of the provinces balking at the idea. He began an intense campaign, garnering formal acceptances from all of the individual powers across his realm by 1722, on the condition that their privileges and powers would be guaranteed under his chosen heir. He negotiated similar agreements with external jurisdictions throughout Europe, offering significant concessions but ultimately obtaining the full list of signatories by 1738. In his mind, Maria Theresa's tenure was secured.

This was not the case at his death in October of 1740. Before the end of the year, Frederick II of Prussia successfully invaded Silesia, the richest province in the Austrian Empire. He arrogantly offered the new young empress his support for her husband's bid for the crown of Holy Roman Emperor and a promise to intrude no further into Austrian territories if she would accept his possession of Silesia. To his surprise, she refused and began assembling an army that would attempt to regain the territory in the spring. At least one historian has speculated that Maria Theresa's femininity partially informed the Prussian attitude in the Silesian conquest. Frederick was an overbearing husband with a notoriously poor opinion of women, and it seems likely that he let his assumptions about the empress' gender blind him into thinking she would meekly submit to his insolent demands.[15]

Though the mission to regain Silesia failed, Maria Theresa's determination to hold the imperial throne carried her through the War of the Austrian Succession that followed, from 1741–1748. She began to build a staff of advisors, including Count Anton von Kaunitz. In the aftermath of the peace of 1748, Kaunitz convinced her that an alliance with France, Austria's traditional enemy, would be a wise strategic move against Prussia. After the outbreak of the Seven Years' War (1756–1763), Austria secured the support of the Imperial Diet (the first time in many years that the Holy Roman Empire had agreed to help Austria fight one of its own members), Russia, and France. Despite this remarkable achievement, the Austrian Empire was crippled by the wars, and Maria Theresa again failed to recover Silesia.

Nonetheless, the empress had revealed her tenacity and had at the very least quashed the uncertainty that pervaded the early days of her assumption of the throne. She remained as leader of the empire until her death in 1780.

A host of domestic problems beset the young empress at the start of her reign, and she launched a series of dramatic reform programs in response. With the help of her advisors, Maria Theresa attempted to centralize government and extend royal power over Bohemia. She also launched substantial reforms to the tax-collection system to begin to fill the empire's coffers, which were empty when she took the throne. The empress also changed Austrian military culture, offering more substantial rewards for sons of nobles to join the army and developing training academies to improve their preparation for command. The year 1757 saw the advent of the prestigious new "military order of Maria Theresa," which recognized "[b]rave deeds, bold personal decisive initiatives and prudent advice in battle," which came with a pension and automatic noble status.[16] She addressed the problems of religious division as well, with a zeal befitting her Jesuit education. She had the dubious distinction of being the final European ruler of the eighteenth century to actively persecute her Jewish subjects, expelling the Jews of Bohemia in 1745 and refusing settlement to Jews in Vienna in 1777. In her single-minded quest to consolidate Catholicism in the empire, she also exercised "very harsh" policies towards Protestants within her realm.[17]

Her attitude towards the peasantry was much more sympathetic. In the course of her reign, Maria Theresa passed several new regulations governing serfdom in the Austrian Empire. Operating from the Enlightenment principle that the old feudal system was crippling economic development in the empire, she set an example by abolishing it completely within her own Austrian lands. Her hopes that the Hungarian and Bohemian lords would voluntarily follow in her footsteps were soon dashed. However, the peasants within these territories gained hope from her overtures and began to resist lords' demands with growing vehemence throughout the 1770s, believing their empress would support them. "Colourful tales" of Maria Theresa's progressive attitudes had spread from village to village in the distant countryside.[18] There is evidence that she saw herself as "mother of her people" in her endeavor to bring an end to serfdom, though ultimately she felt compelled to quash Hungarian peasant resistance with the Austrian army and their lot remained little better than in previous centuries.[19]

In fact, most of Maria Theresa's biographers have highlighted her maternity as a central part of her identity. This is not surprising, considering the fact that she had a dozen children and wrote hundreds of affectionate motherly letters to them. Indeed, Maria Theresa seemed to revel in the time-honored feminine roles of mother and matchmaker in dynastic politics. When her eldest son became a widower and wanted to adhere to his late wife's wish that he marry her younger sister (Princess Louise of Parma), the empress tried to use her influence to bring about the match. She wrote to the head of the girl's family, the Bourbon King of Spain, with a sincere entreaty befitting any mother of the Enlightenment:

> Both as mother and as sovereign I ardently desire his remarriage, but I also desire his happiness. . . . His wishes are centred on Princess Louise of Parma out of respect for the memory of his wife and at her advice. . . . Your Majesty's wish that she might marry your son should prevent me from thinking of it, and I realize my indiscretion. But put yourself in my place. The happiness of my son and my peoples depends on it, so I look to you to restore a stricken family.[20]

Her conduct during a visit by the Mozart family also attests to her desire to present herself as a mother. Leopold Mozart recounted her discussing "my children's smallpox" with great "familiarity" with Mrs. Mozart, affectionately "strok[ing her] cheeks and press[ing] her hands."[21]

Recent studies have sought to shift the focus to the ways that Maria Theresa clung to her power as empress and walked a very careful tightrope because of her gender. This is visible, for example, in the architecture of her residence at Schönbrunn Palace. Her husband Francis bore the title of emperor, but real authority rested with the empress. Nonetheless, she maintained a separate suite of rooms from her husband which were "located and decorated to accord with her secondary status" as a woman compared with that of Francis as a man.[22] Rather than chafing at the subordination dictated by her gender, Maria Theresa worked within it. The empress was careful to maintain, throughout her reign, an external appearance of appropriate femininity while ultimately wielding considerable political power.

She married for love, and at the untimely death of Francis in 1765, she descended into a widowhood reminiscent of that of Britain's Queen Victoria in the following century. She reportedly donned a widow's cap over newly shorn hair and adopted a somber wardrobe devoid of jewelry.[23] It was customary for European noblewomen to withdraw from society and take up more contemplative spiritual pursuits after their husbands' demise, so it is not particularly remarkable that Maria Theresa's widowhood bore similar patterns. What is noteworthy is that she did so while continuing to govern and reform the Austrian Empire. Her son, Joseph, assisted her as co-regent after his father's death and was especially involved in foreign policy, but Maria Theresa continued to ardently pursue her domestic improvements. It has even been suggested that her status as grieving widow provided a welcome pretext for Maria Theresa to withdraw from the duties of state, which she had always found burdensome, and focus on the real business of government.[24]

RUSSIAN GYNECOCRACY

In the same way that Charles VI sparked a major shift in the succession policy of the imperial throne in Austria, so too did Peter the Great in Russia. The efforts of both resulted in the unprecedented possibility of female reign. Though Charles had a specific woman in mind, Peter was motivated more by his greater agenda of modernizing and Westernizing Russia. In 1722, he issued a succession law that disrupted the traditional practice of sons inheriting the Russian throne from their fathers. From that point forward, Tsar Peter decreed, each monarch would be empowered to designate an heir based on his or her own opinion of the individual's merit, rather than on any dynastic claims. This followed Enlightenment principles that privileged knowledge and education over birth.

Notwithstanding the likelihood that Peter preferred male leaders, the new succession policy brought a chain of women monarchs to Russia. In the two years following his death in 1725, his widow ruled as Catherine I. After a brief interval where Peter II occupied the seat of power, Anna became empress for a decade, starting in 1730. The infant Ivan VI, Anna's nominated successor, held the throne only fleetingly before being deposed and imprisoned for the rest of his tragic life. His captors supported Elizabeth, daughter of Peter the Great, who assumed power from 1741 until her death in 1762. She designated her nephew to take over as Peter III, but he was quickly deposed in favor of his wife, who became Empress Catherine II, eventually known as Catherine the Great. Her reign lasted until her death in 1796.

Traditional histories of Russia in the eighteenth century have thus viewed it as a "gynecocracy," when the country had fallen under the control "of a series of weak women with low morals."[25] More recent work has, of course, added considerably more nuance to this picture, and has tended to celebrate many of the contributions of Catherine the Great, in particular. In many ways, Catherine I, Anna, and Elizabeth seemed often to be uninterested in state affairs and to have left the true business of governance to others. Russia transformed in these years, however, and the empresses at least tacitly approved the reforms, which were based on distinct Enlightenment principles.

Elizabeth bears the merit of having abolished capital punishment, though the overall benefit to her people remains dubious because of the growth in the oppressiveness of serfdom during her reign.[26] She followed her father in his desires to Westernize Russia, and she made great progress in increasing the cause of education, which had been especially dear to his heart. It seems likely that her sex has prompted chroniclers to focus upon her extravagance in dress and finery—she was reputed to own more than fifteen thousand gowns alone. Yet her rule built upon the economic developments begun by her father, and Russia maintained a pattern of overall economic growth that was to be continued by Catherine. Empress Elizabeth was also a passionate opponent of Frederick the Great of Prussia in the Seven Years' War and—like her ally Maria Theresa—refused to bow to his threats. She simply turned his portrait to face the wall and readied her armies.

She was passionately religious and believed it her role to suppress the opponents of the true church. This included the Old Believers, the dissenters who refused to comply with the reforms to the Russian Orthodox Church in 1667 and who were especially known for their long beards. Elizabeth reintroduced the tax on beards and ardently pursued those who continued defiance. There followed a tragic series of self-immolations, as it was customary for groups of Old Believers to gather together in churches at the approach of Elizabeth's troops and set the building aflame, from the conviction that they would rather burn in this world than in the afterlife. Though this happened into the nineteenth century, the empress Elizabeth has the unfortunate reputation of having presided over more burnings than any other Russian leader. Several hundred burned themselves in 1751 alone. According to one fairly reliable chronicler, another single incident of self-immolation during her reign took 6,000 lives.[27]

The empress was also known for her massive building projects, however. She made extensive renovations to her palaces in the most elaborate Baroque style. She had a love of music and theatre and brought many artists to Russia. Credited by some with founding Russian romance music, she also introduced the horn orchestra, invented in 1748 by a Czech hornist.[28] She revitalized the Academy of Sciences, establishing the worthy Cyril Razumovski as its president, who fostered talents such as that of Lomonosov. The brilliant son of a fisherman, Lomonosov's research on icebergs, meteorology, and geology continued alongside his experimentation in mosaic portraiture and poetry writing in true Enlightenment fashion.[29] Elizabeth steadfastly pursued the policies begun by her illustrious father throughout the two decades of her reign.

Catherine II was to become an even more renowned empress than her predecessor. She had great ambitions for her beloved adopted nation (she was born in Germany, but came to Russia at the age of fifteen for her betrothal). She conducted several large campaigns to attempt to broaden the empire. Under her rule, the Russian Empire expanded into Poland and captured huge territories from the Ottomans. Herself probably an atheist in keeping with her Enlightenment values, Catherine paid lip service to the Russian Orthodox church and is widely reputed to have indulged in a quiet game of solitaire at a hidden table during the long worship services she attended regularly. She introduced a fair measure of religious toleration to Russia, allowing Old Believers to practice their faith without persecution.

She founded the first Russian school for girls in 1769 to educate the daughters of Russia's wealthiest citizens.

An avid reader and letter writer, Catherine the Great left volumes of correspondence attesting to her Enlightenment sympathies, including a prolonged and enthusiastic correspondence with Voltaire. Shortly after assuming the imperial throne, Catherine penned a treatise on law reform inspired by her reading of celebrated Enlightenment legal theorists Montesquieu and Beccaria. Building on foundations laid by Elizabeth's previous government, Catherine established a commission on writing a new legislative code, the first session of which was held in 1767. Again following in the footsteps of the previous empress, Catherine set up new statutes for the Academy of Fine Arts. She placed it in one of a series of fine new neoclassical buildings she had commissioned in the Russian capital, making it the largest of its kind in Europe.[30] Catherine the Great's enthusiasm for Enlightenment ideals was already visible in the first few weeks of her reign, when she offered to publish the *Encyclopédie* for Diderot, who was having trouble finding a publisher in France.

Though there were many of the qualities of the *philosophes* in the actions of the Russian empresses, there were also cruel autocratic elements to their time in power. This is particularly visible when studying the condition of serfs under the reigns of Elizabeth and Catherine II. Dar'ia Nikolaevna Saltykova, a Russian noblewoman reputed to have tortured at least seventy-seven of her serfs to death for her own sadistic pleasure, operated without hindrance under Elizabeth, despite countless petitions against her.[31] Catherine ensured that Yemelyan Pugachev, a Don cossak who led a massive serf uprising in the eastern territories, was executed by quartering in exemplary fashion to make sure that none of her other subjects gained the courage to overthrow the feudal system. Indeed, serfdom in eighteenth-century Russia became tantamount to slavery. There is general historical agreement, however, that Catherine and Elizabeth, like Maria Theresa, regarded this fact without relish, as the necessary price of power. All three women knew that their rise and hold on the throne was contingent upon the support of the landed gentry.

Not surprisingly perhaps, the peasants blamed the empresses' femininity for their worsening circumstances. Whisperings that "grain does not grow, because the feminine sex is ruling," became popular in the eighteenth-century countryside.[32] Detractors included a monk who was heard to complain, while very drunk, of Russia's unfortunate situation of being under the rule of *babi*, or women. He was whipped and removed from the monastery in punishment.[33] Frederick II, safe from the clutches of the Russian legal system, could freely remark that "Elizabeth, Maria Theresa and Madame de Pompadour [the powerful mistress of French King Louis XIV] are the three first whores of Europe."[34]

Casting aspersions on one's chastity was a favorite way to insult women of all classes in early modern Europe, and Elizabeth's propensity to take attractive young men into her bed only fueled her detractors (though male leaders across Europe indulged the same appetites with impunity). Catherine, too—boasting a series of younger lovers throughout her reign—was the target of sexual insults. Feeling the threat as Catherine enlarged the Russian Empire to the south and west, English political cartoonists depicted her as a "Europe-devouring whore."[35] Another attack by the English press presented her as Katherine in the Shakespearian play *The Taming of the Shrew*. A host of males representing France, the Holy Roman Empire, England, Prussia, Holland, and the Ottoman Empire were present at her "taming."

Even in direct personal interactions, the empresses' gender played a pivotal role. Maria Theresa's son, Emperor Joseph II of Austria, wrote this revealing observation of Catherine in 1782:

> Whoever has to deal with her [Catherine] must never lose sight of her sex nor forget that a woman sees things and acts differently from one of our sex.... When she expresses a wish for a thing that can be granted..., indulge her with that complaisant attention which is ever due to a lady; but when she insists on what ought not to be complied with, indicate that though she may often lead she cannot drive. In this manner one may hope to live upon a fair footing with her, guarding her against the heat and impetuosity of her feelings....[36]

Elizabeth's feminine weakness was known to be her vanity. Even as her looks began to fade with age, she "wanted everyone to play the role of the Chinese ambassador admiring her beauty as ardently as ever."[37] Courtiers and foreign ambassadors were able to exploit this vulnerability in the aging empress.

Like Maria Theresa, the Russian empresses were often depicted as mother to their people, but unlike their Austrian counterpart, they do not seem to have reveled in the personal experience of motherhood. Indeed, there is some indication that the birth of her first child reminded Catherine very acutely of the limitations of being a woman in early modern Europe. Within moments of Catherine delivering the infant Paul, the then reigning empress Elizabeth gleefully bore him away to her apartments. Catherine's husband Peter caroused in celebration with his male companions in his separate apartments, and the exhausted Catherine remained in the now empty birthing chamber, cold, thirsty, and alone. According to her memoirs, "I had been in tears ever since the birth had taken place, particularly because I had been so cruelly abandoned, lying in discomfort after a long and painful labour."[38] She was not allowed to see her baby until more than a month had passed, and even then she had only limited access at the sporadic

Catherine II cowers before English statesman William Pitt as Don Quixote and Petruchio. Pitt symbolically rides an emaciated horse representing King George III of England. Also on the horse behind Pitt are the King of Prussia and Sancho Panza (representing Holland). Selim III kisses the horse's tail. Catherine's arms are supported by Holy Roman Emperor Leopold II and a very thin French gentleman symbolizing the old order in France. Taming of the Shrew: -Katharine & Petruchio; -The modern Quixotte, or, what you will, engraving published in London in 1748. (Courtesy of Library of Congress)

whim of the empress. This was the lot of many aristocratic women in eighteenth-century Europe, women whose main role was to bear sons. Even as empresses, the women of Europe could never entirely escape the constraints of their gender.

Throughout their reign, Elizabeth and Catherine the Great were faced with the daunting task that confronted all women in power in patriarchal societies. They had to navigate the cultural minefield of being in a position of power while possessed of a subordinate gender. This is what prompted the archbishop at Elizabeth's coronation to stress the extreme circumstances that had forced the girlish empress "to forget the delicacy of her sex ... to act as a leader and a cavalier of fighting men" in the fateful storming of the Winter Palace that gained her the throne.[39]

SEXUALITY AND POLITICS

Elizabeth and Catherine the Great were not the only targets of sexual insult due to their political activities in Enlightenment Europe. Marie Antoinette, wife of King Louis XVI, has the dubious distinction of figuring in the surprising amount of pornography published in revolutionary France. The groundswell of antipathy towards the queen, building in the summer before the revolution of 1789 and growing in the 1790s, culminated in shockingly explicit images of her engaged in various perverse sexual acts. Along with the illustrated literature portraying Marie Antoinette in compromising situations with both male and female lovers, there were also a host of plebeian depictions in songs and poems, and even in puns (*calembours*) that passed through the populace in *ancien régime* and revolutionary France.[40]

Queen Marie Antoinette was vilified for doing almost exactly what women of her status were expected to do in eighteenth-century political life: obey the dictates of family. Her mother, Maria Theresa, had carefully orchestrated Marie Antoinette's marriage to the French king to ensure that she would advance the interests of the Austrian government within the French royal court. Almost at once, she fell under fire from her new subjects for influencing the king in favor of his old enemy. As was done to her Russian counterparts, the French queen was made the butt of sexual insult for being a political threat.

Hatred of the queen was far from the sole driving force of revolutionary fervor. The poor fiscal state of the monarchy, its high taxes, and the fear of foreign incursions fanned the flames of revolution much more than did the supposed sexual proclivities of Marie Antoinette. It is nevertheless remarkable that the queen "was, without question, the favourite individual target of pornographic attacks both before and after 1789."[41] Without any real foundation, the rumor mill and the printing press cooperated in churning out images of the queen as a lesbian, indulging in secret trysts in the parks outside the palace with her ladies-in-waiting, seducing her son, and—possibly the most insidious by early modern notions of the inviolability of class—fornicating with her valet after she was imprisoned by the revolutionary government.

The butcher-kissing duchess can also join the French queen as an example of the way in which eighteenth-century culture used sexual imagery to denigrate political women. Georgiana, Duchess of Devonshire, was drumming up votes for her favorite political candidate in the English national election of 1784. In an age when the franchise did not even extend to all men, the borough of Westminster—with its large cross-section of male voters (all men with the status of freeholders resident in the borough)—was the "chief battleground."[42] It was here in the spring of 1784 that the duchess was reputed to have kissed a butcher in return for his pledge of support for her candidate.

It may not have been Georgiana herself who actually kissed the butcher (she denied it).[43] By going to the butchers, however, the Duchess of Devonshire and her friends had moved out of the "safe" territories for those of their class and gender. Georgiana was not limiting her efforts to her own family seat in the countryside, nor was the political candidate any relation. Regardless, her activities were not entirely atypical for one of her class and gender. English noblewomen's involvement in campaigns had become fairly common by the eighteenth century. Canvassing involved much more than knocking on doors in this period. It quite often entailed long conversations over drinks or dances, with much flattery imparted from the lady in question to the prospective voter.[44]

The caricatures of the incident reflect a shock and distaste far greater than that merited by the act itself. In one image, entitled "The Duchess Canvassing for her Favourite Member," Georgiana is lasciviously fondling the butcher. Like Marie Antoinette, the English duchess is portrayed as sexually available to even the most common orders, represented not only by the butchers, but also by the chimney sweep who has taken the chance to sneak a peek up her skirts.[45] The extensive stream of caricatures of the kissing episode present it as a symbolic warning against female involvement in politics. The butcher is a thinly veiled representation of England, under threat of emasculation by the dominant, sexually aggressive, unfeminine duchess.

Though there were some fairly prominent examples of female political activity in eighteenth-century Europe, public reaction could be swift and merciless, and often involved sexualizing the woman perceived as a threat. Both Marie Antoinette and Georgiana were participating in ways that had been generally accepted as appropriate to their class and gender, yet their opponents constructed them as depraved whores. The technique was effective: the English duchess confined her future canvassing to her drawing rooms, and the French queen was guillotined in front of a jeering crowd.

NOTES

1. Janet L. Polasky, "Women in Revolutionary Belgium: From Stone Throwers to Hearth Tenders," *History Workshop* 21 (1986), 87.

2. See Theresa Ann Smith, *The Emerging Female Citizen: Gender and Enlightenment in Spain* (Berkeley: U of California P, 2006).

3. John Lawrence Tone, "A Dangerous Amazon: Augustina Zaragoza and the Spanish Revolutionary War, 1808–1814," *European History Quarterly* 37, no. 4 (2007), 553.

4. Albert C. Cizauskas, "The Unusual Story of Thaddeus Kosciusko," *Lituanus* 32, no. 1 (Spring 1986), http:/www.lituanus.org/1986/86_1_03.htm (accessed September 1, 2009).

5. Marianne Henn, "The Other Voice: The Reaction of German Women Writers to the French Revolution," *Occasional Papers in German Studies* 8 (February 1996), 5.

6. Katherine Aeslestad, "Republican Traditions: Patriotism, Gender, and War in Hamburg, 1770–1815," *European History Quarterly* 37 (2007), 586–87.

7. Helen Maria Williams, *Letters Written in France, in the Summer 1790, to a Friend in England; Containing Various Anecdotes Relative to the French Revolution*, ed. Neil Fraistat and Susan S. Lanser (Peterborough, On.: Broadview Press, 2001), 148.

8. Kathryn Gleadle, "British Women and Radical Politics in the Late Nonconformist Enlightenment," in *Women, Privilege, and Power: British Politics, 1750 to the Present*, ed. Amada Vickery (Stanford, CA: Stanford UP, 2001), 124.

9. Olwen H. Hufton, *Women and the Limits of Citizenship in the French Revolution* (Toronto: U of Toronto P, 1992), 50.

10. Darline Gay Levy and Harriet Branson Applewhite, "Women and Political Revolution in Paris," in *Becoming Visible: Women in European History*, 2nd ed., ed. Renate Bridenthal, Claudia Koonz, and Susan Stuard (Boston, MA: Houghton Mifflin, 1987), 298.

11. Etta Palm d'Aelders, "Adresse des citoyennes françoises à l'Assemblée Nationale" (July 1791), quoted in *Women, the Family, and Freedom: The Debate in Documents, Volume One, 1750–1880*, ed. Susan Groag Bell and Karen M. Offen (Stanford, CA: Stanford UP, 1983), 103.

12. Olympe de Gouges, *Les Droits de la femme* (Paris, 1791) quoted in Bell and Offen, 105.

13. Hufton, 46.

14. Sara Maza, *Private Lives and Public Affairs: The Causes Célèbres of Prerevolutionary France* (Berkeley: U of California P, 1993), 208.

15. Walter Oppenheim, *Habsburgs and Hohenzollerns 1713–1786* (London: Hodder & Stoughton, 1993), 59.

16. Michael Hochedlinger, "Mars Ennobled: The Ascent of the Military and the Creation of a Military Nobility in Mid-Eighteenth-Century Austria," *German History* 17, no. 2 (1999), 169–70.

17. W. R. Ward, "'An Awakened Christianity': The Austrian Protestants and Their Neighbours in the Eighteenth Century," *Journal of Ecclesiastical History* 40, no. 1 (1989), 66.

18. Rebecca Gates-Coon, *The Landed Estates of the Esterházy Princes: Hungary during the Reforms of Maria Theresia and Joseph II* (Baltimore, MD: Johns Hopkins UP, 1994), 104–5.

19. Oppenheim, 97.

20. Quoted in G. P. Gooch, *Maria Theresa and Other Studies* (Archon Books, 1965), 16.

21. Quoted in Jane Glover, *Mozart's Women: His Family, His Friends, His Music* (London: Pan Macmillan, 2006), 30.

22. Michael E. Yonan, "Modesty and Monarchy: Rethinking Empress Maria Theresa at Schönbrunn," *Austrian History Yearbook* 35 (2004), 27.

23. Gooch, 18.

24. Yonan, 42.

25. James F. Brennan, *Enlightened Despotism in Russia: The Reign of Elizabeth, 1741–1762* (New York: Peter Lang, 1987), 11.

26. Though this was never codified into law, it became common practice to commute all capital sentences into permanent exile.

27. Brennan, 125–26.

28. Evgenii Viktorovich Anisimov, *Five Empresses: Court Life in Eighteenth-Century Russia*, trans. Kathleen Carroll (Westport, CT: Praeger, 2004), 208.

29. Philip Longworth, *The Three Empresses: Catherine I, Anne and Elizabeth of Russia* (New York: Holt, Rinehart and Winston, 1972), 194.

30. Allen McConnell, "Catherine the Great and the Fine Arts," in *Imperial Russia 1700–1917: State, Society, Opposition*, ed. Ezra Mendelsohn and Marshall S. Shatz (DeKalb: Northern Illinois UP, 1988), 38–39.

31. Evgenii Viktorovich Anisimov, *Five Empresses: Court Life in Eighteenth-Century Russia*, trans. Kathleen Carroll (Westport, CT: Praeger, 2004), 232 and Brennan, 62.

32. James H. Billington, *The Icon and the Axe: An Interpretive History of Russian Culture* (New York: Vintage Books, 1970), 199.
33. Brennan, 223.
34. Frederick II, quoted in Oppenheim, 67.
35. Monika Greenleaf, "Performing Autobiography: The Multiple Memoirs of Catherine the Great (1756–96)," *Russian Review* 63, no. 3 (2004), 423.
36. Letter from Emperor Joseph II of Austria to Robert Keith, British Ambassador in Vienna (1782), quoted in Gooch, 114–15.
37. Anisimov, 195.
38. Dominique Maroger, ed., *The Memoirs of Catherine the Great*, trans. Moura Budberg (New York: Collier Books, 1961), 178.
39. Quoted in Anisimov, 177.
40. Vivian R. Gruder, "The Question of Marie-Antoinette: The Queen and Public Opinion before the Revolution," *French History* 16, no. 3 (2002), 280.
41. Lynn Hunt, "Pornography and the French Revolution," in *The Invention of Pornography: Obscenity and the Origins of Modernity, 1500–1800*, ed. Lynn Hunt (New York: Zone Books, 1996), 324.
42. Amelia Rauser, "The Butcher-Kissing Duchess of Devonshire: Between Caricature and Allegory in 1784," *Eighteenth-Century Studies* 36, no. 1 (2002), 25.
43. Amanda Foreman, *Georgiana, Duchess of Devonshire* (New York: Random House, 1998), 140.
44. Elaine Chalus, " 'That Epidemical Madness': Women and Electoral Politics in the Late Eighteenth Century," in *Gender in Eighteenth-Century England: Roles, Representations and Responsibilities*, ed. Hanna Barker and Elaine Chalus (New York: Longman, 1997), 166–78.
45. Rauser, 29–30.

SUGGESTED READING

Anisimov, Evgenii Viktorovich. *Five Empresses: Court Life in Eighteenth-Century Russia*, translated by Kathleen Carroll. Westport, CT: Praeger, 2004.
Brennan, James F. *Enlightened Despotism in Russia: The Reign of Elizabeth, 1741–1762.* New York: Peter Lang, 1987.
Foreman, Amanda. *Georgiana, Duchess of Devonshire.* New York: Random House, 1998.
Godineau, Dominique. *The Women of Paris and Their French Revolution*, translated by Katherine Streip. Berkeley: U of California P, 1998.
Gooch, G. P. *Maria Theresa and Other Studies.* Archon Books, 1965.
Hufton, Olwen H. *Women and the Limits of Citizenship in the French Revolution.* Toronto: U of Toronto P, 1992.
Hunt, Lynn, ed. *The Invention of Pornography: Obscenity and the Origins of Modernity, 1500–1800.* New York: Zone Books, 1996.
Levy, Darline Gay, and Harriet Branson Applewhite. "Women and Political Revolution in Paris." In *Becoming Visible: Women in European History*. 2nd ed. Edited by Renate Bridenthal, Claudia Koonz, and Susan Stuard. Boston, MA: Houghton Mifflin, 1987, 279–306.
Madariaga, Isabel de. *Russia in the Age of Catherine the Great: A Short History.* New Haven, CT: Yale UP, 1991.

Maza, Sara. *Private Lives and Public Affairs: The Causes Célèbres of Prerevolutionary France*. Berkeley: U of California P, 1993.
Oppenheim, Walter. *Habsburgs and Hohenzollerns 1713–1786*. London: Hodder & Stoughton, 1993.
Smith, Theresa Ann. *The Emerging Female Citizen: Gender and Enlightenment in Spain*. Berkeley: U of California P, 2006.

4

Women and Law

Eighteenth-century legal reforms had a varied impact on European women. Some enjoyed the chance to speak on their own behalf in the courtroom, a right they had never before possessed. Reforms offering more state assistance in detecting and prosecuting crime helped female victims launch complaints, where before they might have kept silent or sought extra-legal solutions. Torture and violent execution ill fitted criminal justice systems reformed on the basis of "reason." This, combined with the fact that elites felt less threatened by demonic magic, was of special benefit to those women who might have faced witchcraft charges in earlier centuries. Women tempted to commit infanticide benefited from Enlightenment demographic concerns that offered better alternatives to dispose of bastard children.

Not all Enlightenment legal reforms held feminine interests uppermost, however. Some further cemented women's formal subjugation to husbands and fathers by continuing to allow the latter to speak on their behalf. As the poorest members of society, female offenders were less able to avoid lengthy prison sentences by paying fines, and felt the brunt of harsher legislation against property crime. Many rape victims continued to be silenced by cultural understandings of sexuality that colored virtually all penetrative sex as consensual. Female legal experts, who often offered a perspective more sympathetic to women in the courtroom, began to lose credibility with male physicians. The new French republic trumpeted gender and class equalities before the law, but the revolutionary tribunals issued a summary justice with striking similarities to the worst of the *ancien régime.*

LEGAL IDENTITIES

As in the previous centuries, much of women's legal identity in eighteenth-century Europe was connected to their marital status. Many civil law courts refused to consider married women as individuals separate from their spouses. The English common-law principle of coverture and the French notion of *feme couvert* placed wives and their property firmly under husbands' control. In Germany, gender guardianship (*Geschlechtsvormundschaft*) had the power to make all women the legal equivalent of children by giving them a male guardian to oversee and take responsibility for all of their commercial activities. Gender guardianship underwent a process of erosion during the Enlightenment period, placing the onus for their own business enterprises upon the women themselves, but simultaneously reducing wives' protection from liability for their husbands' financial indiscretions.[1]

There were also ways around coverture, and these deviations were practiced more and more by the eighteenth century. Families might have legally settled property on an Englishwoman prior to her marriage, for example, or a wife could conduct business in her own name under the status of a *feme sole* trader. French wives, too, enjoyed the possibility of running their own enterprises with the legal designation of *marchande publique*.[2] In Poland, Magdeburg Law protected wives' dowries, so that husbands could not use dowries to pay off their debts, and widows were granted exclusive access to these funds upon their husbands' deaths.[3] These advantages could only be enjoyed by propertied women; poorer women lacked the funds to pursue such avenues through the legal system.

Enlightenment legal reforms had mixed results for the women of Europe. By mid-century, all Russian women, including serfs, could initiate lawsuits and speak on their own behalf as plaintiffs and defendants in Russia's courtrooms.[4] The women of the Dutch republic were free to launch legal proceedings in their own right as well.[5] Prussia, by contrast, further cemented wives' subordination. When Frederick II commissioned a new legal code in 1750—celebrated for its basis in "reason"—it continued to stipulate that a husband should "defend his wife, as well before the judge as elsewhere; wherefore also he may appear in a judicature for her ... and she shall ratify what he does."[6] In other words, a husband could speak for his wife in the courts, and she would be expected to accept and confirm his actions, regardless of her private views.

In the eyes of many European civil courts, women—married, widowed or single—continued to have no legal identity. The Italian civil courts and the

Chetmno Law courts of Poland heard only male litigants, and women with relevant business there needed a man to speak for them.[7] For married women, this was their husband; single women would have their father or another male associate represent them. As one Polish historian notes, women deprived of the right to bear legal witness were placed in the same category "as the lunatics, mentally deficient, dumb, deaf or blind people, and heretics."[8]

Occasionally this principle worked to women's advantage. Married Englishwomen who committed certain crimes could theoretically seek refuge in the defense of marital coercion, because of their "civil subjection" to their husbands. In practice, this tactic required extensive evidence for proof and had uncertain results.[9] The civil protections afforded Frenchwomen did not extend to the criminal law at all. When a Bordeaux woman on trial for infanticide in 1723 tried to defend herself by saying that she had strangled her daughters at her husband's insistence, the court nonetheless found her criminally responsible.[10] German women, too, often failed to benefit from the protections of gender subordination. The prerogatives of *Geschlechtsvormundschaft* that had allowed German women to avoid creditors fell under siege throughout the eighteenth century, culminating in their complete abolition in the early decades of the nineteenth century.[11]

The women of the French Revolution enjoyed access to temporary local arbitration courts (so-called *tribunaux de famille*: family tribunals, or family courts) set up by the National Assembly in 1790. For the next decade, this institution provided some measure of redress for women seeking to take advantage of the new laws passed by the revolutionary government. The radical reformers offered new opportunities for divorce (see Chapter 1), but they also introduced laws allowing equal inheritance to offspring, whether male or female, legitimate or illegitimate. In this burgeoning spirit of equality, the *tribunaux de famille* even allowed the disputants to select their own arbiters from among their family and friends, though many chose someone with formal legal training anyway. Regardless, women took advantage of the family tribunal as an avenue for enjoying their newfound rights within civil society, and these courts' reputation for fairness and accessibility to French women has stood the test of time.[12]

In the rest of Europe, the ecclesiastical courts remained one of the most common of Europe's legal institutions for female litigation. Rather than acting in a purely repressive manner, the church courts addressed many feminine concerns of the eighteenth century. They were a popular refuge for the middling and elite women who could afford the cost, because they dealt with issues of morality, and particularly with marriage. Wives in Spain, for example, came before the ecclesiastical courts seeking solutions to sexual problems within their marriages, and often found satisfaction.[13] The popularity with eighteenth-century women of the Bishop of London's Consistory

Court was so great that it led one chronicler to dub it, "A Women's Court." While masculine resort to ecclesiastical justice had all but disappeared in this century, female Londoners continued to bring suits to protect their reputations from sexual slander.[14] Though mediated through lawyers, it is clear that women's voices and interests were recognized by the church courts of Enlightenment Europe.

FEMALE CRIMINALS

The eighteenth century saw a number of changes to the punishment of criminals which had a significant impact on women. Rulers imbued with Enlightenment ideals were eager to make their imprint upon their nations' justice systems. Russia, for example, long known for its harshness towards its lawbreakers, experienced a comparative softening under the enlightened despots of the eighteenth century. Empress Elizabeth attempted to ban the death penalty, as did Grand Duke Leopold of Tuscany and several other European leaders.

Elizabeth also made special concessions to female convicts, making nostril slitting exclusive to male felons and reducing the punishment for mariticide (the murder of a husband by his wife). Formerly, Russian women found guilty of killing their husbands, regardless of their reasons for doing so, were buried up to their necks and left to die slowly. Under the reformed penal system, these women were simply beheaded.[15] In England, too, the sentence for this crime (known as petty treason) was reduced from burning at the stake to hanging in 1790.[16] Men who killed their wives had always experienced the lesser penalty; the reduction of women's sentences reflects the reform mentality of the eighteenth century.

This reform mentality did not eliminate class privilege, however. In the feudal states of Enlightenment Europe, nobles still maintained a hegemonic control of the courts, and it was very difficult for a peasant plaintiff to succeed in a lawsuit against her overlord. In nonfeudal states, elitism still existed, only in a more subtle form. Even England, celebrated by residents and visitors alike for the freedom and equality of its people, gained infamy for its "bloody code" of the eighteenth century. This refers to a series of new statutes that were passed in the course of the century that made a remarkably wide variety of property offenses punishable by death.

In practice, most convicted thieves received lighter sentences or pardons, but the bloody code served to keep the poor in a constant state of fear. Periodically, women like milliner Hannah Dagoe, "a wild, light-headed Girl, of disobedient Temper" who had stolen a watch, were hanged as examples to their peers of the dangers of pilfering.[17] This has generally been interpreted as a product of the rise of mercantile interests at the expense of the working class. Norway, too, experienced a similar elitist policy, reinstating capital punishment for theft in 1690. It hung over the heads of property offenders for most of the eighteenth century (until its abolition in 1771) though no one was likely ever executed.[18] In France, the proportion of food thieves awarded prison or galley sentences rose from 15 to 45 percent over the period from the start of the century to the eve of the French Revolution.[19] Women, as frequent offenders in shoplifting and pilfering crimes across Europe, felt the impact of such legislative shifts.

Executions did not disappear from the landscape of Enlightenment Europe, but they took on a less grisly form that was more in tune with the civilizing ethos of the time. As with all Enlightenment-inspired reforms, reason, rather than humanity, was the driving force. Thus, the traditional practices of torture or prolonged executions were examined for their basis in reason, and found wanting. In the words of Italian legal theorist Cesare Beccaria in 1764:

> The purpose of punishment... is nothing other than to dissuade the criminal from doing fresh harm to his compatriots and to keep other people from doing the same. Therefore, punishments and their method of inflicting them should be chosen that, mindful of the proportion between crime and punishment, will make the most effective and lasting impression on men's minds and inflict the least torment on the body of the criminal.[20]

The guillotine, as a machine that neatly decapitated its victims and—unlike human executioners—would not administer differing degrees of force depending on strength or sentiment, fit these principles nicely.

An even more serious deterrent, Beccaria argued, was the sentence of lifetime incarceration. Where the effects of capital punishment are felt only at the moment of execution, he argued, "life at hard labor" stands as a "constant example" of the results of indulging in criminal activity.[21] While Beccaria's book was banned in Spain and condemned by prominent figures in France and England, many European powers strove to implement its ideas.

There was a visible growth in the use of incarceration to punish offenders in the eighteenth century. Female prisoners were crowded in with men, increasing their vulnerability to sexual assault or other forms of violence. The poor air and sanitation further compounded the dangers to inmates. Anna Elizabeth Muller, sent to a Leipzig correctional center in 1708 for stealing, suffered convulsions with a white and bloody discharge from her mouth.[22] Prisons of the modern version with single cells and gender separation took much longer to appear in most of Europe. In Sweden, for example, the first such structure was built in the 1840s.[23]

Lifetime imprisonment was not the only alternative to the death penalty in eighteenth-century Europe. There were a number of ways for a capital sentence to be commuted, and these varied techniques became popular with the reform-minded judiciary of the Enlightenment. In France, Spain, and Italy, galley slavery served as a substitute for execution. Another possibility was transportation to a penal colony. This had the added benefit of contributing much-needed workers to the new settlements overseas. Britain was the most prominent jurisdiction to use this option, though some German offenders found themselves in North America as slaves, and France transported some offenders as well.[24] While only men could receive a galley sentence, women could and did get transported.

Punishment in eighteenth-century Europe was often different for men and women, not always to the latter's advantage. Hungarian men were immobilized in the stocks, but women faced the *korbács* (whipping) in the manorial courts of Esterházy lands.[25] Female thieves in Sweden were birched, where men were flogged.[26] The public whipping of women fell into increasing disfavor as the century wore on, particularly in England. The illustration entitled *Whipping John of Islington*, printed in 1748, depicts a wife being whipped while a lascivious onlooker peeps through the door. The exposure of the female posterior, and the violence of the act itself, were becoming more distasteful to the growing middle class of eighteenth-century England. In London in 1783, for example, a woman found guilty

Whipping John of Islington, an etching from 1748 showing the evils of whipping women, and wives in particular. (Courtesy of Library of Congress)

for stealing a pork ham was sentenced to be "severely and privately whipped, in the presence of females only."[27]

In some cases, gender distinctions of punishment were not legislated, but existed in practice. In jurisdictions across Europe, a range of crimes was punishable by fines. Those who could not pay had to serve the penalty in some other way, usually spending a term in jail or undergoing some form of corporal punishment, or both. This latter scenario more often applied to women, while their male counterparts were able to escape the harsher punishments, because they had sufficient means to pay the fine. This accounts for the disproportionate levels of women in European prisons, such as the "surprisingly high" numbers of female thieves found incarcerated in a study of the Dutch republic.[28]

One particular category of female criminals may have experienced distinct advantages in the eighteenth century. The crime of infanticide attracted government attention for a variety of reasons. The murder of newborn babies had always been considered a reprehensible act, yet the unwed mothers who were typically guilty of the offense had little other recourse to avoid the shame or financial burden of a bastard baby. With the rise of concerns about demographic growth preoccupying many nations in Europe (see Chapter 1), attitudes towards unwed mothers also began to soften.

These factors combined to create a relaxation of judicial attitudes towards infanticide across Europe during this period. The Croatian courts were more likely to suspend trials and let suspects go free in eighteenth-century infanticide cases.[29] More often, authorities acted to reduce the likelihood of the crime occurring at all. Sweden actually introduced new legislation in 1778 allowing bastard-bearing women to give birth "in an unknown place ... without action being taken or enquiries made."[30] Spain, too, passed a law in 1796 that protected anyone "carrying a child which they say is to be exposed in a hospital or hospice" for *expósitos* (foundlings).[31] In the Austrian Empire, where the crime had traditionally been punished by decapitation, emperor Joseph II also reduced the penalties and passed a number of laws in 1780 to shield unwed mothers from social censure. These sorts of measures, it was hoped, would ensure a healthy population of citizens in the years to come.[32]

Unlike infanticide, the courts' attitudes towards prostitution differed little from previous centuries. Though French women's groups called for new laws that would result in education and rehabilitation for prostitutes, the Republic paid only lip service to their demands. A decree was issued—with the ostensible goal of improving the moral purity of the new republic—to incarcerate all women caught publicly soliciting. However, prostitution itself remained legal; if prostitutes continued their trade quietly behind the scenes, they were not hindered.[33] The sex trade was essentially considered a necessary evil, and the women involved were either ignored or punished, not helped in any way.

In this, at least, revolutionary France was similar to its European counterparts. In 1765, the priest and parishioners of the Hungarian village of Haratschon demanded the expulsion of three women who were selling sex to the soldiers quartered nearby. As they told the estate manager, they were "afraid that God will visit yet more misfortune upon [the parish] because of the evil way of life of these persons."[34] Without regard for the circumstances that might have driven these women (a schoolmaster's widow and her two grown daughters) to such an enterprise, the courts enacted the order for exile. A Liepzig correctional center operated on related principles, arresting large numbers of prostitutes and locking them up, so that "the common weal will be cleansed of them."[35]

FEMALE VICTIMS OF CRIME

The women of Enlightenment Europe fell victim to a wide variety of offenses but were disproportionately vulnerable to rape and other violent crimes. Their subordinate cultural, economic, and legal position left them often unable to prosecute offenses, so historians can only guess at the looming "dark figure" of unreported crimes. Many interesting studies have been done of those that were reported, however. They show that some European women, at least, could seek redress for crimes against them.

There was an overall decline in homicides throughout Europe by the eighteenth century. It has been theorized that early modern Europe underwent a slow "civilizing process" that culminated in an overall antipathy to violence in the Enlightenment age. As a result of this "civilizing process," Europeans—especially those of the middle class—were less likely to indulge in physical aggression in general public interaction.[36] Detailed studies of the Netherlands and England show a marked decrease in homicides in the eighteenth century, and it seems likely that this is the case for much of Europe.

The decline had less of an impact upon female victims. The types of violent crime most commonly targeting women—domestic violence, or violence against intimates, as opposed to strangers—continued to occur at relatively the same rates in this as in subsequent centuries.[37] By the Enlightenment, however, more women may have felt justified in bringing their attackers to justice. A large outcry followed London Judge Buller's assertion that it was acceptable for a husband to use a rod against his wife provided its diameter did not exceed that of his thumb. He was derided in the press, most famously by his countryman James Gillray's 1782 caricature, *Judge Thumb*.

The Dutch Republic "severely frowned upon" wife-beating, and abused women could go before the courts on their own behalf and initiate a

Judge Thumb, or –patent sticks for family correction: warranted lawful! (London, 1782). This etching by James Gillray depicts Judge Buller holding a bundle of rods—each with a diameter less than his thumb—asking, "Who wants a cure for a nasty wife?" while, in the background, a husband beats his wife. She pitifully cries out "Murder for God sake, Murder!" (Courtesy of Library of Congress)

prosecution that would see their husbands fined on the first instance, with escalation of punishments for subsequent infractions.[38] Christian V, King of Denmark and Norway until 1699, passed a law making a husband who "acts tyrannically and unchristianly against his wife" punishable by imprisonment with hard labor, and there was a clear decline in legal acceptance of any physical chastisement of wives by Norwegian husbands throughout the eighteenth century.[39]

Wives sought aid and refuge from a range of community members, and this included—but was definitely not confined to—legal officials. When they did appeal to the courts, some battered women expected little more than "protection and some support in their everyday life"; they did not expect their husbands to be incarcerated for any length of time.[40] Others, such as those in the Netherlands, watched their husbands suffer serious reprisals. Dutchman Elias Crammer's letter to his wife reflects the power her prosecution had over him, but also the disadvantages she faced by having her husband incarcerated. Writing from jail, he warned her that further prosecution could result in "the eternal destruction and ruination of me and of you and of all ours" and entreated her to withdraw her complaint so that he would not face the ultimate penalty of banishment. If that were to happen, he argued, "we won't keep a penny in the world, and what will thou begin when I am gone?"[41] His entreaties worked; Elias was eventually released from prison, much chastened, one would assume, after being reminded of the repercussions for abusing his wife.

In all types of crimes, female prosecutors benefited from the Enlightenment trend towards more centralized government. Previously, many nations had entirely private prosecution systems, where the victim of a crime bore the financial and personal burden of investigating the offense, locating the suspect, and bringing him or her before the judge. The Enlightenment era saw a slight shift of the prosecutorial burden over to the state. In Sweden, for example, local constables and sheriffs assisted private plaintiffs more often, even in cases of theft or violence, prompting one historian to acknowledge that, by this century, "the embryo of a modern police force and prosecutor's office had come into being."[42]

Simultaneously, informal means of resolving disputes began to lose their effectiveness in the increasingly anonymous urban environments of eighteenth-century Europe. In the absence of the unofficial arbitration of the local curate or priest, lord or *seigneur*, citydwellers turned more frequently to the courts. Eighteenth-century legal officials in many towns throughout Europe heard a growing number of assault, defamation, theft, and general nuisance complaints. As a significant component of the migrants to cities, women were among those seeking satisfaction through formal channels for interpersonal disputes. The increasing use of state funds in aid of private prosecutions began to break down the financial barriers that commonly prevented women from accessing the machinery of justice.

Other limitations remained, however, and this was most visible in prosecutions for rape. Very few rapes ever found their way into the courts of early modern Europe. Russia is the exception. A 1715 military statute in Petrine Russia raised the penalty for rape from exile to execution and disallowed defendants from impugning the victim's character. As a result, Russian women stood out as "energetic and persistent litigants" in eighteenth-century rape trials. Here, lack of consent was comparatively easily established, and cases of "he said, she said" so common to rape narratives were often decided in favor of the female plaintiff.[43]

Most other European women, however, inculcated from the cradle to be chaste, silent, and obedient, were ashamed to admit that they had been the victims of such an indecent assault, or they lacked the vocabulary necessary to prove that the crime had occurred. Early modern descriptions of licit sex portrayed women as being "used," "occupied," or "known" by men. There were simply no words in the eighteenth-century lexicon for rape. Any description of penetrative sex necessarily recounted female submission—the very characteristic that prevented it from being understood as nonconsensual.[44] The *philosophes* themselves denied the physical plausibility of rape. Voltaire offered the example of the impossibility of putting a sword into a moving scabbard, saying "it is the same with rape as with impotence; there are some cases which ought never to come before the courts." [45]

In such an atmosphere, consent was difficult to disprove. Anything less than all-out screaming resistance by the most innocent young girl was deemed to indicate consent. Indeed, only the latter type of victim had a chance at convincing a jury. Children were treated differently in the Enlightenment age (as discussed in Chapter 1); childhood innocence was protected much more vigilantly. It is thus not surprising that young girls became almost the only rape prosecutors in this era. As early as the first decade of the century in Holland, for example, a group of impoverished orphan girls independently charged a wealthy and connected man with assaulting them. The only prosecution testimony was theirs, that he had raped them for a prolonged period while they were in the Rotterdam poorhouse, with no other witnesses. The court found him guilty and sentenced him to death.[46] Many jurisdictions experienced a visible rise in prosecutions for child rape by at least the second half of the eighteenth century.

This did not leave adult women entirely without recourse against their rapists. Female prosecutors' goals were not limited to seeing their sexual assailant executed or incarcerated. Marie Peraud and Marie Salgues of eighteenth-century Bordeaux initiated rape proceedings because their fiancés had impregnated and then jilted them. Launching a criminal charge of rape encouraged the accused men to marry the women. Indeed, "a prompt marriage ceremony in the chapel of the Palais de l'Ombrière" indemnified the men and reinstated their brides' honor.[47]

When marriage was impossible, as in cases where the rapist was already married, money could go a long way to reduce the social impact of rape. Women and their families customarily agreed to abandon rape charges upon payment of a financial settlement. These could be quite substantial, the most notorious being the 2,400 *livres* received by Rose Keller, victim of a violent rape by the Marquis de Sade. Keller made only 350 *livres* a year in her trade as a spinster, so this represented a substantial sum indeed.[48] Compensation to the victim and her family was common in Russian culture as well, whether the rape was settled in or out of court.[49] In the same vein, Spanish victims of ravishment or defloration (*estupro*) sought significant damages that would compensate for their forcible seduction and resulting loss of status on the marriage market. Such plaintiffs had the advantage of a justice system that was fairly inexpensive in relation to many of its European counterparts.[50]

WOMEN AS EXPERT WITNESSES

From the time of the middle ages, Continental courts paid midwives and physicians for their testimony in a wide variety of cases. Midwives' opinions were sought in establishing physical proof of the presence or loss of virginity, pregnancy, female impotence, and a variety of other issues related to female genitalia. They provided medical observation of fetuses in cases where women claimed to have experienced miscarriages from assaults, or where mothers charged with infanticide claimed that a natural stillbirth had occurred.

Women's presence as experts on these matters was long established, part of the Roman law used in many jurisdictions, and accepted in German law as early as the sixteenth century.[51] All European courts ascribing to the Roman law tradition prohibited the execution of pregnant women. According to common practice, authorities summoned a jury of matrons to determine a condemned woman's lack of pregnancy before she underwent the death sentence, to ensure that an innocent fetus would not perish along with its mother.

All women, not just midwives, were considered to have a specialized knowledge of the female body. It was an established tradition that the fishwives of Paris, known as the *poissardes*, had to be present when the queen gave birth to attest to the legitimacy of the infant.[52] In England, many parishes employed "searchers," elderly women who were called in to investigate corpses and report to the coroner's jury on probable causes of death.[53] Croatian authorities required two women to inspect "all the women of fertile age" to locate a suspect in the case of a possible infanticide.[54] Russian courts traditionally sent married or widowed women to check for signs of rape on victims' bodies. Their testimony clearly carried weight, as was seen in the 1689 case of the rape of 13-year-old Feklitsa, where three womens' observations of blood on her shirt and evidence of a sexual attack swayed the court against the defendant's denial, even though there were no witnesses to the rape itself.[55]

By the Enlightenment era, physicians and surgeons had already begun to appropriate many of the midwives' traditional duties (as discussed in Chapter 2), but the judges of early modern Europe continued to call upon these women even after male professionals challenged their credibility.[56] Female medical testimony became contested terrain in the Enlightenment age. A case from Italy illustrates this point. A Roman court sent three midwives and a surgeon to examine a woman named Matthia, charged with infanticide, who claimed that the bloody rags and stains neighbors had found in her home had come from a sudden return of her menses. Two of the midwives attributed the physical evidence to a pregnancy, while the third midwife and surgeon supported Matthia's story that she was only heavily menstruating and was thus innocent of infanticide. The court called in a renowned physician from the university who—without having directly examined Matthia—dismissed the two midwives as ignorant and upheld her innocence. A detailed study of the incident shows the lack of medical knowledge surrounding the signs of pregnancy at this time and the prolonged assault to which female legal experts were subjected by medical professionals.[57]

In 1799, Swiss legislators abolished the requirement that midwives act as servants of the court in commanding unwed mothers to name the father while in the throes of labor. The end of this official duty was symptomatic of an overall decline in midwives' courtroom functions. For much of Europe, the eighteenth century marks the last in which women were considered the only true interpreters of the female body.[58]

Women often took the responsibility of preparing bodies for burial, and this function frequently brought them before the courts in homicide cases. For female victims of violent crime, a feminine observer who could testify to their wounds and understand their circumstances added a sympathetic voice to the courtroom. This was certainly the case with Mary Goynes, murdered by her husband in 1739. As she languished near death from the wounds he inflicted, she anticipated his murder trial and told her friend that she wanted her to be the one to "lay her out" so that she could see and attest to "what she had gone through."[59] In a slightly different example, a Frenchman might have escaped a rape trial if it was not for the midwife with whom his victim consulted regarding injuries from the attack. She pushed the girl and her family to prosecute him and helped them get additional medical evidence against him.[60] The female expert witnesses did far more than just passively list their observations in Europe's courtrooms.

This direct action did not always work in women's favor. Their reproductive knowledge led many European women to police their peers. They watched their feminine relations, neighbors, and co-workers for signs of pregnancy or recent childbirth. The surveillance could be as subtle as sideways glances at growing abdomens or observations of telltale stains in laundry and bedding, or as overt as squeezing breasts and lifting petticoats. Croatian Anica Šabadinka's neighbor testified at her infanticide trial that she "stripped her breasts naked and saw the dark circles indicative of a pregnant woman."[61] A Stockholm woman named Brita who lost a substantial amount of girth after a short illness was observed and reported on by her female neighbors in 1765.[62] In the eyes of the woman on trial at least, female witnesses did not always serve feminine interests.

DECLINE OF WITCHCRAFT

The eighteenth century saw the last executions for witchcraft in most countries in Europe, but prosecutions had been on the wane for a considerable period. At the height of the early modern witch-hunts in the sixteenth century, many states had employed legal officials who actively initiated witchcraft prosecutions and would bring charges based simply upon the "ill fame" of an individual. This fell out of fashion by the Enlightenment era. In 1682, for example, France's Louis XIV stopped such practices in his realm, as did Prussia in 1728, followed by England and Scotland in 1736.[63] By the early 1700s, therefore, accusations of witchcraft relied solely upon the initiative of private citizens, and the number of prosecutions dropped visibly.[64] Anna Göldi was the last witch to be executed by judicial authorities in Europe in Glarus, Switzerland, in 1782.[65] Though Portugal executed its last witch more than 150 years earlier, it—along with Würtemburg and Spain—held witch trials into the nineteenth century.[66]

Though twenty-first-century depictions of witches tend to consider them all to be women, witchcraft could also be a male offense. Iceland and Finland had very high percentages of men—more than 90 percent in the former, in fact—charged with witchcraft.[67] Nonetheless, across early modern Europe as a whole, approximately 80 percent of the accusations of witchcraft targeted women.[68] In most of these cases, the feminine suspects were already marginalized figures in the community—elderly, decrepit, single or widowed, and poor. Countries like Poland, where there was a shortage of men in this period, saw remarkably few witch trials, probably because every woman had a vital place as a worker in the community.[69]

Studies of the decline in witchcraft prosecutions stress that edicts against persecuting witches did not completely dismiss the possibility of demonic magic. In 1766, for example, Empress Maria Theresa of Austria issued a government patent to suppress witchcraft trials within her domain. While she stressed the "well-known fact" that "the mania of sorcery and witchcraft was grossly exaggerated in earlier times" and thus all allegations must be viewed with skepticism in the courts, she left open the possibility for genuine cases.[70] Across Europe, the appetite for witch trials among legal officials declined, not because of a complete disbelief in demonic powers, but instead because of a growing skepticism in the ability to uncover the necessary proof of the crime.[71] Decriminalization had a sporadic and varied impact across Europe. Hungarian and Prussian legislation put a visible end to state witch-hunts, while in places like England and Denmark, decriminalization came after prosecutions had already disappeared.[72]

Witches who were convicted in eighteenth-century Europe nonetheless experienced the effects of the reforming spirit of the age. Penalties took on a more Enlightenment flavor. Where witches in Italy, Spain, and Portugal had formerly been put to death for the crime, they were now subjected to the alternatives of corporal punishment or imprisonment.[73] Russian judges, under the enlightened despots of the eighteenth century, sentenced witches to beheading and after 1770 could issue only noncapital penalties.[74] English witches were hanged, but the last person found guilty of witchcraft (Jane Wenham in 1712) received a reprieve from execution.[75]

Even after witchcraft was decriminalized or prosecutions through the courts had all but disappeared, fear and belief in witchcraft persisted among the populace. A case from the Netherlands illustrates this point. Rijntje Boom, a widow residing with a young couple, was suspected of causing an illness in their seven-week-old infant in 1746. They believed that she had bewitched the baby, and with the help of some neighbors, they beat her to death in the process of trying to persuade her to remove her enchantment.[76] Another widow in Palermo, Italy, was believed to have supernatural powers and was tried for murder in 1788–89, after six people bought a potion from her and used it successfully to kill their enemies. They and she received guilty verdicts. Though the locals saw her as a witch, the courts treated her as a murderess.[77]

The swimming of witches, whereby suspects were bound and immersed in water to see whether they floated (by which their guilt was considered to be proved), was still practiced in Hungarian municipal courts during the Enlightenment age, though officials in much of the rest of Europe had abandoned the practice. Villagers continued to subject putative witches to their own forms of justice in all parts of Europe throughout this century, however.[78] Indeed, a particularly lurid account of 1751 Hertfordshire tells of an English couple subjected to a swimming ordeal that was witnessed by 5,000 people. A local publican believed the wife had bewitched his cows and persuaded several friends to help him seize the husband and wife and throw them into the water on a rope. The wife drowned and the publican was hanged for murder.[79]

A Danish woman in her early fifties, a spinster in marital status and by trade, was suspected to be a witch by the local populace for many years. When a horse died under suspicious circumstances in 1722, her neighbors tied her down and burned her to death. Though widows and single women attracted the largest percentage of community attacks, married women and men could become objects of vigilante witch-hunts as well. In fact, in Denmark, attacks on men actually rose during the next century.[80] In any case, witchcraft remained a reality in the lives of certain women in eighteenth-century Europe long after the courts had lost interest in the crime.

WOMEN BEFORE THE REVOLUTIONARY TRIBUNAL

The execution of Louis XVI in 1793 was the beginning of a spate of decapitations in France which was to last for several years. Many women found themselves before the legal machinery of the Terror, and accounts have survived of some of the more renowned. Helen Williams, an English novelist and poet who had traveled to France full of enthusiasm in the early days of the fall of the old regime, was more muted as she watched Queen Marie Antoinette on trial. She was especially moved at the queen's reaction to the charge of "having committed the most shocking crime" (presumably referring to the allegations that she had committed incest with her son). According to Williams, Marie Antoinette "turned with dignity towards the audience," and quietly asked if there was any mother who would not "shudder at the idea of such horrors."[81] Though her conduct obviously won Williams's sympathy and approval, it neglected to sway judgment in her favor, and she followed her husband to the scaffold.

Charlotte Corday, the moderate republican who assassinated Jean-Paul Marat in the belief that it would end the Terror, presented a formal defense at her trial, in contrast to the queen who had refused to recognize the charges against her and called no witnesses on her own behalf. Williams's account of Corday's trial depicts the jury deliberating and the presence of the defense counsel with whom Corday consulted. The revolutionary tribunals and executions were public spectacles, where the conduct of the women facing judgment was carefully scrutinized and recorded by observers like Williams. The latter remarked upon Corday's courage and composure on her way to the scaffold, deeming it so powerful as to silence "the women who were called furies of the guillotine . . . who had assembled to insult her on leaving the prison."[82] The British press conveyed a similar image of the trial in the sketch by James Gillray, depicting a serene and beautiful Corday surrounded by simian-faced officials.

Charlotte Corday faces the tribunal separated by the body of Marat. The caption reads "The heroic Charlotte la Cordé, upon her trial, at the bar of the Revolutionary Tribunal of Paris, July 17, 1793, for having rid the World of that monster of Atheism and Murder, the Regicide MARAT . . ." Etching by James Gillray (London, 1793). (Courtesy of Library of Congress)

Other accounts of prominent women who faced the tribunal depict similar theatre. The public trials allowed little, if any, defense testimony. Judges interrupted Jeanne-Marie Roland—another moderate revolutionary—during her impassioned defense speech in 1793, found her guilty, and sentenced her to death. Executions were carried out within twenty-four hours of issuance; the condemned were given no possibility of appeal. Roland's exclamation at the fatal moment of her execution encapsulated the irony of the proceedings: "O Liberty, what crimes are committed in thy name!"[83] Her memoirs, penned during her time in prison, exhibit a calm sense of the inevitability of the guillotine in Robespierre's regime. "I do not dread going to the scaffold," she wrote; "it is disgraceful to live in the midst of ruffians."[84]

Théroigne de Méricourt, another proponent of the republic who was later declared its enemy, actually escaped the guillotine due to her obvious insanity. Nonetheless, the Revolutionary Committee of the Le Peletier *section* that came to arrest her in the spring of 1794 left a report that illustrates the events that preceded a tribunal hearing:

> Having climbed up to a room on the fourth floor we informed her [Méricourt] of the aforesaid order, and ... we proceeded with a vigorous inspection of all her papers, which we have deposited in two box-files, bearing the numbers one and two, upon which we have placed our seals, together with those of citizeness Théroigne; we have also put our seals on a case containing some papers, so that all of these things may be taken to our committee and checked in the presence of citizeness Théroigne.[85]

The committee was composed of reputable citizens, who acted in response to a denunciation that Méricourt had "made suspect remarks." Despite its appearance of meticulous bureaucracy, the legal machinery of the tribunal was all too hurried for many who came before it.

As the revolution progressed, so too did the speed at which justice was meted out by the republic. An infamous law passed on 22 Prairial Year II of the revolutionary calendar (June 10, 1794)—shortly after Méricourt's arrest—allowed counterrevolutionary suspects to be condemned without the chance to provide any evidence in their defense. The government placed the onus on every citizen to seek out sedition. According to the legislation,

> The proof necessary to convict the enemies of the people is every kind of evidence, either material or moral or verbal or written.... Every citizen has the right to seize conspirators and counterrevolutionaries and to arraign them before magistrates. He is required to denounce them when he knows of them.[86]

The period that followed saw an escalation in the paranoia of the Terror. The slightest deviation from the norm offered a pretext for denunciation, and both women and men were vulnerable to the summary justice meted out by the revolutionary tribunals. While some fell victim to the harsh surveillance, others seized the opportunity to serve the republic.

Women were among the most vigilant in denunciations during the Terror. One particularly zealous woman, responsible for multiple denunciations, befriended the nuns who had cared for her during a period of illness in a Parisian hospital. Suspecting their counterrevolutionary sympathies, she pretended to be a royalist herself, so that they would feel safe expressing antigovernment sentiments, and then she turned them into the tribunal.[87] Though it may seem repugnant for modern minds to acknowledge the significant feminine participation in the Terror, it was a matter of pride to the republican women themselves. Indeed, most women who turned in neighbors and associates to the tribunals did so out of genuine patriotism and a desire to make their mark in the progress of the revolution. As one historian indicates,

> For women who could not bear arms, denunciations were an important way to participate in the welfare of the homeland and help their companions who fought against the enemies on the borders or in the Vendée.... In addition, their professional or homemaking activities in the streets of the city enabled women to notice even the most slightly suspicious act.[88]

Any discussion of the women who died on the scaffold must also acknowledge the many Parisian women who zealously pursued the enemies of the revolution and celebrated the effects of the guillotine.

NOTES

1. Robert Beachy, "Women without Gender: Commerce, Exchange Codes, and the Erosion of German Gender Guardianship, 1680–1830," in *Family Welfare: Gender, Property, and Inheritance since the Seventeenth Century*, ed. David R. Green and Alastair Owens (Westport, CT: Praeger, 2004), 195–215.

2. See Lloyd Bonfield, "Developments in European Family Law," in *The History of the European Family, Volume One: Family Life in Early Modern Times 1500–1789*, ed. David I. Kertzer and Marzio Barbagli (New Haven, CT: Yale UP, 2001), 120–23, and Beachy, 197.

3. Maria Bogucka, *Women in Early Modern Polish Society, against the European Background* (Aldershot, Hampshire: Ashgate, 2004), 14.

4. Natalia Pushkareva, *Women in Russian History from the Tenth to the Twentieth Century*, ed. and trans. Eve Levin (New York: M.E. Sharpe, 1997), 177.

5. Manon van der Heijden, "Women as Victims of Sexual and Domestic Violence in Seventeenth-Century Holland: Criminal Cases of Rape, Incest, and Maltreatment in Rotterdam and Delft," *Journal of Social History* 33, no. 3 (2000), 635.

6. *The Frederician Code* (Edinburgh, 1761), part I, book I, Title VIII (translated from German printing of 1750), quoted in *Women, the Family, and Freedom: The Debate in Documents, Volume One, 1750–1880*, ed. Susan Groag Bell and Karen M. Offen (Stanford, CA: Stanford UP, 1983), 32.

7. Bogucka, 14, 43, and Maura Palazzi, "Female Solitude and Patrilineage: Unmarried Women and Widows during the Eighteenth and Nineteenth Centuries," *Journal of Family History* 15, no. 4 (1990), 450.

8. Bogucka, 14.

9. Dierdre Palk, *Gender, Crime and Judicial Discretion, 1780–1830* (Woodbridge, Suffolk: The Boydell Press, 2006), 21–32.

10. Rebecca E. Kingston, "Criminal Justice in Eighteenth-Century Bordeaux, 1715–24," in *Crime, Punishment, and Reform in Europe*, ed. Louis A. Knafla (Westport, CT: Praeger, 2003), 7.

11. Beachy, 208–9.

12. Suzanne Desan, *The Family on Trial in Revolutionary France* (Berkeley: U of California P, 2004), 6, 154–55.

13. Edward Behrend-Martínez, "Female Sexual Potency in a Spanish Church Court, 1673–1735," *Law and History Review* 24, no. 2 (2006), 297–330.

14. Tim Meldrum, "A Women's Court in London: Defamation at the Bishop of London's Consistory Court, 1700–1745," *London Journal* 19, no. 1 (1994), 1–20.

15. James F. Brennan, *Enlightened Despotism in Russia: The Reign of Elizabeth, 1741–1762* (New York: Peter Lang, 1987), 208–9, 224.

16. Ruth Campbell, "Sentence of Death by Burning for Women," *Journal of Legal History* 5, no. 1 (1984), 55–56.

17. The Ordinary's *Account*, May 4, 1763, quoted in Peter Linebaugh, *The London Hanged: Crime and Civil Society in the Eighteenth Century* (Cambridge: Cambridge UP, 1993), 303.

18. Ferdinand Linthoe Naeshagen, "Private Law Enforcement in Norwegian History: The Husband's Right to Chastise His Wife," *Scandinavian Journal of History* 27, no. 1 (2002), 27 n49.

19. Clive Elmsley, *Crime, Police, and Penal Policy: European Experiences 1750–1940* (Oxford: Oxford UP, 2007), 36.

20. Cesare Beccaria, *On Crimes and Punishments, Translated from the Italian in the Author's Original Order* (1764, reprinted Indianapolis: Hackett, 1986), 23.

21. Beccaria, 50–51.

22. Tanya Kevorkian, "The Rise of the Poor, Weak, and Wicked: Poor Care, Punishment, Religion, and Patriarchy in Leipzig, 1700–1730," *Journal of Social History* 34, no. 1 (2000), 176.

23. Jan Sundin, "For God, State, and People: Crime and Local Justice in Preindustrial Sweden," in *The Civilization of Crime: Violence in Town and Country since the Middle Ages*, ed. Eric A. Johnson and Eric H. Monkkonen (Urbana: U of Illinois P, 1996), 180.

24. Michael R. Weisser, *Crime and Punishment in Early Modern Europe* (Bristol: The Harvester Press, 1979), 141.

25. Rebecca Gates-Coon, *The Landed Estates of the Esterházy Princes: Hungary during the Reforms of Maria Teresia and Joseph II* (Baltimore, MD: Johns Hopkins UP, 1994), 91.

26. Sundin, 179.

27. *Old Bailey Proceedings* June 1783, Trial of Mary Siddon alias Field, quoted in Robert Shoemaker, *The London Mob: Violence and Disorder in Eighteenth-Century England* (London: Hambledon and London, 2004), 93.

28. Herman Diederiks, "Punishment during the *Ancien Régime*; the Case of the Eighteenth-Century Dutch Republic," in *Crime and Criminal Justice in Europe and Canada*, ed. Louis Knafla (Waterloo, On.: Published for Calgary Institute for the Humanities by Wilfred Laurier UP, 1981), 292–93.

29. Nella Lonza, "'Two souls lost': Infanticide in the Republic of Dubrovnik (1667–1808)," trans. Vesna Bace, *Dubrovnik Annals* 6 (2002), 104.

30. Quoted in D. Bradley, "Unmarried Cohabitation in Sweden: A Renewed Social Institution?" *Journal of Legal History* 11, no. 2 (1990), 320.

31. Murcia, *Discurso político*, apéndice tercero, xiv, article xxii, quoted in Joan Sherwood, *Poverty in Eighteenth-Century Spain: The Women and Children of the Inclusa* (Toronto: University of Toronto Press, 1988), 186.

32. Gates-Coon, 152.

33. Dominique Godineau, *The Women of Paris and Their French Revolution*, trans. Katherine Streip (Berkeley: U of California P, 1998), 14.

34. Estate Manager Zöchmeister to regent, August 4, 1765, Lackenbach, quoted in Gates-Coon, 143.
35. Kevorkian, 167, n16.
36. Norbert Elias, *The Civilizing Process: Sociogenetic and Psychogenetic Investigations* [1939], rev. ed., trans. E. Jephcott (Oxford: Blackwell Publishing, 2000).
37. Pieter Spierenburg, "Long-Term Trends in Homicide: Theoretical Reflections and Dutch Evidence, Fifteenth to Twentieth Centuries," in *The Civilization of Crime*, 94–95.
38. van der Heijden, 633.
39. Chr. V 6, 5, § 7, 1687, quoted in Naeshagen, 20.
40. Joachim Eibach, "The Containment of Violence in Central European Cities, 1500–1800," in *Crime, Law and Popular Culture in Europe, 1500–1900*, ed. Richard McMahon (Portland: Willan Publishing, 2008), 65.
41. Quoted in van der Heijden, 635.
42. Sundin, 175.
43. Daniel H. Kaiser, "He Said She Said: Rape and Gender Discourse in Early Modern Russia," *Kritika: Explorations in Russian and Eurasian History* 3, no. 2 (2002), 202, 204, 206 n37.
44. Garthine Walker, "Rereading Rape and Sexual Violence in Early Modern England," *Gender and History* 10, no. 1 (April 1998), 6.
45. F. M. Arouet dit Voltaire, *Prix de la justice de l'humanité* (1777), quoted in Georges Vigarello, *A History of Rape: Sexual Violence in France from the 16th to the 20th Century*, trans. Jean Birrell (Cambridge: Polity Press, 2001), 43.
46. van der Heijden, 626–27.
47. Kingston, 5 and 30 n20.
48. Vigarello, 69.
49. Kaiser, 210 n45.
50. Renato Barahona, *Sex Crimes, Honour, and the Law in Early Modern Spain: Vizcaya, 1528–1735* (Toronto: U of Toronto P, 2003), 118–56.
51. E. H. Ackerknect, "Midwives as Experts in Court," *Bulletin of the New York Academy of Medicine* 52, no. 10 (December 1976), 1225–26.
52. Darline Gay Levy and Harriet Branson Applewhite, "Women and Political Revolution in Paris," in *Becoming Visible: Women in European History*, 2nd ed., ed. Renate Bridenthal, Claudia Koonz, and Susan Stuard (Boston, MA: Houghton Mifflin, 1987), 283.
53. Kevin Siena, "Searchers of the Dead in Long Eighteenth-Century London," in *Marginality and Gender in Pre-Modern Europe*, ed. Kim Kippen and Lori Woods (Toronto: Centre for Reformation and Renaissance Studies, forthcoming).
54. Lonza, 104.
55. Kaiser, 209–10.
56. Silvia De Renzi, "Medical Expertise, Bodies, and the Law in Early Modern Courts," *Isis: Journal of the History of Science in Society* 98, no. 2 (2007), 318.
57. Silvia De Renzi, "Witnesses of the Body: Medico-Legal Cases in Seventeenth-Century Rome," *Studies in History and Philosophy of Science* 33A, no. 2 (2002), 229–32.
58. Ackerknect, 1228.
59. Old Bailey Proceedings, September 1739, trial of Edward Goynes, quoted in Jennine Hurl-Eamon, "I Will Forgive You if the World Will": Wife Murder and Limits on Patriarchal Violence in London, 1690–1750," in *Violence, Politics, and Gender in Early Modern England*, ed. Joseph P. Ward (New York: Palgrave Macmillan, 2008), 231.
60. Vigarello, 80.

61. Lonza, 94n.

62. Maria Kaspersson, "Prosecution and Public Participation—the Case of Early Modern Sweden," in *Crime, Law and Popular Culture*, 108.

63. Edmund M. Kern, "An End to Witch Trials in Austria: Reconsidering the Enlightened State," *Austrian History Yearbook* 30 (1999), 170.

64. Brian Levack, "The Decline and End of Witchcraft Prosecutions," in *Witchcraft and Magic in Europe: The Eighteenth and Nineteenth Centuries*, ed. Brian Levack, Marijke Gijswijt-Hofstra and Roy Porter (London: The Athlone Press, 1999), 32.

65. Marijke Gijswijt-Hofstra, "Witchcraft after the Witch-Trials," in *Witchcraft and Magic in Europe*, 173.

66. Levack, "The Decline and End," 77–78.

67. Gijswijt-Hofstra, 151.

68. J. A. Sharpe, *Instruments of Darkness, Witchcraft in England, 1551–1750* (Philadelphia: U of Pennsylvania P, 1997), 169.

69. Bogucka, 33.

70. *Artikel von der Zauberey, Hexerey, Wahrsagerey, und dergleichen* (*An Article on Sorcery, Witchcraft, Divination, and Similar Activities*), (1766), Section 3, quoted in Kern, 171.

71. Levack, "The Decline and End," 7–33.

72. Bengt Ankarloo and Stuart Clark, "Introduction," in *Witchcraft and Magic in Europe*, 4.

73. Brian Levack, "General Reasons for the Decline in Prosecutions," in *Witchcraft and Magic in Europe*, 25.

74. Brennan, 209.

75. E. J. Burford and Sandra Shulman, *Of Bridles and Burnings: The Punishment of Women* (New York: St. Martin's Press, 1992), 218.

76. Gijswijt-Hofstra, 106.

77. Ibid., 141.

78. Levack, "General Reasons," 25.

79. Sharpe, 1–4.

80. Gijswijt-Hofstra, 152–53.

81. Helen Maria Williams, *Letters Written in France, in the Summer 1790, to a Friend in England; Containing Various Anecdotes Relative to the French Revolution*, ed. Neil Fraistat and Susan S. Lanser (Peterborough, On.: Broadview Press, 2001), 173.

82. Ibid., 172.

83. Gita May, *Madame Roland and the Age of Revolution* (New York: Columbia UP, 1970), 281–88.

84. Jeanne-Marie Roland, *The Private Memoirs of Madame Roland*, ed. Edward Gilpin Johnson (Chicago: A. C. McClurg., 1901), 326.

85. Quoted in Elizabeth Roudinesco, *Madness and Revolution: The Lives and Legends of Théroigne de Méricourt*, trans. Martin Thom (London: Verso, 1991), 145–46.

86. James M. Anderson, *Daily Life during the French Revolution* (Westport, CT: Greenwood Press, 2007), 227.

87. Godineau, 238.

88. Ibid., 235–36.

SUGGESTED READING

Anderson, James M. *Daily Life during the French Revolution*. Westport, CT: Greenwood Press, 2007.

Barahona, Renato. *Sex Crimes, Honour, and the Law in Early Modern Spain: Vizcaya, 1528–1735*. Toronto: U of Toronto P, 2003.

Bonfield, Lloyd. "Developments in European Family Law." In *The History of the European Family, Volume One: Family Life in Early Modern Times 1500–1789*, edited by David I. Kertzer and Marzio Barbagli. New Haven, CT: Yale UP, 2001.

De Renzi, Silvia. "Medical Expertise, Bodies, and the Law in Early Modern Courts." *Isis: Journal of the History of Science in Society* 98, no. 2 (2007): 315–22.

Desan, Suzanne. *The Family on Trial in Revolutionary France*. Berkeley: U of California P, 2004.

Elmsley, Clive. *Crime, Police, and Penal Policy: European Experiences 1750–1940*. Oxford: Oxford UP, 2007.

Johnson, Eric A. and Eric H. Monkkonen, eds. *The Civilization of Crime: Violence in Town and Country since the Middle Ages*. Urbana: U of Illinois P, 1996.

Levack, Brian, Marijke Gijswijt-Hofstra, and Roy Porter, eds. *Witchcraft and Magic in Europe: The Eighteenth and Nineteenth Centuries*. London: The Athlone Press, 1999.

Palk, Dierdre. *Gender, Crime and Judicial Discretion, 1780–1830*. Woodbridge, Suffolk: The Boydell Press, 2006.

Vigarello, Georges. *A History of Rape: Sexual Violence in France from the 16th to the 20th Century*, translated by Jean Birrell. Cambridge: Polity Press, 2001.

5

Women and Arts and Sciences

Only wealthy middle-class and aristocratic women could afford the cost and leisure to amass even the most basic degree of knowledge necessary to gain recognition in the arts and sciences. Those within this privileged group still faced the barrier of accessing the same level of formal education afforded their male counterparts. Even when they had overcome these obstacles to become highly skilled, they were often deprived entrance into professional associations for which they were more than qualified. These women also lived in a time when the very act of publishing one's writing or exhibiting one's artistic talents placed one at risk of being considered bold and unfeminine.

Despite these obstacles, a surprising number of women left their mark upon the artistic and scientific culture of the Enlightenment age. The difficulties they faced gave these women many characteristics in common. It was no coincidence that some of the most talented female painters had fathers or husbands who were painters. In the same way, female scientists gained much of their knowledge by assisting a male scientist and using his library. Women with natural talents who did not live in households with men of a similar bent would have been virtually unable to develop their skill beyond a rudimentary level. The few women who rose to prominence in literary, scientific, or artistic fields contrived as much as possible to work in domestic, rather than public, spheres. Nonetheless, an impressive number of female writers, researchers, performers, and illustrators emerged from the eighteenth century. Beyond these more notable women was a still larger group that acted as nurturers of talent and arbiters of taste, deciding the direction of scientific, artistic, and literary expression in very important ways.

SALONNIÈRES

The tradition of the salon gathering predated the Enlightenment. In the words of one historian, "the Enlightenment did not appropriate the salons. It is probably more accurate to say that the salons appropriated the Enlightenment."[1] The French tradition of gathering in the domestic setting of the salon to engage in intellectual conversation had been in existence since the seventeenth century, but it underwent a growth and formalization in the eighteenth century that gave an even greater role to its female host, the *salonnière*. *Salonnières* were elite women who wished to increase their own and others' understanding of the newest ideas, and they did so by inviting leading intellectuals into their homes for social gatherings that—by the mid-eighteenth century—were governed by very specific programs set by the hostess.

Salonnières required distinct talents to succeed in the Enlightenment milieu. Contemporaries likened their skills to those of musicians or artists in their ability to bring the appropriate individuals together to discourse upon stimulating topics. They had to navigate the rough terrain of opposing viewpoints, encouraging healthy debate while at the same time easing tensions. Parisian salons became institutions where rising *salonnières* served informal apprenticeships that sometimes lasted for decades. When a leading *salonnière* died, her legacy passed to the woman at the forefront of the next generation of hostesses. Thus, upon Mme de Lambert's death, her guests then gathered at Mme de Tencin's salon. The latter's protégé, Mme Geoffrin, took up the mantle of the leading *salonnière* at her demise, followed by Mme Necker. Mme de Lambert is credited with having begun the tradition of a regular salon schedule. She received guests twice weekly, and by the end of the century, various Parisian *salonnières* had established their own consistent day and time, making the *philosophe*'s life in the French capital "a sequence of conversations."[2]

The Enlightened thinkers of Spain (*ilustrados*) also enjoyed the exchange of ideas in a domestic atmosphere. *Tertulias*, as Spanish salon gatherings were known, contributed to the state's Enlightenment reform agenda, but they also aided in broadening the education of their female hosts and attendees. The Count-Duchess of Benavente invited an impressive range of intellectuals from across Europe to her *tertulias* in her family's elaborate palace at the Alameda de Osuna. Her surviving correspondence, including letters from leading *ilustrados*, authors, musicians, and scientists—often seeking her opinion or sharing newfound knowledge—indicates the diversity of her interests. The Marquise of Sarría's *tertulia* focused on poetry in the period of its existence between January 1749 and April 1751. It became known as the *Academia Poética* of Spain for its depth and influence in that area of Spanish literature.[3]

The Italian states boasted a rich salon culture as well, aided by the growing fashion of the Grand Tour—the tradition among wealthy Europeans to visit the sites of antiquity. Clelia Borromeo (1684–1777), who had a literary and scientific salon in Milan, boasted, among her many remarkable talents, fluency in Arabic. In keeping with the cultural interests that brought Europe's elite to Italy, Roman salons typically focused upon creative topics in the realm of literature, theatre, music, and the visual arts. Maria Pizzelli Cuccovilla's home became celebrated as a gathering place for those with literary talents. Her influence and erudition was such that she was known as "the oracle of those who aspired to the rank of author."[4]

The *salonnières* of London were arguably more associated with feminism than any other European group. The English gatherings tended to have more women than in other nations—some were even exclusively composed of women. London *salonnières* were also more likely to be published authors in their own right than their European counterparts. These London women became quite vocal in their claims to equality and gradually earned the name "bluestockings." The term has been attributed a variety of origins, but it essentially refers to the cheaper blue wool stockings worn by working class men and women. Its invocation was intended to draw to mind the contrast between the cheaper blue hosiery and the white silk variety associated with gentry and aristocracy. By demanding blue wool stockings instead of conventional silk apparel, London *salonnières* sent a subtle message that their evening gatherings were different from other fashionable social affairs.

From 1757 to 1775, the bluestocking circle was a very small group of serious women, but the meetings became larger and more inclusive after the widowed Elizabeth Montagu built her elegant home in Portman Square. Other prominent hostesses included Ireland's Elizabeth Vesey, who began an evening salon in her London mansion in the early 1750s and hosted all of England's leading intellectuals. The men and women who graced her receptions "mix[ed] the rank and the literature, and exclude[d] all beside."[5] Elsewhere in Europe, titled aristocracy mixed with lower bourgeois intellectuals with relative ease, but it took the growth of the spa culture in mid-century to create the same dynamic in Britain. It had become popular to take the waters at fashionable spas like Tunbridge Wells, where the bright women of the bluestocking circle had the opportunity to rub elbows with leading male intellectuals and titled nobility. In hosting larger gatherings, women like Montagu and Vesey brought the spa atmosphere to London and expanded the bluestockings' opportunities for knowledge and connections.

German salons were less prolific than the English and French variety and only came into existence in the last quarter of the century. Henriette Herz is recognized as Berlin's first *salonnière*. The Jewish doctor's wife was a celebrated beauty whose intellect, wit, and capacity for friendships combined to ensure her success in creating a vibrant literary salon in 1780s Berlin. Her husband expounded upon science and medicine in one room of their home, while Henriette held court in the other, which was instead devoted to literary topics. The cost of entertaining the German intelligentsia on such a regular basis consumed all of the Herz's resources, forcing Henriette to close the salon upon her husband's death in 1803. Among Herz's list of accomplishments was an incredible proficiency with languages. She mastered English, French, Latin, Hebrew, Portuguese, and Danish, and was also familiar with Turkish, Malayan, and Sanskrit.[6] In 1770s Hamburg, Elise Reimarus and her sister-in-law established a regular evening tea table with the desire of spreading their passion for the ideals of the Enlightenment.

Despite their extension of intellectual life to women, the salons of eighteenth-century Europe remained exclusive to a select group of wealthy urban bourgeois. Public lectures, however, were often able to engage a broader swath of society. Renowned intellectuals traveled Europe giving talks to eager audiences, among which were more than a few women. These venues drew listeners such as Ann Taylor and her sister, daughters of an English engraver. They and their working-class friends participated in free monthly lectures in Colchester covering "astronomy, geography, geometry, mechanics, general history and anatomy."[7]

AUTHORS

A whole host of European women wrote letters, poems, and fictional prose throughout the eighteenth century. Many did so only for a small audience, but a surprising number saw their work circulate in print. Of these women, only some are named here, and they are not necessarily the most important. The female authors of the Enlightenment enjoyed a greater freedom in publishing than did their seventeenth-century forbears. Though the fame of publication still constituted a slight breach of feminine modesty and many women prefaced their writing with an apology for their sex, the leading female novelists, playwrights, and poets of eighteenth-century Europe did not suffer the sexual slurs faced by seventeenth-century English author Aphra Behn and other writers of previous centuries.

Poetry was perhaps the most intimate form of authorial expression for Enlightenment women. At the same time, however, they used this medium to convey rather public messages about the need for female social and political equality. Princess Ekaterina Sergeevna Urusova authored many poems in support of the key role for women as a civilizing force in Russian culture. Keraskova had, until recently, been recognized only as the wife of the more prominent author Mikhail Kheraskov. She was a passionate and accomplished poet herself, however, and interacted with some of the most creative minds of Russian literature at the time. From the appearance of her first published poem in the journal *Poleznoe Uveselenie* (*Useful Entertainment*) in 1760, Keraskova went on to publish many more poems, all with themes of remarkable sophistication.

Hamburg's Elise Reimarus was one of the first women to write in epigrams—a poetic form traditionally used only by men—yet she considered poetry a private medium of expression. In her mind, "poems ... absolutely belong only into[sic] the closer circle in which they originated."[8] Even when writing for the stage, women felt the need for anonymity. Luise Adelgunde Gottsched and Charlotte von Stein are two such examples. The former authored the highly controversial *Die Pietisterey im Fischbein-Rocke* (*Pietism in a Whale-Bone Corset*) in 1739, which was banned in Königsberg and Berlin for its satire of the Pietist religion. Von Stein's first play, *Rino*, was published in 1776, and she went on to write several more dramas, all anonymously. Her work often tackled controversial themes, such as female subordination and the relative merits of male versus female reign.

Though the previous century must be credited with the birth of the novel, the eighteenth century saw its growth into a full-fledged and popular genre. This can at least in part be explained by the growing ranks of middle-class readers. They had not only literacy but also sufficient income and leisure to allow them to consume fiction to a far greater degree than the vast majority of their forbears. The distinct middle-class culture stressing industry over idleness and piety and morality over licentiousness had a visible influence on the direction of novelists' creativity. The development of the sentimental novel by mid-century brought with it many more women authors. This was partially due to the greater receptiveness of publishers and editors, who needed to meet the demands of a rising readership, but also to female authors' greater comfort with topics of sensibility and domestic settings, which they saw as safely feminine terrain.

Isabelle de Charrière, a Dutch aristocrat who spent much of her life in Switzerland, tried her hand at a variety of literary genres, including novels and poetry, with considerable success in all. She is perhaps most remembered for the series of epistolary novels written in the 1780s, beginning with *Lettres de Mistriss Henley publiées par son amie* in 1784. Her work offered a penetrating glimpse into her contemporary society. It was a literary criticism of female subordination, Christian piety, and aristocratic privilege.

French novelist Marie-Jeanne Riccoboni had a similar mastery of the epistolary novel. She wrote several books, starting with *Lettres de Mistress Fanny Butler* in 1757. A decade before, Françoise d'Issembourg d'Happencourt, better known as Mme de Graffigny, gained notoriety for her novel in the same style, entitled *Letters d'une Péruvienne*. Until recently, Françoise de Graffigny was remembered only for her close friendship with Voltaire, but she has since been celebrated in her own right. Like de Charrière and Riccoboni, de Graffigny was lauded for her artistry, her ability to capture an interior feminine voice, and her moral sensibility.

Eliza Haywood wrote a few plays but is most remembered as a novelist. Daughter of a London tradesman, she married young and was forced to support herself and two young children by her pen after her husband's abandonment. Within her long career, she successfully shifted her novel-writing style from the earlier licentious flavor to the more moralizing didacticism that became popular by mid-century. Fanny Burney published *Evelina* anonymously in 1778 to rave reviews from the London reading public. A naturally shy person, Burney felt awkward with the adulation once her identity was revealed, but it was perhaps the very insularity of her existence that made the character of Evelina appear so real and so unlike any previous heroine in English literature. Burney went on to publish *Cecelia* in 1782, *Camilla* in 1796 and *The Wanderer* in 1814.

Sophie Von La Roche anonymously published *Geschichte des Fräuleins von Sternheim* in 1771. She wrote it in the epistolary style popularized by England's Samuel Richardson and it exemplified the sentimental qualities of late eighteenth-century novels across Europe. *Geschichte des Fräuleins von Sternheim* is distinct, however, in being the first German *frauenroman* (woman's novel). Though possessed of a greater than normal education for an eighteenth-century woman, Von La Roche was nonetheless visibly conscious of her subservient role and placed masculine wishes above her own, not the least of which being her father's desire that she marry a man who was not her first choice. It is likely that her book would never have seen the light of day had it not been for another man, Wieland, who edited the text and insisted it be printed.[9]

The Russian Empress Catherine II was an author in her own right. In addition to her political and philosophical writings, she churned out an incredible volume of plays—modeled on Shakespeare—and several libretti that were set to music by court composers. Her work has since been accorded little literary value, but her enthusiasm for Russian drama undoubtedly inspired other contemporaries, whose work greatly enriched the Russian culture of the Enlightenment age.

Almost all of the female authors named—and an enormous assemblage who remain unnamed—made additional contributions to literature as translators. Working as part of the Enlightenment enterprise of increasing the accessibility of knowledge, these women took upon themselves the monumental task of translating important classical and Enlightenment texts into their own national tongue. Far from a passive or simple act, translation was a creative process in and of itself. The interpretation of an original work into a new language constitutes an original work. At the same time, it often goes unrecognized as such. Translation was thus the perfect project for women seeking to navigate the dangerous waters of Enlightenment femininity. It allowed them to engage with the literary and scientific canons while remaining a secondary figure. Their words could circulate in print without leaving them directly open to public censure. As one historian put it, female translators could hide behind the "protective cover of borrowed words"; another described it as a "shield" that sheltered female authors from the full glare of public scrutiny while at the same time giving them a voice.[10]

Recent investigation into the correspondence between German women and their publishers suggests that their frequently voiced desire to remain anonymous and their apparent reluctance to see their words in print may have been exaggerated. Female authors' letters to publishers bore an assertive style and directness that belied the self-abasement expressed in the more public domain of the printed work. This suggests that women may have often pretended a shyness and insecurity that they did not actually feel, in order to project the necessary social image of modest femininity in print.[11] Venetian Luisa Bergalli Gozzi was a marked exception. She openly published dozens of poems, wrote plays, and produced numerous translations of classical and French theatre. She also rescued a host of other Italian female poets from obscurity, editing a volume of 253 poets' work that went back to the thirteenth century. Far from anonymous, Bergalli demanded recognition and glory for herself and female literary talent in general, vowing "to pave the way" for future aspiring women poets.[12] Her chronicler credits the uniquely receptive culture of the Venetian Republic with having liberated Bergalli from adopting the self-effacing voice of her eighteenth-century counterparts.

PAINTERS AND MUSICIANS

The women of Enlightenment Europe who wished to pursue various artistic endeavors faced many of the same obstacles as in previous centuries. The exhibition of artistic skill—displayed as an object in a gallery or in performance on a stage—went against early modern notions of feminine modesty. Female artistic pursuits outside one's own family home brought a level of public scrutiny considered dangerous and inappropriate, conducive to sexual immorality. Furthermore, women were often formally or informally prevented from acquiring the techniques needed to achieve the highest ranks of a particular art. Most female painters could not afford expensive oil paints and thus were forced to hone their skills in watercolors or pastels, for example. Working with such media forced them into less respected artistic genres, like still-life images and portraits, rather than the more respected large historical motifs favored by the leading male painters.

These masculine artists boasted the additional advantage of extensive training in life drawing. Expectations of feminine modesty kept women away from life classes where they would have had the chance to study the human form in detail. This inability to study live models also prevented women from gaining the necessary skills to be sculptors of any renown. The growing professionalization of artistic work in the seventeenth and eighteenth centuries meant that the best male painters were singled out for special education. They underwent intensive study of Renaissance and classical artistic theories and techniques in order to model themselves after the great masters in history. This posed yet another barrier to artistic women, whose lack of such formal training made it nearly impossible to become one of the greatest artists of their age. The development of art academies across Europe at the same time constituted the final disadvantage to ambitious female painters.

The leading artists of Europe were offered memberships in national academies, which would then provide a host of benefits including venues for exhibiting their work and connections to wealthy patrons, as well as opportunity to interact with and learn from other prominent talents in the field. Most academies officially banned female members, though institutions such as the Académie Royal de Peinture et de Sculpture of France, Rome's Accademia di San Luca, and the Royal Academy of England made exceptions in a small minority of cases. Spain, however, is especially remarkable in its inclusiveness. The Real Academia de Bellas Artes de San Fernando, established in 1752, placed no such ban on feminine membership. Of the 412 members from the Academia's inception to the French invasion in 1808, 34 were women.[13]

María Luisa Carranque's invitation to join the Academia in 1773 made it clear that artistic talent was the central qualification:

> All of the Professors praised highly the skill, intelligence, and quality with which the pastel was worked; and in attention to this and due to the distinguished quality of this Señora, the Señor Viceprotector proposed her for Academic of honor and merit in Painting. And the Council by acclamation and unanimous consent of all its Voices, created and declared her as such Academic of honor and merit in Painting with voice and vote.[14]

Spanish female artists earned their admission in the same way as their male counterparts: on the proficiency of their art alone. Even more illustrative of Spanish inclusiveness, Madrid's first public art exhibition in 1793 featured eleven artists, of which no less than seven were female.[15]

In the more hostile artistic communities outside of Spain, a few talented women nonetheless gained respect as painters. Rachel Ruysch of the Netherlands had the good fortune of being born to a professor of anatomy and botany, who quickly took her to study under a flower painter when he discovered her talent for drawing. She married a portrait painter in 1693 and gained entrance with him into the Hague's Guild of Painters in 1701. The Elector Palatine in Düsseldorf engaged the pair as Court Painters from 1708-1716, but her skill in executing still life images of flowers and insects remains one of the most celebrated of her artistic achievements.[16] Venetian Rosalba Carriera's skill in portraiture elicited commissions from royalty across Europe. Her abilities transformed the miniature from a decorative novelty to a work of art in its own right, and elevated pastels to a respected medium for "serious portraiture." She is additionally celebrated as having made an indelible impact upon the development of the rococo style that was to become so influential in eighteenth-century art.[17]

Angelica Kauffmann tackled the large historical motifs that were traditionally considered the exclusive domain of male painters. Daughter of a Swiss painter who traveled Europe in search of work, Kauffmann learned to draw with pencils and paint at an early age. By sixteen, she had commissions for portraits at the Milanese court. Her travels through Italy with her father allowed her to make the intensive study of Renaissance and classical works of art so vital to aspiring artists in the eighteenth century. The wife of the former English ambassador to Venice met her in that city and invited her to accompany her to London, where she acquired even more commissions and fame as a portraitist. In 1769, she made history as the first female painter to exhibit more ambitious history paintings based on classical mythology, though it is her informal portraits that continue to bring her critical acclaim. One contemporary observer called "the whole world" in 1766 "Angelicamad."[18]

Like Kauffmann, Anna Dorothea Lisiewska-Therbusch learned from her artist father. Of Polish origins but raised in the German states, she was given work at the Württemberg court and later painted for Prussian King Frederick II. Her talent brought her to Paris in 1765–1768, but she eventually returned to Germany and married a painter. Unlike Kauffmann, Lisiewska-Therbusch never fulfilled her dream of exhibiting large historically themed paintings because she—along with most female artists in her time—was unable to make sufficient study of the human form to paint in this more prestigious genre.[19] France's Elisabeth-Louise Vigée-Lebrun, also the daughter of an artist, became famous as official painter for Queen Marie Antoinette. Vigée-Lebrun supported herself quite comfortably through her work at the easel, despite a husband who frittered away much of the household income. Her association with the hated queen forced her into exile with her daughter from 1789 to 1801. She divorced her husband in absentia in 1796 and spent her twelve years of exile traveling from Turin to St. Petersburg, executing numerous commissions and acquiring accolades.

At her death at age 86, she had painted 662 portraits, 15 allegorical history paintings, and more than 200 landscapes.[20]

Music was prominent on the list of most bourgeois girls' accomplishments throughout eighteenth-century Europe. It was so important to Russian daughters' education, for example, that there are accounts of financially constrained mothers taking their children to eavesdrop on wealthier friends' music lessons.[21] Aside from hiring professional music teachers, some fortunate families might make use of a talented servant to give daughters music lessons. Nannerl Mozart was especially lucky to have been born into the household of a prominent Austrian musician and received her father's intensive training alongside her more famous younger brother. In certain exceptional cases, such as the charitable institutions of early modern Venice, working-class girls had access to musical training. Hundreds of girls received instruction in singing and playing an instrument in Venetian orphanages between 1575 and 1797.[22]

There were a variety of venues for female musicians, from the domestic evening among one's own family to more formal public venues with paying audiences numbering in the hundreds. Included within this range were the formal musical evenings held in private homes where highly skilled professionals performed alongside amateurs. Often the small group of listeners held tickets to attend but had only been able to obtain them because they were known to—and considered acceptable by—the hosts. It is thus very difficult to categorize many eighteenth-century women's performances as private or public in the purest sense. Many female musicians walked a very careful tightrope to avoid the stigma that almost inevitably followed a professional woman in the arts.

From the numerous ranks of amateur feminine musicians, a few rose to prominence. Anna Maria della Pietà (given the surname of the Venetian Pietà home for illegitimate children that offered her musical training) became an expert at a variety of stringed instruments. Her proficiency at the violin inspired one poet's wish to bow before her and "kiss the hem of her gown."[23] Renowned Baroque composer Antonio Vivaldi wrote no less than twenty-two violin concertos specifically for this illegitimate girl from Venice. Fellow Venetian Teresa Cornelys (born Anna Maria Teresa Imer) began her career as a soprano at the age of nineteen. She came to London in 1759 and—with the help of several benefactors—bought a house in which to offer small concerts and dancing. Carlisle House, as the venue became known, was only open to a select list of subscribers from among the aristocracy and gentry. Though Cornelys died in poverty, Carlisle House proved a very lucrative and innovative venture while it lasted and stands as a rather surprising example of the variety of opportunities available to eighteenth-century women in music.[24]

Across most of Europe, including France, England, and the Netherlands, audiences preferred women over male castratos to sing soprano opera roles. Wolfgang Amadeus Mozart's first great love, Aloysia Weber, traveled throughout Europe as a famous opera singer in the last decade of the eighteenth century. The English artist Thomas Rowlandson's drawing, *Vaux-Hall*, depicts Elizabeth Weichsel Billington singing from the elaborate outdoor stage to a large illustrious crowd at the famous Vauxhall public gardens. She began as a pianist, but gained greater fame in vocal music after marrying her singing instructor, James Billington, in 1783.

Professional female soloists often had the additional complications of pregnancy to contend with. Portuguese singer Luisa Rosa Todi—celebrated as the "Canatrice de la Nation" in France in 1789—delivered her first child in Lisbon in 1772, then embarked on a concert tour of England and had her second child in 1773. Her eldest child died at age eighteen after an abrupt illness while accompanying his mother on tour in The Hague in 1790. Despite her grief, La Todi performed with little outward sign, save one audience member's record that "her voice was a little affected by a cold, especially in the lower register."[25]

Of female composers, often little is known. Maria Antonia Walpurgis Symphorosa, Electress of Saxony, has been credited with having written and set to music the opera entitled *Il Trionfo della fedeltà*, among an impressive list of other musical endeavors.[26] England's Ann Young's book

Vaux-Hall (1785), etching and aquatint of drawing by Thomas Rowlandson. (Courtesy of Library of Congress)

of harpsichord lessons, first published in 1790, was one of the few openly female-authored pedagogical works of music. Young's book made use of more female composers than most other work of its kind, which must be attributed to its author's gender, and she was a prolific composer.[27] Venetian Lombardini-Sirmen was one of the most famous women composers of the Enlightenment age. Like Young, she gained her fame largely as the result of a music lesson book, this time on how to play the violin. The book was very popular, published in a dozen editions across Western Europe.

In Lombardini-Sirmen's case, notoriety came not because she authored the book, but because she was one of its main subjects. The author was one of Europe's leading violin masters, Giuseppe Tartini, who wrote it in the form of a letter to his then prize pupil, Lombardini-Sirmen. Her resulting fame and natural talent as a violinist spawned requests for performances in cities from Moscow to London. Lombardini-Sirmen entered one of Venice's charitable institutions (*ospedali*) at the age of seven in 1753 and was singled out as a musical prodigy. She went on to compose violin concertos and chamber music, leaving behind hundreds of prints of scores which remain to this day.[28]

SCIENTIFIC WOMEN

Though feminine interest in the sciences did not begin in the eighteenth century, a much larger proportion of women indulged in scientific pursuits in the Enlightenment age than in previous centuries. Nonetheless, even by the end of the century, justifications for feminine studies of science remained closely connected with women's domestic role. Maria Edgeworth, who wrote with her father on the importance of science in the early education of children, explicitly listed mothers' pedagogical responsibilities as the primary reason for women to be exposed to the sciences. The female author of *An Introduction to Botany* (1796) stressed that it was a way for aristocratic women to channel their energies in a useful direction, away from "levity and idleness."[29]

Another English author, Hester Chapone, encouraged women to study science because it would help them find a husband. In her 1773 *Letters on the Improvement of the Mind addressed to a Young Lady*, Chapone argued that interest in science would help girls avoid more frivolous pastimes that would do little to increase their attractiveness to the opposite sex.[30] Italian anatomist, surgeon and obstetrician Tarsizio Riviera, contributor to the education that allowed a laborer's daughter, Maria Dalle Donne to earn a prestigious medical degree in 1799, believed that "a woman's imagination was vivid, but empty, full of images, but poor in thought."[31] Women could thus benefit from academic pursuits, but only to a limited degree.

Regardless of the basis of its justification, amateur female scientific study had become fairly fashionable by the eighteenth century. *Female Rights Vindicated, or the Equality of the Sexes Morally and Physically Proved*, authored anonymously in 1758 by "a lady," attributed an inherent scientific prowess to women, particularly in physics and medicine. When John Tipper wrote an almanac specifically for women in 1704, he was surprised by the deluge of letters he received from feminine readers. They requested that he discard much of the housekeeping and homemaking content in favor of articles on science and mathematics. This very inexpensive twenty-leaf volume advertised microscopes and other scientific instruments to its female subscribers.[32]

Several men began the movement to present scientific theories in a format that would be more accessible to women. The first, French Author Bernard le Bovier, Sieur de Fontenelle, published *Entretiens sur la pluralité des Mondes* in 1686, which was translated as *The Theory or System of Several New Inhabited Worlds* in 1688, and underwent numerous subsequent printings. Fontenelle wrote in a literary style with a fictitious heroine who had a thirst for scientific knowledge but boasted little or no formal education. Italian Francesco Algarotti wrote a very useful explication of the Newtonian theory of optics that was specifically directed at women in 1737, entitled *Il Newtonianismo per le dame*. Though these books helped to expand the ranks of feminine scientists, already some European women were gravitating towards scientific fields of study.

One of these was the German Maria Winkelmann. A nearby farmer introduced her to astronomy in her girlhood. Her enthusiasm for astrological observation led her to marry Germany's leading astronomer, Gottfried Kirch, though he was thirty years her senior. They worked as partners, maintaining an unwavering record of the night sky, often in shifts. On one notable evening, Winkelmann became the first woman to observe a previously unknown comet, known as the Comet of 1702, for the year in which she spotted it. Winkelmann's sex probably prevented her from being credited with the discovery for many years. Gottfried Wilhelm Leibniz, the famous seventeenth-century mathematician, wrote a glowing letter introducing Winkelmann to the Prussian court in 1709 where he called her "a most learned woman" who would not "easily find ... her equal in the science in which she excels."[33] At her husband's death the following year, Winkelmann presented herself as a candidate for his vacant position in the Berlin Academy. Guildsmen's widows often took over leadership of their husband's business, and Winkelmann was careful to stress her subservient role as assistant astronomer, assuring the Academy that she was not so "bold as to suggest that I take over completely the office [of astronomer]."[34] Nonetheless, her repeated requests fell on deaf ears.

Pious bourgeois Italian daughter Maria Gaetana Agnesi was the first woman to publish a book in mathematics. A child prodigy, Agnesi regaled Milanese salons at the age of nine with a Latin treatise (probably written by her tutor) on the values of education for women. She was quickly disenchanted with the glamorous *soirées* of Milan's leading families and persuaded her father to allow her to lead a semi-reclusive life. Math studies fit her antisocial tendencies, being "the only province of the literary world where peace reigns."[35] In 1748, Maria Agnesi published *Instituzioni Analitiche*, a book on calculus designed to introduce beginners to this important mathematical field. Agnesi chose to write in the vernacular, rather than the customary Latin, and is credited with developing the first thorough compendium of Italian terminology for calculus. Her focus on the usefulness of calculus in solving geometrical problems caused her name to be associated with a particular curve, known in the Anglo-Saxon literature as the "witch of Agnesi."[36] The death of Agnesi's father signified the end of her last connections with academic life and allowed her to devote herself more fully to the charitable work with Milan's poor that she believed her true Catholic duty. Her extreme piety clearly transcended her delight in mathematical pursuits. "I hope my studies have brought glory to God, as they were useful to others, and derived from obedience, because that was my father's will," she told her friends. "Now I have found better ways and means to serve God, and to be useful to others."[37]

Botanic and entomological pursuits, in particular, drove feminine researchers to the farthest reaches of the globe. Dutch naturalist Maria Sybylla Merian has been credited with having made "the first long-term zoological discovery and an unprecedented body of work," at a time when most books on animals still contained "medieval bestiaries" like dragons, unicorns, and mermaids.[38] Far more than just a passive illustrator, Maria Merian captured insects, bred them in captivity, and conducted experiments. Her thirst to observe living insects led her to Surinam in South America where she spent two years exploring the rain forest in search of new entomological and botanical varieties. Merian then prepared the magnificent volume *Metamorphosis Insectorum Surinamensium*, containing sixty colored plates and lengthy explanation, which she published at her own expense in 1705. Biological studies of flora and fauna intertwined science and art, and this intersection offered a special niche to women like Merian.

Another such intersection occurred with anatomical modeling. The lack of available cadavers in eighteenth-century Europe forced medical researchers to find creative ways of observing and understanding human anatomy. Wax models that accurately reflected the color, texture, size, and shape of the internal organs were used extensively in the teaching of physiology, obstetrics, and surgery. Although Madame Tussaud has had more lasting fame for her artistry with wax, women such as Italy's Anna Morandi and Marie Marguerite Bihéron of France made valuable contributions to medical science with their skills as anatomical modelers. To do their work properly, they needed to understand complex Latin texts on the appearance and workings of the body and then recreate and assemble the organs as realistically as possible in wax. They also dissected cadavers to ensure that they could communicate the appearance and function of the specimens as clearly as possible.

Morandi probably gained her skills with her marriage to anatomist Giovanni Manzolini in 1740. Though she could not write or speak in Latin (but clearly read the language), and thus was not qualified to teach or engage in debate within a university classroom, her anatomical models were vital to the obstetrics and surgery professors in instructing future physicians, surgeons, and midwives on the internal workings of the human body. Despite being banned from formal pedagogy in the university, Anna Morandi conducted numerous workshops in her home for groups of men interested in her techniques of dissection and preparation of anatomical parts. Her vast experience was invaluable, sought by experts such as Germano Azzoguidi, a physician at the university who recorded his relief at having Morandi confirm an inaccuracy in a textbook that had long perturbed him.[39]

What Spain's *Academia de Bellas Artes* was for artistic women, Italy's Bologna University was for women in the sciences. Here, Laura Bassi could rise through the ranks to become one of the highest-paid professors, and the first woman in Europe to teach at a university. She was named professor of experimental physics in 1776. Among her contributions to the field were some discoveries in electricity that coincided with—if not predated—those of Benjamin Franklin.[40] Even Bassi experienced the constraints of her sex, however. Eager to engage in debate and probe Newton's theories on light and color, Bassi invited colleagues to her home early in her career. Rather than regarding Bassi as a professional sharing ideas with other professionals, however, her contemporaries saw only a single woman entertaining men away from public view, and salacious gossip ensued. Because she relied on the Vatican's beneficence to continue in her work, Bassi chose marriage as a way of silencing the rumors. It was very clear that pragmatism trumped romance in her decision. "I have chosen a person who walks my path in the arts and who, through long experience, I was certain would not impede me from following mine," Bassi wrote in 1738.[41]

Scientific women outside of Italy were forced to seek recognition more indirectly. French scientist Emilie du Châtelet has gained international fame as the lover of the renowned *philosophe* Voltaire, but she was a remarkable intellectual in her own right. As a woman, du Châtelet was unable to gain admission into the French Academy of sciences. This deprived her of direct access to discussion and debate with the leading intellects of the day, not to mention opportunities for experimentation and publishing that were generally reserved for members only. Châtelet had to find creative ways to circumvent the obstacles posed by her lack of standing in the Academy, but her persistence met with some success. In 1737, du Châtelet secretly wrote an essay on the nature of fire, which she submitted along with Voltaire's essay in an anonymous competition held by the French Academy of Sciences. Neither Voltaire nor du Châtelet won, but the latter's essay evoked tremendous praise when its author's identity became known, and both papers were published in response to public demand. She published other pieces at her own expense to ensure that her work could reach a wider audience.[42]

While amateur interest in the sciences continued for women in the nineteenth century, the eighteenth century marked the end of women's ability to engage more formally in scientific study. Even within this period, the most renowned women experienced the impact of their gender. International praise of both Anna Morandi and Laura Bassi included their fecundity—their role as mothers in producing new citizens—in the list of their significant accomplishments.[43] It is unlikely that the same would have been said of their male counterparts. It was clear in other ways, too, that gender constraints had not been lifted by the feminine forays into science in the eighteenth century. By the early nineteenth century, active exploration, investigation, and experimentation had again become a male bastion, and many, many years would pass before another woman would attain the privileged status of those eighteenth-century women offered university teaching posts or memberships in the Science Academy.

FEMALE PATRONS

Patronage was vital for anyone to engage fully in the arts and sciences in early modern Europe. Patrons thus had considerable influence over the direction of creativity and research. Europe's leading *salonnières* played a significant role in fostering the talents of various authors and researchers and seeing their work reach a wider audience. Many aristocratic and wealthy bourgeois women could influence the leading intellectual and artistic talents of their age by acting as their patron.

In many cases, that influence was greater than one might think. The Austrian Empress Maria Theresa had an enormous impact on Viennese musical life. Her patronage of the leading composers and players came with strict stipulations that affected every aspect of musical creation and performance. In one letter to composer Giovanni Paisiello of Naples, the Empress asked that he "set to music the opera... *La corona del merito, o sia Il Torquato Tasso.*" Though her tone was very respectful and flattering, Maria Teresa included a list of very specific parameters to govern his work, including the venue in which it was to be performed, the main instruments it should feature, and the bass singer who would take the role of Gherardo. In parting, she added that "other observations that might occur to me will be communicated to you later."[44] Such meticulous oversight was bound to leave an irrevocable imprint on Viennese opera. Its nineteenth-century shift to embrace modern French drama is clearly attributable to Empress Maria Theresa's influence.

Catherine the Great also made her mark through her patronage of Europe's artists and thinkers. She funded an extensive program of translating into Russian the leading works of literature of the time, which in turn inspired new directions for Russian poetry and novels. Among other international efforts, Catherine invited Diderot to transfer the printing of the *Encyclopédie* to Riga in August of 1762, when he was experiencing royal opposition in France. The Empress's contributions to the fine arts are most notably in her acquisition of paintings and drawings—numbering in the tens of thousands—from across Europe. She stored this tremendous repository in her Hermitage, where one contemporary complained that he was frequently denied entrance because "the sovereign comes at all moments of the day" to gaze upon the marvels of her collection.[45] She did, however, keep the Hermitage's doors open to the members of the Academy of Fine Arts, which was an incredible boon to their skill development.

Madame de Pompadour, mistress of King Louis XV of France, took no less an Enlightenment figure than Voltaire under her wing. Her patronage allowed the young poet to become the Historiographer of France with a salary of 2000 livres, and the position of Gentleman-in-ordinary of the Bedchamber, which he was then allowed to sell for considerable profit. At her death, Voltaire assured a friend "that true men of letters, true philosophers, ought to mourn for Madame de Pompadour. Her opinions were in harmony with ours; no one knew it better than myself. She is in truth a great loss."[46] Many Enlightenment men of letters numbered among her protégés, and she also sponsored an enormous cadre of painters, sculptors, engravers and architects. Indeed, the king's mistress can be credited with having fostered and left an indelible stamp upon a substantial output of French art and literature during her period of influence.

Female patronage went beyond art and literature. Queen Maria I of Portugal founded the first Portuguese scientific academy, the Royal Academy of Sciences of Lisbon, and also began the first school providing technical education. The Opening Address, read on 7 June 1780, declared the academy the remedy for Portugal's current international reputation as a "centre of ignorance."[47] The academy boasted multiple committees focused on agricultural and industrial innovation, and a physics laboratory filled with the latest and best instruments available from across Europe. Another queen,

Sophie Charlotte, Queen of Prussia, funded the Berlin observatory that opened in 1706. The thirst for scientific knowledge was also shared by the grand duchess of Tuscany, Queen Christina of Sweden and Christina of Lorraine, whose consumption and patronage of leading Enlightenment theories was of international renown.

Patronage was not the exclusive purview of queens and leading aristocrats. The wealthier widows of Old Poland were active patrons of the arts.[48] England's Harriet Fox Lane aggressively promoted certain musicians in whom she saw special talent. The exclusivity and high quality of the concerts she offered in her London home made beggars out of the wealthiest music lovers. As one contemporary described it,

> Whenever a benefit was in contemplation for one of her *protégés*, taking care of the honour of her guests, she obliged them to behave with due gratitude and munificence on the occasion. "Come!" would she often say to her friends, "give me five guineas,"—a demand as implicitly obeyed as if made on the road.[49]

Fox Lane could promise her guests an intimate setting and proximity to the performers that could not be equaled by a more public venue. To the musicians themselves, she offered connections to the wealthiest members of London society, who could then become their pupils or patrons. The Spanish Count-Duchess of Benevente not only inspired the dedication of playwright Tomàs de Iriarte's late eighteenth-century play, *El don de gentes*, she also built a theatre to stage it and ensured that the production respected the author's original vision.[50] Saxony's Maria Antonia Walpurgis Symphorosa's enthusiastic patronage of musicians and composers ensured that Dresden's artistic community and opera house survived and prospered despite the ravages of the Seven Year's war.

Any discussion of feminine patronage should include the role that male patrons played in the lives of female artists, authors, and scientists. Female scientists were especially indebted to Prospero Lambertini, a Bolognese archbishop (later Pope Benedict XIV) who felt strongly that women could and should hold university positions. He believed that by establishing the reputation of church-controlled University of Bologna as the most progressive institute of higher learning in Europe, it would reveal the progressive and enlightening qualities of the Catholic faith as a whole. His patronage of the leading female academics aided him in such a quest. Through his influence, Laura Bassi, Maria Gaetana Agnesi, and Anna Morandi Manzolini were offered teaching posts at the University of Bologna. Six memberships in the Italian Academy of Sciences went to Christina Roccati, Faustina Pignatelli, Emilie du Châtelet, Anne-Marie du Bocage and Marguerite le Compte, along with Bassi. When widowed Anna Morandi

Manzolini faced the prospect of having to take a post abroad in order to support herself, she appealed to Pope Benedict. He used his influence to arrange an appointment as a modeler through the chair of anatomy at the University of Bologna. Morandi's worklife changed little; she continued to practice her art from home but had secured a salary of 300 lire for the rest of her life.[51]

NOTES

1. Steven Kale, *French Salons: High Society and Political Sociability from the Old Regime to the Revolution of 1848* (Baltimore, MD: Johns Hopkins UP, 2004), 35.

2. Kale, 19.

3. Theresa Ann Smith, *The Emerging Female Citizen: Gender and Enlightenment in Spain* (Berkeley: U of California P, 2006), 41–50.

4. Cesare Stasi, "Elogio," in *Academica poetica* (1808), 14, quoted in Maria Pia Donato, "The Temple of Female Glory: Female Self-Affirmation in the Roman Salon of the Grand Tour," trans. Matthew Sneider, in *Italy's Eighteenth Century: Gender and Culture in the Age of the Grand Tour*, eds. Paula Findlen, Wendy Wassyng Roworth, and Catherine M. Sama (Stanford, CA: Stanford UP, 2009), 71.

5. Fanny Burney's diary, ca. 1768–1778, quoted in Sylvia Harcstark Myers, *The Bluestocking Circle: Women, Friendship, and the Life of the Mind in Eighteenth-Century England* (Oxford: Clarendon Press, 1990), 250.

6. Deborah Hertz, *Jewish High Society in Old Regime Berlin* (New Haven, CT: Yale UP, 1988), 97–100.

7. Patricia Phillips, *The Scientific Lady: A Social History of Women's Scientific Interests, 1520–1918* (London: Weidenfeld and Nicolson, 1990), 132.

8. Letter from Elise Reimarus to August Hennings, March 5, 1799, quoted in Almut Spalding, *Elise Reimarus (1735–1805): The Muse of Hamburg* (Würzburg: Königshausen & Neumann, 2005), 175.

9. Ruth-Ellen B. Joeres, "'That girl is an entirely different character.' Yes, but is she a feminist? Observations on Sophie Von La Roche's *Geschcte des Fräuleins von Sternheim*," in *German Women in the Eighteenth and Nineteenth Centuries: A Social and Literary History*, eds. Ruth-Ellen B. Joeres and Mary Jo Maynes (Bloomington, IN: Indiana UP, 1986), 137–56.

10. Spalding, 199, and Smith, 178–81.

11. Helen Fronius, "Der Reiche Mann und die Arme Frau: German Women Writers and the Eighteenth-Century Literary Market-Place," *German Life and Letters* 56, no. 1 (2003), 1–19.

12. Luisa Bergalli Gozzi, Poesie itaiane di rimatori viventi non mai per l'addietro stampate... (Venice 1717), quoted in Catherine M. Sama, "'On Canvas and on the Page': Women Shaping Culture in Eighteenth-Century Venice," in *Italy's Eighteenth Century*, 135.

13. Smith, 53.

14. *Juntas ordinaries, generales y públicas desde el año 1770 hasta 1775*, RABA, Legajo 3/83, *junta ordinaria*, April 2, 1773, 193–94, quoted in Smith, 61.

15. Smith, 64.

16. Elsa Honig Fine, *Women and Art: A History of Women Painters and Sculptors from the Renaissance to the 20th Century* (Montclair, NJ: Abner Shram, 1978), 35–36.

17. Sama, 126–28.

18. Letter from Count Schönborn, Danish Ambassador to London, to Klopstock, October 19, 1781, quoted in Angelica Goodden, *Miss Angel: The Art and World of Angelica Kauffmann* (London: Pimlico, 2005), 1.

19. Rozsika Parker and Griselda Pollock, *Old Mistresses: Women, Art and Ideology* (New York: Pantheon Books, 1981), 94.

20. Fine, 48–51.

21. Natal'ia L. Pushkareva, "Russian Noblewomen's Education in the Home as Revealed in Late 18th and Early 19th-Century Memoirs," in *Women and Gender in 18th-Century Russia*, 118–19.

22. Jane L. Berdes, "The Women Musicians of Venice," in *Eighteenth-Century Women and the Arts*, ed. Frederick M. Keener and Susan E. Lorsch (New York: Greenwood Press, 1988), 153–62.

23. Annon., "Sonnet: Concerning the *Putte* in the *Coro* at the Pietà," (ca. 1740), quoted in Berdes, 159.

24. Leslie Ritchie, *Women Writing Music in Late Eighteenth-Century England: Social Harmony in Literature and Performance* (Aldershot, Hampshire: Ashgate, 2008), 64–66.

25. Diary of Nina d'Aubigny, July 8, 1790, quoted in Helen H. Mezelaar, *From Private to Public Spheres: Exploring Women's Role in Dutch Musical Life from 1700 to c. 1880 and Three Case Studies* (Utrecht: Koninklijke Vereniging voor Nederlandse Muziekgeschiedenis, 1999), 40. See also 73.

26. April Lynn James, *Her Highness' Voice: Maria Antonia, Music and Culture at the Dresden Court*, Ph.D. thesis, Harvard University, 2002, 135–38.

27. Ritchie, 44–48.

28. Berdes, 157–60.

29. Marina Benjamin, "Elbow Room: Women Writers on Science, 1790–1840," in *Science and Sensibility: Gender and Scientific Enquiry, 1780–1845*, ed. Marina Benjamin (Oxford: Basil Blackwell, 1991), 39, 51–52.

30. Phillips, 179.

31. Tarsizio Riviera, *Sopra l'indole morale e fisica delle donne* (1796), quoted in Gabriella Berti Logan, "Women and the Practice and Teaching of Medicine in Bologna in the Eighteenth and Early Nineteenth Centuries," *Bulletin of the History of Medicine* 77 (2003), 521.

32. Phillips, 71–72, 98–99.

33. Gottfried Wilhelm Leibniz to Sophie Charlotte, January 1709, quoted in Londa Schiebinger, "Maria Winkelmann at the Berlin Academy," *ISIS: Journal of the History of Science in Society* 78, no. 2 (1987), 183.

34. Maria Winkelmann to the Berlin Academy, August 2, 1710, quoted in Schiebinger, 186.

35. Benenuto Robibio, *Disgrazie di Donna Urania, ovvero degli studj femminili* (1793), quoted in Massimo Mazzotti, "Maria Gaetana Agnesi: Mathematics and the Making of the Catholic Enlightenment," *Isis: Journal of the History of Science in Society* 92, no. 4 (2001), 671.

36. Mazzotti, 676.

37. Frisi, *Elogio di Agnesi* (1799), quoted in Mazzotti, 682.

38. Sharon Valiant, "Maria Sibylla Merian: Recovering an Eighteenth-Century Legend," *Eighteenth-Century Studies* 26, no. 3 (1993), 468.
39. Logan, "Women and the Practice," 512–14, 516.
40. Gabriella Berti Logan, "The Desire to Contribute: An Eighteenth-Century Italian Woman of Science," *American Historical Review* 99, no. 3 (1994), 807.
41. Letter from Laura Bassi to Giovanni Bianchi, April 26, 1738, quoted in Logan, "The Desire to Contribute," 795.
42. Vesna Petrovich, "Women and the Paris Academy of Sciences," *Eighteenth-Century Studies* 32, no. 3 (1999), 384–85.
43. Lucia Dacome, "Women, Wax and Anatomy in the 'Century of Things,'" *Renaissance Studies* 21, no. 4 (2007), 529–30.
44. Letter dated July 18, 1802, quoted in John A. Rice, *Empress Marie Therese and Music at the Viennese Court, 1792–1807* (Cambridge: Cambridge UP, 2003), 188–89.
45. Fortia de Piles, *Voyage de deux Français dans le Nord de l'Europe . . .* (1796), quoted in Allen McConnell, "Catherine the Great and the Fine Arts," in *Imperial Russia 1700–1917: State, Society, Opposition*, ed. Ezra Mendelsohn and Marshall S. Shatz (DeKalb: Northern Illinois UP, 1988), 49.
46. Quoted in Noel Williams, *Madame De Pompadour* (New York: Harper and Brothers, 1902), 244.
47. Teodoro de Almeida, quoted in Ana Simões, Ana Carneiro, Maria Paula Diogo, "Constructing Knowledge: Eighteenth-Century Portugal and the New Sciences," in *The Sciences in the European Periphery during the Enlightenment*, ed. Kostas Gavroglu (Dordrecht: Kluwer Academic Publishers, 1999), 17.
48. Maria Bogucka, *Women in Early Modern Polish Society, against the European Background* (Aldershot, Hampshire: Ashgate, 2004), 28.
49. Charles Burney, *A General History of Music* (London, 1776), vol. IV, 671–72, quoted in Ritchie, 62.
50. Smith, 49.
51. Logan, "Women and the Practice," 507, 514–15.

SUGGESTED READING

Cocalis, Susan L., and Ferrel Rose, eds. *Thalia's Daughters: German Women Dramatists from the Eighteenth Century to the Present.* Tübingen: Franke Verlag, 1996.
Findlen, Paula, Wendy Wassyng Roworth, and Catherine M. Sama, eds. *Italy's Eighteenth Century: Gender and Culture in the Age of the Grand Tour.* Stanford: Stanford UP, 2009.
Fine, Elsa Honig. *Women and Art: A History of Women Painters and Sculptors from the Renaissance to the 20th Century.* Montclair, NJ: Abner Shram, 1978.
Hertz, Deborah. *Jewish High Society in Old Regime Berlin.* New Haven, CT: Yale UP, 1988.
Kale, Steven. *French Salons: High Society and Political Sociability from the Old Regime to the Revolution of 1848.* Baltimore, MD: Johns Hopkins UP, 2004.
Keener, Frederick M., and Susan E. Lorsch, eds. *Eighteenth-Century Women and the Arts.* New York: Greenwood Press, 1988.
MacCarthy, B. G. *The Female Pen: Women Writers and Novelists, 1621–1818.* New York: New York UP, 1994.

Mezelaar, Helen H. *From Private to Public Spheres: Exploring Women's Role in Dutch Musical Life from 1700 to c. 1880 and Three Case Studies.* Utrecht: Koninklijke Vereniging voor Nederlandse Muziekgeschiedenis, 1999.

Myers, Sylvia Harcstark. *The Bluestocking Circle: Women, Friendship, and the Life of the Mind in Eighteenth-Century England.* Oxford: Clarendon Press, 1990.

Ritchie, Leslie. *Women Writing Music in Late Eighteenth-Century England: Social Harmony in Literature and Performance.* Aldershot, Hampshire: Ashgate, 2008.

Schiebinger, Londa. *The Mind Has No Sex?: Women in the Origins of Modern Science.* Cambridge, MA: Harvard UP, 1989.

Spalding, Almut. *Elise Reimarus (1735–1805): The Muse of Hamburg.* Würzburg: Königshausen & Neumann, 2005.

6

Women and Religion

Generally, the Enlightenment brought increased religious toleration to Europe. A variety of faiths emerged and matured in this more fertile atmosphere, which simultaneously offered more opportunities to their female adherents. The Enlightenment ideal valuing education for all was not absent from the religious schools of the age, and European and colonial girls attained some benefit from this. Even in the supposed absence of faith—in the de-Christianization movement of revolutionary France—women found prominent roles to play. Jewish women gained more freedom to associate with their Christian neighbors and enjoyed more equality under the law than in previous centuries.

If the religious atmosphere of eighteenth-century Europe opened some doors to women, it also closed some. Because they were among the first to embrace the most radical forms of Christianity of the era, women were also often the first to feel the effects of the reprisals. Mysticism—long a route to spiritual authority for women—faced the increasing onslaught of Enlightenment rationalism throughout the century. Despite new civil liberties, Jewish women continued to feel alienated and find advantages in converting to Christianity. The European missions across the globe posed significant dangers to many women, though it also granted a select few the chance to travel and take pride in a spiritual vocation.

ENLIGHTENMENT SECULARISM

As much as a century before the Enlightenment, murmurings could be heard among a few scientists and theologians that raised doubts about the authority of scriptural revelation and the role of the supernatural. Rather than a physical presence imposing judgments and effecting miracles in daily life, God was instead considered a divine Creator, who had devised the wonderfully complex natural systems of the Earth and left them to operate in fixed mechanical ways.

This formed the basis of Deism, similar to Christianity in accepting the existence of God as the Creator, but different in its denial of the possibility of an afterlife, the importance of organized religious observation, the existence of Satan, and a host of other central tenets of Christianity. Voltaire was the most prominent *philosophe* to embrace such reasoning as it gained ground in the Enlightenment, and it helped to justify principles of religious toleration and separation between church and state. Deism was concentrated in England and France. Elsewhere in Europe, Enlightenment-inspired opposition to established churches tended to retain its Christian roots.

The attempt at de-Christianization in revolutionary France is perhaps the most visible example of Deist principles in practice. The remains of the movement's most vocal proponent, Voltaire, were transferred to the Church of St. Genevieve in 1789, which now became the Panthéon to the heroes of the revolution. The relics of the saint for whom the church was named were unceremoniously tossed into the Seine. Thus began a national movement to secularize churches and clergy, where organized and spontaneous groups engaged in acts of iconoclasm and expressions of anti-clerical sentiment. At the same time, the Republic sponsored new observances celebrating the divine gifts of reason, law, truth, equality, and the like. Robespierre reacted against the most vehement de-Christianizers by establishing the Cult of the Supreme Being, which returned some elements of Christianity to revolutionary spirituality. On 20 Prairial (June 8) 1794, the Convention government celebrated the festival of the *Être Suprême* with processions and feasts across the country.

The elaborate ceremonies often included a "Mountain of Reason" and a "Goddess of Reason." The latter presented a significant opportunity for Frenchwomen. Hundreds of women vied for the opportunity to play the goddess in festivals across the country. Only the most beautiful were chosen, such as citeness Cussy who appeared as the goddess in the Besançon festival of the Supreme Being. She rode a wagon surrounded by the "fruits of the earth" and bearing the inscription "The French people recognizes the Supreme Being and the immortality of the soul."[1] One Frenchman reminisced over the legions of "superb women" parading through the streets "enthroned on antique chariots" and hailed by "beautiful young girls throwing flowers."[2] Women's support of the festivals of Reason and the Supreme Being was more than superficial. They demonstrated this by naming their babies after the heroes of the revolution, abandoning traditional biblical names to show their distaste for *ancien régime* Catholicism.[3]

Often, however, women appeared among the most vociferous opponents of de-Christianization. While many monks accepted the order to disband and entered secular society, their female counterparts remained with their fellow nuns as long as they possibly could. Laywomen, too, clung passionately to their Catholic faith. The women of Avallon stationed themselves in Saint-Julien's bell tower for days on end, and held up crucifixes against those threatening to destroy it, saying "Here, see our master who chases you!"[4] Countless other women participated in similar acts against de-Christianization.

A number of factors contributed to their passionate defense of Catholicism, not the least being their perception of their role as moral guardians of their families. Also, however, it was often the parish women who cleaned the buildings and sacred objects within the church, so they felt a stronger obligation to protect them. Even after the revolution, when missionaries tried to draw lapsed Catholics back into the fold, there was a measurable

Le Déménagement du Clergé (ca. 1790). (© Gianni Dagli Orti/CORBIS)

"feminization of piety" in rural France. Women were twice as likely to begin attending Communion as their male counterparts.[5] Among noblewomen in particular, the revolutionary violence elicited a personal search for solace in faith. In 1792, Mlle de Mussay wrote, revealingly: "I, who am not very pious, I lift my soul up to God to pray 'Turn away the blows which could fall on my father!' "[6]

Enlightenment secularism placed a particular stigma on female mystics. As early as the seventeenth century, skeptics raised doubts about the plausibility of witchcraft and supernatural possession, phenomena that were frequently—though not exclusively—associated with women. There was a general decline in legal prosecution of witches by the eighteenth century, informed at least in part by elite skepticism of the veracity of most allegations of witchcraft (see Chapter 4). On the surface, this certainly would seem a positive shift for women, since they were less likely to face criminal persecution as a result. In other respects, however, the decline in belief in the supernatural among the intellectual elite brought with it a decline in one source of feminine authority.

This is particularly visible in the literature on ventriloquism, where Enlightenment thinkers attempted to dispel the myth of demonic possession using the experimental method. In 1772, Johannes Baptista de La Chapelle published *Le Ventriloque, ou l'engastrimythe*. The book included numerous accounts of skilled ventriloquists deceiving naïve observers into believing they had heard supernatural voices. In true Enlightenment fashion, La Chapelle then disabused them of their belief by explaining exactly how the ruse was constructed. In the process of constructing a scientific explanation for demonic possession, however, La Chappelle and his contemporaries removed the authority of spiritual voices from female territory to male. Where several early modern women and girls had gained a measure of authority as vessels through which divine (or diabolical) utterances could be heard, their eighteenth-century counterparts began to lose that authority. Viewed through the eyes of Enlightenment proponents of a secular, rational world, female mystics began to appear as frauds, or worse, as dupes.[7]

PROTESTANT REVIVALISM

The Enlightenment views of femininity (outlined in Chapter 1) that held that women were biologically intended to act as nurturers and moral compasses of the household also considered them more naturally capable of intense piety and spiritual dedication. In many ways, therefore, the more radical forms of religious devotion held a special attraction to eighteenth-century women. Female Nonconformists (those who did not adhere to the official Church of England) outnumbered men by at least a third, for example.[8]

The roots of eighteenth-century Protestant revivalism ran deep. At least a century before, English Protestants decided that the reformation had not gone far enough and began to pursue even more introspective forms of worship. The Pietism movement began in central Europe at the end of the seventeenth century as an objection to Lutheran formalism. By the 1730s, John Wesley had begun the English movement that would later evolve into Methodism by organizing "united societies" within the Anglican Church.

Eastern Europe also experienced Protestant revival in the early eighteenth century. The Pietists continually focused upon eastern missionary work, and made significant inroads into Russia and surrounding territories, taking advantage of Catherine the Great's toleration acts of 1762 and 1763. Silesia, the contested territory that became the cause of war between the Austrian and Prussian Empires in mid-century, gained freedom of worship in 1707. Charles XII of Sweden brought his own military might to the cause, and his troops held open-air meetings that presaged the Methodist open-air gatherings in England and America. Contemporary accounts describe passionate night congregations of the faithful, where sermons brought their listeners to tears, and hymns were sung for hours on end.[9]

This spirit of seemingly unprecedented religious fervor brought new opportunities for female preaching and prophesying. The Moravian brand of Pietism stands out for its receptivity to women. It was unique among all European religions in allowing female ordination as Acolytes, Deaconesses, Eldresses and even *Priesterinnen* (female ministers). Offered a haven in southeast Germany after a long period of persecution, Moravian pietism flourished in the 1740s and 1750s. To cultivate an intimate personal relationship with God, Pietists joined together in groups called "Choirs," each of which contained people of like age, gender, and marital status. Where male worshippers tended to gain spiritual understanding by identifying themselves with Christ, female Pietists focused upon the Holy Spirit as a maternal figure or considered themselves the virgin brides of Christ. In this way, Pietism allowed women their own distinct form of worship.

Methodist co-founder John Wesley expressed reluctance to formally sanction female preaching, but he finally conceded the right to Sarah Crosby. Previously, Methodist women had been allowed to publicly read, pray, and exhort the faithful to salvation, but Crosby's exhortations came dangerously close to proselytizing in the absence of a male preacher at a Derby Methodist Society meeting in 1761. A decade later, a number of Englishwomen found themselves in similar situations, and Wesley was finally moved to state that St. Paul's rule forbidding feminine preaching must certainly make room for "a few exceptions" and that a woman who experienced "an *Extraordinary Call*" to preach was indeed correct to heed it.[10]

Crosby was one of many prominent Methodist women. Joanna Southcott, another Wesleyan Methodist, experienced a divine revelation in 1792 of the

Second Coming of Christ. Though she was ultimately spurned by both the Church of England and the Methodist leaders themselves, she gained a substantial following among English men and women that numbered in the 1000s. They were overjoyed in 1814 at the confirmed pregnancy of their 64-year-old leader, who had predicted her own role as mother of Shiloh, "the Second Christ," twelve years earlier, but she died before the prophecy could be fulfilled.[11]

Women's presence in the front lines of eighteenth-century Protestant revivalism left them vulnerable to the reprisals of official churches and mainstream society. An Irish Methodist woman threw herself in the path of an angry mob in order to protect a preacher as he began to broadcast the Methodist message. The crowd proceeded to whip her so violently that she later died of the blows. Thanks to her selflessness, the man survived to continue his ministry.[12] One of the most famous examples from Eastern Europe is that of the wife and daughters of evangelist Joseph Schaitberger. A Salzburg miner, Schaitberger publicly professed his faith after having secretly worshipped as a Protestant for many years. He and his wife were expelled as a consequence but were forbidden to bring their two young daughters with them into exile. Schaitberger's wife never recovered from the pain of this forcible separation and died soon after, begging her husband until the very end to get their children back. The girls were raised as Catholics and never returned to their father's home.[13]

Women's prominence among those spearheading Protestant evangelical movements was often used against the movements themselves. One of Methodism's denigrators depicted Methodist minister George Whitfield surrounded by a host of female supporters in symbolic garb, in a print entitled *Enthusiasm disply'd*. Other detractors called it a movement of "silly women" or "sour, disappointed old maids, with some others of a less prudish disposition."[14] The latter hint at sexual impropriety crops up again and again in attacks on radical Protestantism. Luise Adelgunde Gottsched's *Die Pietisterey im Fischbein-Rocke* (*Pietism in a Whale-Bone Corset*) underscored the hypocrisy of German Pietist circles. The male Pietist character vociferously condemned carnal desire while secretly lusting after a young female follower. Though the work was ill-received by many Germans for its strong antipietist message, it was not alone in criticizing the movement by depicting Pietists as secretly lascivious.[15] A similar taint of hypocrisy surrounds Welsh Methodist Howell Harris' extraordinarily close relationship with Madam Sidney Griffith, with whom he traveled and praised as a "prophetess" and "a Mother in Israel." The hint of scandal in their relationship remains to this day.[16]

In virtually every branch of Protestant revivalism, feminine participation and power was most visible in the earliest years, when each respective faith was struggling to gain a foothold. Once it had established itself, it fell under

Enthusiasm display'd: or, the Moor Fields congregation (1739), engraving of Methodist minister George Whitefield preaching at Moorsfield in London. His right leg stands on a woman labeled "Hypocrisy," holding a mask; his left on "Deceit." The woman in the right foreground is "Folly" and holds a jester's staff and is accompanied by a monkey. (Courtesy of Library of Congress)

patriarchal control and its female adherents were silenced. Certainly, the door that had opened to female preachers with Protestant revivalism closed quickly. As early as 1802, a Conference of Wesleyan Preachers found female proselytizing "contrary to both scripture and prudence."[17] Moravian Pietists made the shift even earlier, at their General Synod of 1764. Practices according women a wide variety of official roles in the church "as was the case before," they decreed, were now "deemed not good."[18]

CATHOLIC ENLIGHTENMENT

Catholic churches across Europe also felt the influence of Enlightenment ideas. The term "Catholic Enlightenment" is misleading in that it suggests a single program; the reality was a complex and varied range of attitudes among the Catholic states of Europe. In some forms, Catholic Enlightenment actions simply furthered the changes to the Roman Church begun with the Counter-Reformation of centuries before. In other ways, however, Enlightened Catholicism reacted against the Baroque emotionalism of these earlier reforms, and often clashed with the Jesuit order that had been so prominent a part of Counter-Reformation Catholicism.

The Jesuit emphasis on Latin as the language of instruction, their rigid intolerance of any deviation from Catholic orthodoxy, as well as their being unanswerable to any authority save that of the Pope made the order an anathema to Enlightenment Catholicism. Portugal expelled the Jesuits from all of its territories and withdrew Portuguese subjects from the Papal States in 1760 in order to more aggressively pursue an Enlightenment agenda. The Parisian *Parlement* officially abolished the Jesuit order in 1762, an act repeated by provincial *parlements* across France over the next few years.

Many devout Catholics embraced Enlightenment rationalism, the experimental method, and the ideal of universal education. They eagerly pursued astronomy studies in order to discredit astrology. A Polish clergyman described a path of learning that began with Italy in the sixteenth century and spread through France, England, Germany, Poland, Sweden and Russia by the eighteenth century. In a glorifying tribute to the age, he wrote that "nations which were first enlightened now learn together with those which they had taught. Exquisite taste spreads ever wider, and almost all the nations of Europe contribute to their mutual enlightenment."[19]

The Catholic Enlightenment had a significant impact on female members of the flock, not the least of which being its general support for the equal education of women. The pontificate of Benedict XIV set a prominent example of the potential of women in the sciences by fostering the careers of a number of prominent European women, including Milan's Marie Gaetana Agnesi and Laura Bassi of Bologna (see Chapter 5). Such women fit well within an agenda seeking to reveal the Catholic Church as the center of the most innovative research and broadest education program of the age.

Women were victims as well as beneficiaries of the Catholic Enlightenment. The Portuguese inquisition, for example, which reached its peak between 1715 and 1760, prosecuted over five hundred magical healers, both male and female. Portugal was unique throughout Europe in launching a prolonged assault on cunning men and women in this period. This was undoubtedly the result of a prominent group of university-trained physicians entering the official ranks in the Holy Office, who consciously sought to implement rationalistic medicine. Though no one was executed, female healers were silenced by this systematic attempt at suppression.[20] The varied decline in the power of female mysticism all over Europe is attributable, at least in part, to reform-minded Catholics like those in Portugal's Holy Office.

Enlightenment women were also visible among the Jansenists of eighteenth-century Europe. Jansenism began as an offshoot of Catholicism, gaining most of its followers in the seventeenth century. Jansenism veered from Catholic orthodoxy in allowing no room for free will in the acceptance of divine grace; supplicants needed genuine contrition, but they bore no other role in obtaining salvation. The sect also advocated the reduced authority of the Pope. Jansenism gained most of its popularity in eighteenth-century France and Italy. It was declared heretical by the Catholic Church, but the Jansenists had always seen themselves as Catholics. One historian has suggested that Jansenism suffered an unusually high level of persecution because its rise came on the heels of Protestantism, the most wounding attack the papacy had ever known.[21]

Jansenism held particular attraction for the women of France. Unlike their Catholic counterparts, Jansenist bishops offered laywomen the opportunity to gain a higher level of spirituality than they were ordinarily accorded. Devout women unable to afford the entrance dowries to convents who wished to engage in charitable works now had an outlet:

> They have no vows but those of their baptism ... They have no cloister, but live in a manner similar to nuns.... They go to church in the parish.... They are engaged to establish little schools and to teach Christian doctrine to members of their sex throughout the diocese.... They sleep in dormitories.... They have a common room where they say the daily office.... They dress in secular clothing but very modestly, completely covering the lower arm.[22]

Jansenists encouraged both women and men to seek spiritual illumination through education, and provided schools for both girls and boys. They allowed women equal participation in the liturgy and access to scriptures. The papal reprisals against Jansenism are particularly visible against the nuns of Port-Royal, who were forcibly deported from the convent in 1706. In 1708, French King Louis XIV ordered the structure razed; the task was accomplished so completely that even deceased nuns' remains in the cemetery were dug up and reburied in a common grave.[23]

Seventeenth-century French noblewoman Mme de Sévigné was one of the most prominent laywomen to embrace Jansenism. Her letters to her daughter, published for a wide readership in the 1720s and in several subsequent editions up to 1775, made her Jansenist sympathies visible. She had many friends among the sisters of Port-Royal. In her later years, she underwent a "conversion" to the Jansenist way of life and found it a great comfort in dealing with the loss of her daughter. Her letters went on to a new round of popularity in the century following the French Revolution, when Jansenism was no longer a threat and they could be read only as expressions of maternal love and simple piety.[24]

The Catholic churches of Eastern Europe also experienced external assaults in the eighteenth century. The Austrian Emperors were almost constantly plagued by fears of a Protestant uprising in the various territories of their domain. Catholic missionaries were dispensed into the countryside, instructed to search for infidels by trapping young children into admissions that would reveal the heresy of their parents. It is even rumored that the

Two Jansenist nuns in the seventeenth century. After The Ex-Voto of 1662 by Philippe de Champaigne. (© Leonard de Selva/CORBIS)

daughter of Joseph Schaitberger—held back and raised as a Catholic after her famous evangelist father was expelled from Salzburg—went to him at age twenty-five to attempt to convert him to Catholicism, but failed.[25] In the highest echelons of Hungarian society, Catholic noblewomen heeded the church's call to promote Roman Catholicism. An Esterházy princess devoted considerable resources to the cause by sponsoring a Jewish woman's conversion. With sums considered "excessive largess" by her husband, the Princess paid for the new convert's room and board at an Ursuline convent in Ödenburg and later for clothing and household goods to facilitate her marriage to a Christian man.[26]

CHRISTIANITY AND EMPIRE

Missionary activity was rife among the faithful in eighteenth-century Europe. The Catholics of France, Spain and Portugal considered the promotion of the faith a key goal of colonial expansion and continued to send men and women to their outposts in various parts of the globe. Pietists tended to focus on the east—though not exclusively—making evangelical forays into Russia which resulted in the establishment of schools in Moscow, St. Petersburg, Narva, Astrakhan and Tobol'sk. Though all were short-lived ventures, they taught oriental languages to promote future missionary expansion into Asia.[27]

Radical Protestants from England had taken refuge in the British North American colonies since the past century, and their influence on North American culture remains to this day.

There are many examples of the latter, but one of the most colorful is that of the founder of the New Lebanon Society near Albany, New York. Mother Ann Lee was an Englishwoman who had joined the Protestant radical sect known as the Shakers in 1758 and received a revelation twelve years later that she was the new female messiah. As she told her credulous audience "it is not I that speak but Christ who dwells in me."[28] Within four years, she led a group to America to form the New Lebanon Society, which acquired 1,000 members by the time of her death in 1784. Her association bore many similarities to Catholic monastic life, particularly in its emphasis on celibacy and a shared community of goods, and attracted a markedly high proportion of women, especially those who were single, widowed, or unhappily married and sought out the New Lebanon Society as a refuge from conventional wedded life. The society grew to 6,000 but declined by the late nineteenth century.[29]

Not surprisingly, nuns were very prevalent among Catholic female spiritual ambassadors to the new world. Mother María Rosa, a Spanish Capuchin nun, became Prioress of a new convent in Lima, Peru. She later wrote of her three-year adventure in traveling from Madrid to Buenos Aires, which included a Dutch attack, to finally inaugurate the convent in May of 1713.[30] Marguerite Bourgeoys of Troyes, France, came to the North American city of Montreal in 1658 and founded the institute of the Congrégation de Notre-Dame, accepted with a formal constitution by the bishop in 1698. Like their Ursuline counterparts, the sisters of the Congrégation taught local girls religion, reading, writing, some arithmetic, and domestic skills. Just as significantly, these women helped to buttress resistance to English invasion during the War of Spanish Succession in 1711 by setting the example of calm faith in a French victory. Records of the order show that most of the eighteenth-century sisters came from the surrounding settlements, but some, such as Catherine Bony (Rouen), Claude Durand and Thérèse Rémy (Paris), Élisabeth de la Bertache (Dijon), and Marie-Madeleine de la Corne de Chaptes, sailed from France.[31]

Though there is little evidence of Muslim women on European soil in the eighteenth century, it is clear that Europeans ventured into Islamic territory. The most prominent account of Muslim women in the eighteenth century comes from Lady Mary Wortley Montagu. As the wife of the English ambassador to Turkey, Lady Montagu had a unique opportunity to view the role of women in Ottoman culture, and she wrote many descriptive letters of her experience between 1716 and 1718. In contrast to previous observations by male European visitors that lamented Turkish women's oppression, Montagu said " 'Tis very easy to see they have more liberty than we have."[32]

A Deist, Montague had no interest in trying to convert Ottoman women to Christianity and returned to Europe with admiring accounts of the East that purported to divulge the "secrets" of the harem. She befriended many elite Muslim women and wrote many accounts of Ottoman culture that were published, without her authorization, in 1763. Aside from the considerable literature on Montagu's fascination with the Muslims of the East, however, there are few, if any, accounts to connect Islamic women with eighteenth-century Europe.

Moravian Pietist communities existed around the world, including Western Europe, Greenland, and North and South America. One of its foremost figures was Anna Nitschmann, who led a group of female believers into a ceremonial covenant with Christ at the young age of fourteen. Later becoming the head Eldress of the Moravian Pietists, Nitschmann was required to visit all of the outlying colonies in person. The Single Sisters' Choir in Bethlehem, Pennsylvania, accorded Nitschmann elite status within the movement. Their 1761 celebration called her "our blessed and unforgettable Mama, the originator of this covenant with the Savior."[33] At the height of their movement, female Pietists played a key role in spreading their faith around the globe.

The Christian missionaries of the eighteenth century also had a substantial impact upon indigenous women as sexual predators. Priest Bachiller Luis Antonio de Echazarreta's ministry to New Spain resulted in a 1780 court case where his Mayan parishioners brought numerous allegations of rape and immorality. Francisca Cauiche testified that he had told her that "I have permission and a license to have relations with anyone, even a young virgin like you.... I should be the first to taste of the fruits that will soon belong to those *cabrones*." Her reply, "My Lord, I cannot have relations with you because you are Christ on earth!," fell on deaf ears.[34]

Indigenous women who refused to embrace Christianity faced even more conflicts with colonizers. María Savina, a single mestiza (mixed race) woman in colonial Guatemala was denounced to the Inquisition by a wealthy Spanish Catholic woman who had recently given birth to a "monster." She claimed that Savina had bewitched her and caused her to hear the croaking of a toad through her last four months of pregnancy, which led her to give birth to a creature "with a toad-like head and long arms that reached almost to the infant's feet."[35] This was commensurate with early modern notions of the causes of monstrous births (see Chapter 1), but it is interesting that neither the wronged mother nor the priests who testified attributed the birth to a divine judgment or to natural causes. In focusing on Savina's guilt, they simultaneously accorded the mixed-race female sorcerer supernatural powers. Reprisals against colonial heathen were guided as much by fear as by a sense of Christian righteousness.

Interactions between Christians and colonial peoples were not always adversarial. One marked example illustrates the fascinating opportunities occasionally presented by European Christianity. Black freed slave Rebecca Protten was inspired to join the Moravian Pietists after meeting one of the earliest Moravian missionaries in 1736 in the Dutch colony of St. Thomas. Already a literate Christian working as a house servant, Protten now spent her off hours working tirelessly to deliver God's message to slaves all over the island. Many accepted the fellowship, literacy, and sense of equality that Moravian Christianity offered. By her death in 1780, Rebecca Protten had traveled to Europe and Africa, bringing the Pietist message to both black and white women and is "apparently, the first black woman ordained in western Christianity."[36] Though in some ways her race set her apart from her fellow worshippers (the Moravians labeled Rebecca and all Pietists of color "Moors," despite their diverse Asian and African origins), her ordination as a deaconess during her years in Europe gave the black woman spiritual authority over her white sisters, qualifying her to lead even the highest born among them in the principles of the faith.

JUDAISM

The Jewish population was scattered throughout eighteenth-century Europe, with the highest concentrations being in Eastern Europe. Prussian Jews had suffered expulsions in the seventeenth century, so their numbers were limited to a few thousand Jews in Berlin, but there were pockets across central Europe in Hamburg, Swabia and elsewhere. Jewish communities were also visible in France, England and Holland. In many ways, the conditions for women of Jewish faith in the Enlightenment age differed little from those of their forbears.

Many still lived in extreme poverty, and a minority enjoyed relative comfort. Not surprisingly, there is much more surviving evidence of the latter despite their lower numbers. The Jewish Berlin *salonnière* Henriette Herz found herself unable to meet the costs of the salon gatherings at her husband's death, but she was still far from destitute (see Chapter 5). She had grown up in a Bourgeois household with parents who could afford to send her to a private day school for girls and teach her at home as well. At the height of their entertaining, the Herz's invited a variety of prestigious guests from among the clients of her husband's medical practice. Her memoirs are vague about their identities, but they were probably gentiles from among Berlin's most respected families. Surviving sources indicate the existence of many other Jewish daughters in the salon circles of central Europe with similarly privileged upbringings.[37]

The hordes of less fortunate Jewish women are largely hidden from history, save for a few vague glimpses. Many Jews were confined to ghettos where strict rules forbade expansion and problems of overcrowding grew to behemoth proportions. One record of Hungarian Jews listed ten to twelve people living in one room.[38] Hermann Samuel Reimarus, father of Hamburg *salonnière* Elise Reimarus, offers another brief glimpse of the living conditions of the most unfortunate Jewish women. His household account books allude to an incident where he was moved to an unusual act of charity in giving—rather than selling, as he intended—"old clothes" to an anonymous Jewish woman. His additional gift of a substantial amount of cash is particularly telling. Though the records do not explicitly account for the extremity of his generosity, it must have been her dire impoverishment in the middle of winter that evoked the gesture.[39]

A petition from a Jewish servant girl in 1774 pleaded for justice after she was unceremoniously dismissed from service and deprived of her possessions. Her submission revealed her "hope to win [the court's] mercy and . . . help in obtaining justice, because I am a servant in foreign lands and have no one who will speak for me."[40] Her mistress answered the petition with a counter charge of theft, and the girl disappeared from history. Theft charges—proven or otherwise—would have raised sufficient doubts about her credibility to destroy her chances of finding other employment in domestic service, and certainly of marriage. Deprived of these avenues of survival, the girl was most likely reduced to abject poverty and had little recourse other than complete beggary. As this example illustrates, most European Jews had very limited networks of protection in eighteenth-century society, but orphaned girls had the least of all.

The Enlightenment did bequeath a few key benefits to eighteenth-century Jews, however. The *philosophes*' move towards secularization motivated Enlightened leaders to issue acts of religious toleration. With Emperor Joseph II's toleration edict 1781, Austrian Jews no longer had to obey a separate set of laws from their Christian counterparts. In contrast to 1745, when an estimated 70,000 Jews had been expelled from Prague, a confessional Jew was awarded a patent of nobility in 1789. In France, the National Assembly agreed to offer Jews full civil rights in 1791, the third year of the revolution. Moses Mendelssohn, one of the most famous Jews of the Enlightenment, enthusiastically embraced Enlightenment rationalism without relinquishing his Jewish faith. His scholarly defense of Judaism contributed to the *philosophes*' arguments for religious toleration. He moved in both Jewish and non-Jewish intellectual circles in his native Germany. Widely published, Mendelssohn gained a reputation as "the German Socrates" and was undoubtedly a source of pride among his people.[41]

This atmosphere of increasing tolerance and pride surrounding late eighteenth-century Judaism nonetheless had significant limitations for Jewish women. Mendelssohn's daughter, Dorothea, was betrothed to a fellow

Eighteenth-century scene depicting a Jewish woman lighting the candles for the Sabbath. (© Chris Hellier/CORBIS)

Jew by her father. She dutifully obeyed his wishes but never found happiness in his choice and left her marriage upon Mendelssohn's death. More than a decade later, she converted to Protestantism, presumably as part of her elusive search for acceptance among her contemporary society.[42] As Berlin *salonnière* Rahel Levin put it:

> It is as if some supramundane being, just as I was thrust into this world, plunged these words with a dagger into my heart: yes, have sensibility, see the world as few see it, be great and noble. . . . But I add one thing more: be a Jewess! And now my life is a slow bleeding to death.[43]

This feeling of ostracism was one of a host of reasons for Jewish girls to convert. The material incentives offered by Hungarian nobles was another. Turning one's back on Judaism was often a pragmatic choice of many young women—to increase their opportunities for marriage or association.

Occasionally, however, it may have been a matter of conscience. This appears to have been the case for two Jewish girls who adopted Catholicism decades after the emancipation of Jews in France. They ran away from the family home with the help of some priests. The eldest sister responded to their father's execrations through an intermediary: "she may be driving herself and the whole Hebrew race to despair, but that does not trouble her," the account read, warning that "all these efforts and those of all Jews to find her would be useless; that consequently she advises her father to keep calm, or rather to imitate her and to embrace, as she is doing, the Christian religion."[44] She later tearfully confronted her father, continuing to defend her spiritual change and attribute it to "grace," rather than priestly coercion.

NOTES

1. John McManners, *The French Revolution and the Church* (New York: Harper & Row, 1969), 103.

2. Quoted in Mona Ozouf, *Festivals and the French Revolution*, trans. Alan Sheridan, (Cambridge, MA: Harvard UP, 1988), 101.

3. McManners, 104.

4. PV de l'administration du district d'Avallon, 7 novembre 1791, quoted in Suzanne Desan, *Reclaiming the Sacred: Lay Religion and Popular Politics in Revolutionary France* (Ithaca: Cornell UP, 1990), 200.

5. Emmet Kennedy, *A Cultural History of the French Revolution* (New Haven, CT: Yale UP, 1989), 388.

6. Fernand Baldensperger, *Le movement des idées dans l'émigration français (1789–1815)*, vol. I, 187, quoted in Margaret H. Darrow, "French Noblewomen and the New Domesticity, 1750–1850," *Feminist Studies* 5, no. 1 (Spring 1979), 54.

7. Leigh Eric Schmidt, "From Demon Possession to Magic Show: Ventriloquism, Religion, and the Enlightenment," *Church History* 67, no. 2 (June 1998), 281–84, 300–301.

8. Bridget Hill, *Women Alone: Spinsters in England, 1660–1850* (New Haven, CT: Yale UP, 2001), 146.

9. W. R. Ward, "'An Awakened Christianity': The Austrian Protestants and Their Neighbours in the Eighteenth Century," *Journal of Ecclesiastical History* 40, no. 1 (January 1989), 63.

10. Letter from John Wesley to Mary Bosanquet, dated June 13, 1771, quoted in Paul W. Chilcote, *She Offered Them Christ: The Legacy of Women Preachers in Early Methodism* (Nashville, TN: Abingdon Press, 1993), 80. Emphasis in original.

11. Hill, 154–55.

12. Chilcote, 30.

13. Ward, 56–58, 63.

14. William Fleetwood and James Lackington (1794), quoted in Chilcote, 25.

15. William E. Petig, *Literary Antipietism in German during the First Half of the Eighteenth Century* (New York: Peter Lang, 1984), 60–61, 86–87, 157–60.

16. Jean Silvan Evans, "Howell Harris: A Welsh Icon and the Two Women Closest to Him," *Journal of the United Reformed Church History Society* 7, no. 10 (2007), 595, 597.

17. Quoted in Hill, 152.

18. Quoted in Beverly Prior Smaby, "Female Piety among Eighteenth-Century Moravians," *Pennsylvania History* 64 (1997), 161.

19. Piotr Świtkowski (1783), quoted in Richard Butterwick, "Between Anti-Enlightenment and Enlightened Catholicism: Provincial Preachers in Late-Eighteenth-Century Poland-Lithuania," *SVEC* (*Studies on Voltaire and the Eighteenth-Century*) (January 2008), 209.

20. Timothy Walker, "Physicians and Surgeons in the Service of the Inquisition: The Nexus of Religion and Conventional Medical Training in Enlightenment-Era Portugal," in *Medicine and Religion in Enlightenment Europe*, ed. Ole Peter Grell and Andrew Cunningham (Aldershot: Ashgate, 2007), 29–48.

21. Marie A. Conn, *Noble Daughters: Unheralded Women in Western Chrisitainity, 13th to 18th Centuries* (Westport, CT: Greenwood Press, 2000), 94.

22. Claude Lancelot, "Relation du voyage d'Aleth" (December 18, 1644), quoted in Conn, 91.

23. Conn, 89, 90–91.

24. Catherine R. Montfort, "Mme de Sévigné and the Jesuits in the *siècle des Lumières*," *SVEC* (*Studies on Voltaire and the Eighteenth-Century*) (December 2001), 167–77.

25. Ward, 58, 69.

26. Rebecca Gates-Coon, *The Landed Estates of the Esterházy Princes: Hungary during the Reforms of Maria Teresia and Joseph II* (Baltimore, MD: Johns Hopkins UP, 1994), 127–28.

27. James H. Billington, *The Icon and the Axe: An Interpretive History of Russian Culture* (New York: Vintage Books, 1970), 277.

28. Quoted in Hill, 153.

29. Ibid., 153–54.

30. María José Álvarez Faedo, *A Bio-Bibliography of Eighteenth-Century Religious Women in England and Spain* (Lewiston, NY: Edwin Mellen Press, 2005), 52.

31. Colleen Gray, *The Congrégation de Notre-Dame, Superiors, and the Paradox of Power, 1693–1796* (Montreal: McGill-Queen's UP, 2007), 29–45, 145–72.

32. Lady Mary Wortley Montagu, quoted in Srinivas Aravamudan, "Lady Mary Wortley Montagu in the Hammam: Masquerade, Womanliness, and Levantinization," *English Literary History* 62, no. 1 (1995), 79.

33. Quoted in Smaby, 160.

34. "Petición y denuncia hecha por Félix Cocom, maestro de capilla del pueblo de Uman contra su cura por abuses que le había hecho" (1781), quoted in John F. Chuchiak IV, "The Sins of the Fathers: Franciscan Friars, Parish Priests, and the Sexual Conquest of the Yucatec Maya, 1545–1808," *Ethnohistory* 54, no. 1 (Winter 2007), 104.

35. Martha Few, "Atlantic World Monsters: Monstrous Births and the Politics of Pregnancy in Colonial Guatemala," in *Women, Religion and the Atlantic World (1600–1800)*, ed. Daniella Kostroun and Lisa Vollendorf (Toronto: U of Toronto P, 2009), 215.

36. Jon F. Sensbach, *Rebecca's Revival: Creating Black Christianity in the Atlantic World* (Cambridge, MA: Harvard UP, 2005), 7.

37. Deborah Hertz, *Jewish High Society in Old Regime Berlin* (New Haven, CT: Yale UP, 1988), 97–111.

38. Gates-Coon, 123.

39. Almut Spalding, *Elise Reimarus (1735–1805): The Muse of Hamburg* (Würzburg: Königshausen & Neumann, 2005), 262.

40. Acta in Sachen Perle Levy von Steinbiedersdorf ca ihre gewesene Dienstmagd Särle Levy, quoted in Claudia Ulbrich, *Shulamit and Margarete: Power, Gender, and Religion in a Rural Society in Eighteenth-Century Europe*, trans. Thomas Dunlap (Boston, MA: Brill Academic Publishers, 2004), 205.

41. Allan Arkush, *Moses Mendelssohn and the Enlightenment* (Albany: State University of New York Press, 1994), xi.

42. Hertz, 105–7.

43. Rahel Levin, quoted in Hertz, 101.

44. Letter found in A. D. Vaucluse, V104, 1818, quoted in Barnett Singer, "A Remnant: the Jews of Vaucluse in the Nineteenth Century," *Jewish Social Studies* 40, no. 2 (1978), 162.

SUGGESTED READING

Barnett, S. J. *The Enlightenment and Religion: The Myths of Modernity*. Manchester: Manchester UP, 2003.

Chilcote, Paul W. *She Offered Them Christ: The Legacy of Women Preachers in Early Methodism*. Nashville, TN: Abingdon Press, 1993.

Conn, Marie A. *Noble Daughters: Unheralded Women in Western Christianity, 13th to 18th Centuries*. Westport, CT: Greenwood Press, 2000.

Desan, Suzanne. *Reclaiming the Sacred: Lay Religion and Popular Politics in Revolutionary France*. Ithaca: Cornell UP, 1990.

Hertz, Deborah. *Jewish High Society in Old Regime Berlin*. New Haven, CT: Yale UP, 1988.

Kienzle, Beverly Mayne, and Pamela J. Walker, eds. *Women Preachers and Prophets through Two Millennia of Christianity*. Berkeley: U of California P, 1998.

Knott, Sarah and Barbara Taylor, eds. *Women, Gender and Enlightenment*. New York: Palgrave Macmillan, 2005.

Kostroun, Daniella, and Lisa Vollendorf, eds. *Women, Religion and the Atlantic World (1600–1800)*. Toronto: U of Toronto P, 2009.

Ozouf, Mona. *Festivals and the French Revolution*, translated by Alan Sheridan. Cambridge, MA: Harvard UP, 1988.
Sensbach, Jon F. *Rebecca's Revival: Creating Black Christianity in the Atlantic World*. Cambridge, MA: Harvard UP, 2005.
Taylor, Charles. *A Secular Age*. Cambridge, MA: The Belknap Press of Harvard UP, 2007.
Ulbrich, Claudia. *Shulamit and Margarete: Power, Gender, and Religion in a Rural Society in Eighteenth-Century Europe*, translated by Thomas Dunlap. Boston, MA: Brill Academic Publishers, 2004.

7

Women and War

Europe's leaders of the eighteenth century were little better than their predecessors at remaining peaceful. For more than half of the one hundred years, various nations were engaged in war with one another, on the continent or in colonial theatres. Enlightenment attitudes to war were condemnatory, fueling an intellectual disdain for military service among some European elites.[1] Prussia's demonstrable military prowess nonetheless inspired many other leaders to transform their armed forces in its image by mid-century. States invested more money in standing armies and initiated or escalated conscription practices. They adopted new battle techniques and encouraged a romanticized image of the officer class that attracted many youth among the nobility and gentry.

European women felt the impact of these changes in a variety of ways. Many dealt with the presence of soldiers in their towns and villages, either acting as reluctant hosts to troops who had been quartered upon them, or living in fear of marauding men cut off from military supply lines. Some fell in love with servicemen and followed them to battle; others stayed behind and attempted to survive at some hand-to-mouth trade. The former situation posed its own difficulties, as the women who traveled with armies often had little official identity and still had to fend for themselves, far from home and under a military administration that deplored their presence. Still other eighteenth-century women experienced the effects of war as massive conscription drives that threatened the men they loved and needed. A celebrated minority of Europe's women—real and imagined—shouldered muskets, wielded a spear, or fired a canon, joining the ranks of warrior women so visible in eighteenth-century iconography.

CAMP FOLLOWERS AND WOMEN ON CAMPAIGN

Generally, fewer women traveled with eighteenth-century armies than had accompanied their seventeenth-century forbears, and fewer still would follow nineteenth-century European troops. There was a visible feminine component to eighteenth-century military encampments nonetheless. German troops, in particular, had a reputation for having a larger "woman-load" than their Italian, Spanish and French counterparts.[2]

Reformers complained of the encumbrance posed by camp followers, and Habsburg authorities set policy in 1756 (further reinforced in 1775) against wives accompanying their husbands on campaign.[3] When Russian hussar Captain Durov's regiment received marching orders in 1783, he brought his wife and infant daughter with him. The daughter's memoirs state that he was finally forced to leave the service four years later, since his quarters were encumbered with "two cradles," and her own little bed. As she put it, "such a family made life on the march impossible."[4] The Convention government of France issued an order in 1793 to send home all "useless" women traveling with the troops, limiting the official count to four per battalion to serve as laundresses. In practice, officials turned a blind eye to the many women accompanying soldiers, save when threatened by a syphilis epidemic.[5]

Despite these negative rumblings, historians often attribute the presence of female camp followers in eighteenth-century wars to improved sanitation, diet, and overall morale.[6] The woman who "followed the drum" put up with many of the same hardships as did the men on campaigns, sometimes with the additional burden of an infant or young child on her hip. Countless descriptions survive of women struggling along with retreating armies, succumbing to the privations of excessive cold, exhaustion, or hunger. The stress and commotion of naval battles was known to bring on labor for expectant women traveling with husbands onboard ship. Many delivered their babies in the heat of the barrage, without privacy, supplies, or assistance.[7]

Few soldiers could afford to pay for laundresses' services, and pay for such work was certainly insufficient for subsistence. A study of mid-eighteenth-century Württemburg found only six women employed to clean for an army ranging from four thousand to sixteen thousand men.[8] Nonetheless, a female camp follower attached to a particular man would certainly have washed his clothing, and perhaps those of his comrades, with or without compensation. Camp women also helped to mend clothing and other necessaries. A subscription fund set up by "some distinguished Female

Characters" in 1790s Britain sent two hundred thimbles to the women following the troops abroad.[9]

Women on campaign also served as nurses. When thousands of colonial soldiers were stricken with smallpox in North America in 1776, a general ordered all of the Pennsylvania regimental women to Fort George (which had become the largest American military hospital) to act as nurses.[10] The British Royal Navy employed female nurses on hospital ships, paying them at the same rate as able seamen; nursing detail in the army garnered only three quarters of what privates were paid.[11] The nurses' reputation for drunkenness was probably merited. One cannot blame them for resorting to drink, however, given the deplorable conditions in which they lived and the dangers of their work, involving frequent proximity to men dying of incurable contagious diseases. Nursing was poorly paid, and both land and sea hospitals were unappealing work environments for eighteenth-century women.[12] The German states officially excluded women from caring for the sick and wounded after 1648, and the British Admiralty banned female nurses from its hospital ships in 1703 "except when circumstances required."[13] In both cases, these rules were often ignored, and women continued to be drawn in to perform medical services.

A few women following the armies earned a living as sutlers, selling provisions to troops on the march. Military authorities placed restrictions on such transactions, including who could act as a vendor and what goods could be sold. This tended to favor male sutlers over their female counterparts. Corrupt associations developed between officers and sutlers who were granted exclusive rights to offer their wares to an encampment at inflated prices. Women who interfered with such liaisons or violated other trade rules risked disciplinary action. One American account depicts a sutler named Lydia Conner being drummed out of camp with another man for selling liquor to the troops in 1797.[14] Evidence about Germany, too, indicates that female sutlers were few and far between even by the eighteenth century. Some female civilian traders offered meals to the troops, but most soldiers worked together in squads numbering at least four to share mess duties.[15]

One of the most notorious sources of employment of eighteenth-century camp followers was, of course, prostitution. Army women's association with the oldest profession was so deeply entrenched that the term "whore" was applied to any woman following the drum, regardless of whether she was affiliated with one particular soldier or many. Historians agree that a significant proportion of European camp followers and wives were actually fairly monogamous and thus did not fit the harlot image of popular perception. The image of soldiers' and sailors' women as promiscuous was fueled in part by the public fascination with military wives being frequently away from husbands' surveillance. Women who sailed with naval ships were even less

134   Women's Roles in Eighteenth-Century Europe

Pretty Polly, say When I was away Did your fancy ever stray To some new Lover? (ca. 1790–1809), watercolor by George Moutard Woodward. (Courtesy of Library of Congress)

likely to be prostitutes; whores generally only came onboard when the ships were in port and the sailors had ready money.[16]

MILITARY WIVES

Most lower-ranking European soldiers were poorly paid, so the many wives denied the opportunity to travel "on the strength" and receive rations had to find alternative sources of employment. A high proportion of men in service had no wives at all, not even the unofficial unions that occurred among the civilian poor. Many states preferred to recruit single men because they could pay them less and hopefully avoid the problem of men deserting to go to their families. This was certainly the case in Spain, whose soldiers—after paying for food—had so little left upon which to survive, they quickly became "dirty, melancholy dwarfs," in the words of one contemporary.[17]

Spain was the first to regulate military marriage, requiring its men to secure royal assent before marrying in 1632. Subsequent decrees in 1701 and 1728 attempted to reinforce these orders. They were often ignored, however, until the 1760s when Charles III issued new marriage statutes with stricter enforcement.[18] By 1700, Germany and France had also implemented strict policies requiring soldiers to obtain their company commander's consent before marrying. In most cases, restrictions included officers. The Prussian king expressed his preference that "an officer should remain single" in his regulations of 1743.[19] By 1789, officers in Würzburg, and later Bavaria and Bamburg, had to pay a large sum to obtain permission to marry. The Austrian Empire attempted to limit military marriages by instating a total prohibition on wives traveling with the troops after 1775.[20]

There was an abrupt shift in favor of a married soldiery in Prussia in 1768, when Frederick decided that wives would help to "populate the country and to preserve the stock, which is so admirable."[21] French *philosophe* Voltaire himself recommended that "soldiers marry [so] they will no longer desert. Bound to their families, they are bound to their countries."[22] Army and navy wives, even left behind at home, helped to preserve the *esprit de corps* so important to an effective fighting force. The solidarity with other regimental wives can be heard in one Life Dragoons lieutenant's letter home to his wife in Finland, when he asked her to "tell the dragoon wives that all are well" and "to greet ... all the dragoon wives [and] tell them that their husbands thank God are still in health."[23]

Though many European military men were single, a significant group evaded marriage restrictions by engaging in clandestine marriages and cohabitant relationships. States, too, relaxed their policies when volunteers were urgently needed. These wives, positioned as they were on the periphery of the military machine with no official claim to rations or other benefits, had to pursue a variety of creative strategies for survival. One London sailor's wife bought gingerbread from a wholesaler and peddled it about the streets.[24] A few of the women of Hessen-Kassel headed households (though meager) by virtue of their association with visiting soldiers. The latter assisted them in acquiring "a cow, a few goats, and some chickens," which they then pastured illegally on the village commons. A woman's lover and his comrades-in-arms—in their periodic visits while on furlough—offered protection from those who might otherwise have objected to her use of common lands.[25] There were a few rare schemes by which military men's wages could be sent to their families, but most pay barely covered the serviceman himself.

Less fortunate wives and associates of absent soldiers and seamen resorted to more desperate measures. A disproportionate number of these women appear in police records as prostitutes in eighteenth-century cities. Some stole to survive. Others sought parish relief or begged in the streets, as was the case with the wives and children of the Enkedrottningens livregemente (Queen Dowager's Life Regiment) in Finland in 1799.[26] In Württemburg, army wives were offered free accommodation in the empty barracks in 1761, but only on the condition that they were to labor in the cotton industry without pay.[27] One Russian soldiers' wife found herself sold into serfdom. Though in theory her husband's military service entitled her to move about the country in search of work, she had little power against an employer's falsehood that she was married to his household serf and was thus his to sell to another noble.[28]

Even the wives traveling "on the strength" who were entitled to rations often received only a portion of the amount given the men. In eighteenth-century Britain, for example, army wives received two-thirds the victuals allotted their husbands. Naval wives were offered no provision at all, and were officially banned from traveling with the ship's company, though they ignored this prohibition and joined their husbands onboard ship with some frequency. Any sailor who brought his wife had to share his meager fare and his hammock with her, as she was allocated neither morsel nor space onboard ship. The differences in treatment between army and naval wives gave rise to unusual situations, such as that during the French revolutionary wars, when an insufficient corps of marines forced the army to provide several regular line regiments to serve as marines onboard naval ships. The army wives received their rations, while the navy wives were offered nothing save what their husbands could give them from their own plates.[29]

The events of 1789 caused a marked shift in how soldiers were recruited and treated in France, which had significant repercussions for their female associates. In the new nationalism of the French republic, women were a significant part of the war effort. In the words of a 1793 proclamation, "the women shall make tents and clothes, and shall serve in the hospitals; children shall tear rags into lint."[30] Male and female, young and old: all had a part to play in the theatre of war. The republic placed great weight on the notion of a national army that fought not for mercenary or feudal loyalties, but for the higher purpose of preserving the ideals of the new French nation.

While *ancien régime* policies generally considered only the welfare of the officer class, the new republic redressed the balance with a number of initiatives focusing on the families of men in the ranks who were invalided or killed in service. They issued a pay scale that dispensed relief in amounts geared towards the severity of injury suffered by the soldiers. Widows, too, received pensions that indiscriminately guaranteed a minimal subsistence income. The republic had set such store by the rights of its citizen soldiery, it was forced to maintain these benefits despite their crippling costs.[31]

Before the French Revolution, pensions still existed, but their payment depended much more upon the status of the recipient and was justified by the older notion of feudal obligations of the minister to his protectors. Women with the right connections stood to receive fairly generous compensation, such as the widow and daughter of military clerk Briquet, who were each sustained through the last years of their lives by his pension.

By 1769, rights to his pension had passed from his widow to his daughter (upon her mother's death), and then finally to his granddaughter's husband.[32]

Early in the century Peter the Great expanded Russia's military pension eligibility to include war widows. Such a woman received cash payments of about one-eighth her husband's salary throughout her lifetime unless she remarried. Noncommissioned officers' widows were additionally offered a small allotment of land (usually on the frontier) and sufficient capital to cover the cost of an initial crop.[33] Military wives who were fortunate enough to have a soldier husband return from service may have suffered more by comparison. Russian veterans from the lower ranks generally came back from the wars infirm and impoverished, yet there were minimal state initiatives to address their needs. Records from the reign of Empress Anna in 1730 show that married veterans received no more aid than their single counterparts.[34]

In England, the families of officers killed in the American Revolution were entitled to pensions, though no similar provisions existed for noncommissioned officers or enlisted men.[35] Widows of low-ranking seamen in the British navy, by contrast, could expect to receive a small pension in the eighteenth century. The Admiralty funded this by adding two fictional "widows men" to a ship's muster and applying their wages to a widows' pension fund. This was sometimes augmented by the proceeds from the sale of her late husband's personal effects, collected by the men onboard and retained for her use.[36]

The Spanish Crown also felt responsible to provide for officers' widows, but it attempted to do so with a law that prohibited officers from marrying undowered women. This provided only partial protection for widows, because the dowries were usually insufficient to cover any children the union had produced. A pension scheme was begun in 1760 that offered relief to officers' wives and children.[37]

Many German states, by contrast, began officially prohibiting officers' widows from receiving pensions, such as Würzburg, which required all potential officers' wives to sign a document renouncing their claims to a pension before the wedding.[38] Though the Finnish army established a pension system for officers in 1757, this did not extend to their widows. In 1784, Finnish army widows and orphans finally received access to funds providing relief (though limited), reflecting the general eighteenth-century trend to increase military widows' eligibility for pensions across Europe.[39]

Even without pensions, however, military widows might find aid from other quarters. London merchants pledged five pounds for each army widow in the American Revolution in 1776.[40] Finnish Colonel Erik Johan Stiernvall's widow, burdened with seven young sons in 1777, roused the compassion of a lieutenant colonel. He traveled to Stockholm and received royal assistance in securing a substantial sum for widow Stiernvall and patronage appointments for the eldest sons.[41]

WOMEN WARRIORS

The history of eighteenth-century warrior women is much broader than the history of women who armed themselves to fight for or against a revolution (see Chapter 3). Contemporary art and literature fed an eager audience with countless depictions of martial women. Some were based on real events; others served a more symbolic purpose.

The Marianne figure of the French republic fits firmly in the latter category. Often used interchangeably with a feminine image of Liberty, Marianne was represented as a militant woman and appears frequently in revolutionary iconography. Bare-breasted in many depictions, she generally held a sword in one hand and a shield in the other, and was surrounded by other revolutionary signifiers, such as the phyrgian cap of liberty and a sash of red, white, and blue for liberty, equality, and fraternity. Her English counterpart, Britannia, had similar warlike qualities, seen in the political cartoon where she stands in defense of English political radical, John Wilkes. Holding spear and shield, she stands at the base of the pedestal upon which Wilkes is perched, and sends her lion against his detractors. Marianne, Liberty, and Britannia went through various incarnations, appearing at other times more virginal and benign.[42]

It was fairly commonplace for female figures to be used as an allegory for a nation or continent in eighteenth-century European iconography, but it is important to read the images within their broader cultural and political context. The popularity of feminine icons in war cannot be equated with a decline in patriarchy. Indeed, the existence of martial female imagery often meant the opposite for real women. It has been argued that a figure like Marianne was "nothing but a picture" to her contemporaries.[43] She existed at the abstract, emotive, visual level, but the true French nation was understood through the written and spoken (male) word.

That being stated, real women could—and did—embrace the female warrior motif as a means of empowerment. Catherine the Great of Russia is an obvious example. As a monarch who gained power through an alliance with soldiers and subsequently pursued strong expansionist policies, Catherine's military connections were unmistakable. The empress' predilection for holding transvestite balls—which she attended dressed as a military officer— was widely known. In the words of the British envoy attached to her court, "a man's dress is what suits her best."[44] One of her favorite portraits, painted by Peter Ericksen in 1765, presents her in such garb, mounted on a magnificent white horse. The foreign press contributed to this image as well.

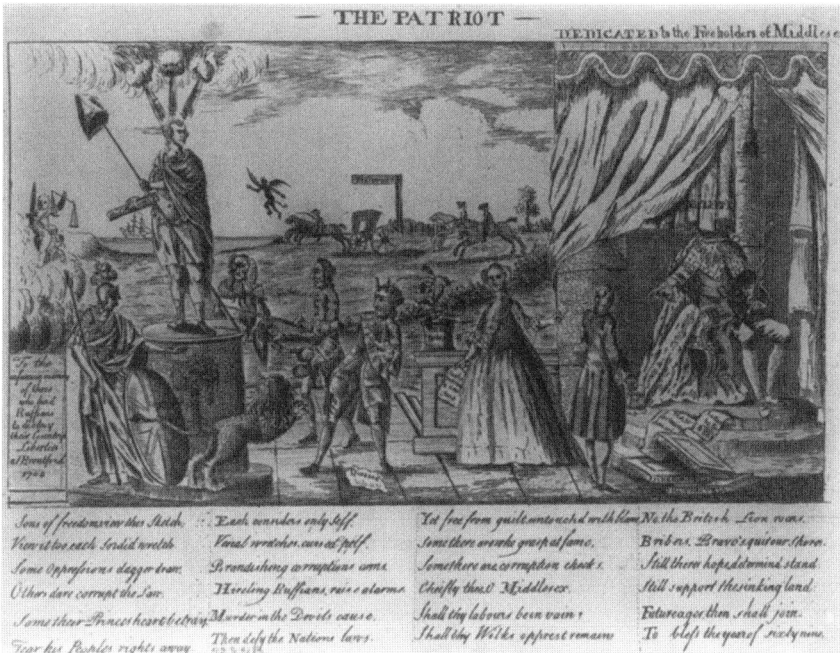

English cartoon depicting Britannia in the lower left foreground, with spear and shield, setting the British lion against those who would attack John Wilkes (standing on pedestal above her). The Patriot—Dedicated to the Freeholders of Middlesex (1769), etching. (Courtesy of Library of Congress)

The Christian Amazon, an English cartoon, represented Catherine sporting a shield and wielding a sword, her dress lifted to reveal men's breeches and boots.

Commoners, too, played the role of warrior woman. Mary Lacy's autobiography, *The History of the Female Shipwright . . . Written by Herself*, published in 1773, has been substantiated by other sources. It recounts the story of a young woman who dressed as a boy and entered the British navy as a carpenter's mate. She served in the Seven Years' War, mainly patroling the seas to maintain the British blockade of French ships. A range of conditions prevailed to ensure that her sex remained secret. The closest point she came to having her sex discovered was when she fell down an open hatch on deck and sustained a head wound:

> When I came to myself I was very apprehensive lest the doctor in searching for bruises about my body should have discovered that I was a woman, but it fortunately happened that he being a middle-aged gentleman, he was not very inquisitive, and my messmates being advanced in years, and not so active as young people, did not tumble me about or undress me.[45]

140   Women's Roles in Eighteenth-Century Europe

English cartoon of Catherine II as an Amazon blocking the bayonet thrust of Turkish foe Selim III while her ally, Joseph II, takes refuge behind her. The Christian Amazon, with her invincible target, Alias, the Focus of Genial Rays, or Dian of the Rushes, to [sic] much for 300,000, Infidels (London, 1787). (Courtesy of Library of Congress)

Lacy's unique career continued after her discharge from the navy. Revealed as a woman, she successfully lobbied to get a comfortable naval pension and finished her life as a speculative homebuilder in Deptford.

The reading public of eighteenth-century Europe eagerly digested stories of women marching off to war, in or out of disguise. The accounts tended to be concentrated in northwest Europe, especially England, Germany, and the Netherlands, but there are traces of female soldiers almost everywhere. The Dutch soldier Maria van Antwerpen was one of the more documented cases. She enlisted as soldier Jan van Ant in 1746 and married a woman a year later who believed her to be a man. Her disguise was not discovered for several years, at which time she became the subject of a popular song and a book entitled *De Bredasche Heldinne (The Heroine of Breda)*. Not broken by her sentence to exile, Antwerpen became Machiel van Antwerpen and married and enlisted again as a soldier in 1762.[46]

The literature on Antwerpen was only part of an entire genre of female warrior stories. A pamphlet entitled "Les femmes belges" recounted the tale of a woman in revolutionary Belgium who married her love and fought with him against Austrian occupation in 1789.[47] That same year, street literature appeared in France showing women boasting that they knew "how to handle other arms than needle and thread."[48] A popular ballad called *The French Amazons*, and mock recruiting posters for a female militia followed soon after. England's fictionalized memoirs of Christian Davies and Hannah Snell, two cross-dressing female soldiers, underwent numerous reprintings from mid-century onward. Across Europe, the eighteenth-century Amazon appeared in engravings, ballads, and other popular fiction.

Whether true or not, these stories carried significant power. The mock poster asking for recruits for a female militia in France actually drummed up a few volunteers. Other Frenchwomen used the images of warrior women to justify their own desires to serve in the republican army.[49] British women came forward to claim a medal for participating in the battle of the Nile in 1798, but were later denied because "it w[ould] leave the Army exposed to *innumerable* applications of the same nature."[50] There is little doubt, however, that tales of feminine exploits in battle more often served as a propaganda tool to fuel male recruitment and patriotism in various European nations.

There were less glorious accounts of female fighters as well that exist only in the private diaries or battle accounts that detail the horrors of war. In 1757, for example, Britain's German dominions fell under French attack. The French soldiers forced German peasants, men and women, to fight against the German armies. One account depicts an officer shooting "a peasant woman dead" for delaying him in his journey to carry a message to the German forces.[51]

Finally, there were "amazons" in other parts of the globe, who existed for eighteenth-century Europeans in traveler's accounts. An English trader visiting King Agaja of Dahomey in Africa in 1727 remarked upon the four women who guarded their leader with muskets, and another man from the Netherlands made a similar observation at Agaja's court six years later. In 1789, French trader Pruneau de Pommegorge depicted an entirely feminine army, "organized as it were into regiments," each with its own officers and numbering in the hundreds.[52] Witness testimonials about these African warrior women continued into the following century.

VICTIMS OF WAR

In 1758, the Swiss-born legal philosopher Emmerich von Vattel published a treatise acknowledging the special status of women, children, the elderly, and the infirm to be spared in war. Because they "offer no resistance," Vattel argued, "the belligerent has no right to maltreat or otherwise offer violence to them, much less to put them to death."[53] At approximately the same time, however, Europe saw a new style of warfare, known as "total war," that made women feel its impact at least as much—if not more—than ever before.

Frederick the Great's campaigns demonstrated the shift to total war tactics in mid-century. This was a change from the siege style of earlier military offensives. The Prussian army advanced quickly and faced its foes in open battlefields. The latter was often achieved by obliterating all structures and vegetation that might have provided cover for the enemy on the eve of battle.[54] This scorched-earth tactic could be extended to include the eradication of all civilians that might fuel future insurrection. The French republic used such a response to an uprising of its own citizens in the Vendée region. Brigadier General Westermann's triumphal report to the committee of public safety claimed to "have crushed children [and] massacred women who at least . . . will engender no more brigands."[55]

Upon mobilization, most European armies quickly found themselves cut off from supply lines and reliant upon the surrounding countryside for sustenance. Even in peacetime, Spanish soldiers received only a miniscule bread ration and were expected to use their daily wages to purchase additional food.[56] Civilian vendors—some of which were women—occasionally benefited by being able to set higher prices in such a captive market. More often, however, the implicit or explicit threat of violence ensured that prices were fair, and occupying armies tended to degenerate into pillaging and plundering for their needs despite official promises to compensate civilians.

European officers could do little to curb the abuses committed by soldiers on campaign, especially when official supplies were thin. A Swiss private's account of his experiences in Saxony in 1756 illustrates the difficulty of reigning in marauding soldiers:

> On the march every man thrust into his pack . . . whatever he could lay his hands on: flour, turnips, spuds, poultry, ducks, etc., and whoever didn't contrive to pick up something was treated to abuse by the others, as indeed was often my lot. What a heck of a din there was whenever we passed through a village from women, children, geese, sucking pigs, etc. Anything we could nab, went. A twist to its neck and into the pack. We broke into all the stables and gardens, belted all the trees about and tore the fruit off, branches and all. It was every man for himself and if you don't somebody else will. . . . So every man jack of us did his duty with a vengeance.[57]

Soldiers goaded one another into perpetrating atrocities on civilians. Any individual scruples were silenced by the group.

The quartering of soldiers was probably one of the most universal sources of military abuse of civilians. A few European nations housed troops in barracks, but most still used the billeting system as their primary means of accommodating armies. Barracks were extremely expensive, and though many European monarchs announced ambitious plans for building barracks, few plans came to fruition. Even in Prussia it was not until the end of the century that barracks began to appear in larger towns.

As proprietors of taverns, inns, and lodging houses, and as domestic help within such institutions, women bore a disproportionately heavy burden in quartering soldiers. Without the collective containment of the barracks, troops were notoriously hard to manage. As one contemporary observer wrote:

> those garrisons which have [barracks] are much more quiet, on account of the convenience which non-commissioned officers have to visit the quarters every evening, and to see that the soldiers are shut up in their quarters, which cannot be done when they are lodged among the inhabitants, where they have the liberty of going out and in whenever they please.[58]

Two Hungarian soldiers quartered in a Deutschkreutz home in 1777 set fire to it in retaliation for a lack of provisions and poor living conditions.[59]

At the very least, quartering soldiers meant putting up with drunken disorderly men who broke crockery, disrupted household routines, and depleted provisions. Mothers gritted their teeth while impressionable sons watched soldiers drink, smoke, curse, and generally behave with unmannerly roughness. One Goettingen matron was called a "sassy, brutal broad" by her unwelcome military guest.[60] Governing authorities were well aware of the popular hatred of the billeting system and often imposed it as a form of punishment on civilians.

Very occasionally, however, armies earned the praise of their hosts, such as the British Fusiliers in 1783. A petition from the Long Islanders expressed rare reluctance to see the troops leave:

> having for some time past had the 23rd Regiment of Troops quartered amongst us, and finding behaviour of both officers and men to be such as affords us the greatest satisfaction from their civil deportment, and carriage, the good order of the troops, and their peaceable behaviour towards the inhabitants in general, [we] cannot but regret their departure from this place.[61]

In Swedish-ruled Finland, too, the people decided in favor of quartering troops over paying an exemption fee in 1803. Obviously the Finnish system, whereby company commanders met with local officials each month to compensate for provision of quartering at a set rate, was sufficiently lucrative as to outweigh any difficulties that arose.[62]

Soldiers were a ubiquitous feature of civilian life in much of Europe. Spanish troops were deployed to work on canals and highways, to bring in harvests, and to capture thieves and smugglers.[63] Here and elsewhere, military forces appeared to suppress riotous crowds, enforce unpopular government initiatives, and the like. The army was a common presence in the civilian life of Peter the Great's Russia, collecting taxes and gathering provisions throughout the countryside.[64] As a permanent figure on the landscape, the European soldier had various and frequent interactions with the local women.

Female civilians also felt the effects of recruitment practices. Growing need prompted military leaders across Europe to adopt or escalate conscription practices. In 1770, Spain solved its recruitment problems by establishing a system whereby each province was required to produce a quota of soldiers from all unmarried young men with good health and standing five feet or more in height. The many men who sought to avoid the *sorteo* (conscription ballot) could do so either by fleeing or by a hasty marriage. In either case, Spanish girls experienced the effects. They were either deprived of an eligible suitor or forced into a premature wedding.[65]

German girls, too, found themselves swept up in conscription-avoidance strategies. In Hesen-Kassel, for example, many lost the chance to marry or were encouraged to marry boys from far outside their village. Families sometimes used resources that formerly would have gone into daughters' dowries to give sons sufficient property exemptions to escape the draft. Conversely, some women played a role in enticing men to volunteer. The newly enlisted men of eighteenth-century Potsdam were housed in a building complete with a dance floor, where young women distracted them from thoughts of desertion as they awaited their unit assignments.[66] One French captain's sister was praised for her efforts on France's behalf. As the marshal said in helpless admiration, "there is not a trick that she does not know" to get men to join the army.[67]

Europe's women were more often passionate opponents of military drafts. Britain's active naval press gangs faced violent resistance from mothers, wives, sisters, and daughters who feared the loss of male breadwinners. French accounts from the end of the century depict women attacking *gendarmes* with knives, axes, stones, and rocks, and even setting their dogs upon them. The ferocity of such resistance frequently resulted in the authorities relinquishing their prey until they could come back with reinforcements.[68]

Rape during wartime was so ubiquitous that it hardly bears mention in many accounts. Raped women were among the casualties listed when rampaging Dutch soldiers wreaked havoc on the village of Rumegis in the Spanish Netherlands in 1709.[69] One contemporary ballad spoke of the "Captain bold in Halifax/Who dwelt in country quarters [and]/Seduced a maid who hanged herself/One Monday in her garters." [70] Rapes also occurred at sea.

A British boatswain's wife—the only woman onboard—was raped after her husband's murder during a mutiny on a naval ship near the Greek coast in 1796.[71]

Even soldiers' consenting sexual partners encountered difficulties when they discovered they were pregnant by men who could not—or refused to—provide for them. The presence of a large number of troops in southwest Scotland has been linked to unusually high rates of infanticide.[72] German soldiers' poor pay and the restrictions on marriage in German armies caused a higher proportion of infanticides in connection with them as well.[73] When battalions received their marching orders, men were forced to abandon any liaisons with local women. The social and economic consequences of an illegitimate pregnancy were often more than some women could bear.

Ultimately, women's experience as victims probably accounts for more of their war-related activities than any other. The fact that the eighteenth century saw so much military aggression only increased the likelihood that few Europeans—male or female—would have been able to avoid feeling the impact of war in one form or another. Though the feminine population rarely fought directly in the front lines of battle, they nonetheless experienced its effects—physically, economically, and emotionally.

NOTES

1. Michael Rowe, "Civilians and Warfare during the French Revolutionary Wars," in *Daily Lives of Civilians in Wartime Europe, 1618–1900*, ed. Linda S. Frey and Marsha L. Frey (Westport, CT: Greenwood Press, 2007), 95–96.

2. John A. Lynn II, *Women, Armies, and Warfare in Early Modern Europe* (Cambridge: Cambridge UP, 2008), 79.

3. M. S. Anderson, *War and Society in Europe of the Old Regime, 1618–1789* (London: Fontana Paperbacks, 1988), 173–74.

4. Nadezhda Durova, *The Cavalry Maiden: Journals of a female Russian officer in the Napoleonic Wars*, (1836) trans. Mary Fleming Zirin (London: Angel Books, 1988), 4.

5. Alan Forrest, *The Soldiers of the French Revolution* (Durham: Duke UP, 1990), 149–50.

6. Richard L. Blanco, "Continental Army Hospitals and American Society, 1775–1781," in *Adapting to Conditions: War and Society in the Eighteenth Century*, ed. Maarten Ultee (n.p.: U of Alabama P, 1986), 165.

7. Suzanne J. Stark, "Women at Sea in the Royal Navy in the Age of Sail," *The American Neptune* 57, no. 2 (1997): 113.

8. Peter H. Wilson, "German Women and War, 1500–1800" *War in History* 3, no. 2 (1996), 155.

9. Catherine Lucas, "Gifts of Clothing to the Troops in 1793–5," *Journal of the Society for Army Historical Research* 55 (1977), 2, 7.

10. Blanco, 158.

11. Paul E. Kopperman, "The British High Command and Soldiers' Wives in America, 1755–1783," *Journal of the Society for Army Historical Research* 60 (1982), 32.

12. Paul E. Kopperman, "Medical Services in the British Army, 1742–1783," *Journal of the History of Medicine and Allied Sciences* 34, no. 4 (1979), 428–55.
13. Wilson, 155. Quotation from Stark, 112.
14. Norman W. Caldwell, "Civilian Personnel at the Frontier Military Post (1790–1814)," *Mid-America* 38, no. 2 (1956): 113.
15. Wilson, 152.
16. Stark, 101.
17. González Carvajal, *Indendente del Ejército* (1810), quoted in Charles J. Esdaile, *The Spanish Army in the Peninsular War* (Manchester: Manchester UP, 1988), 11.
18. Gary M. Miller, "Bourbon Social Engineering: Women and Conditions of Marriage in Eighteenth-Century Venezuela," *Americas* 46, no. 3 (1990), 262–63.
19. Quoted in Wilson, 137.
20. Lynn, 87.
21. *Political Testament of 1768*, quoted in Wilson, 140.
22. Quoted in Reginald Hargreaves, "The Eternal Problem," *Marine Corps Gazette* (April 1973), 48.
23. Letter of Lieutenant Wilhelm Gyllenskiepp to his wife and daughter, (1789), quoted in J. E. O. Screen, *The Army in Finland during the Last Decades of Swedish Rule (1770–1809)* (Helsinki: Finnish Literature Society, 2007), 125.
24. Jennine Hurl-Eamon, "The Fiction of Female Dependence and the Makeshift Economy of Soldiers, Sailors and Their Wives in Eighteenth-Century London," *Labour History* 49, no. 4 (November 2008), 487.
25. Wilson, 147.
26. Screen, 167.
27. Wilson, 156.
28. Elise Kimerling Wirtschafter, "Social Misfits: Veterans and Soldiers' Families in Servile Russia," *Journal of Military History* 59, no. 2 (1995), 229.
29. Commander W. B. Rowbotham, R. N. "Soldiers' and Seamen's Wives and Children in H.M. Ships," *The Mariner's Mirror* 47, no. 1 (1961), 42–44.
30. Quoted in John P. McKay et al., *A History of Western Society, Volume B: From the Renaissance to 1815*, 8th ed. (Boston, MA: Houghton Mifflin, 2006), 711.
31. Forrest, *Soldiers*, 151.
32. Douglas Clark Baxter, "Pension Expectations of the French Military *Commis*," in *Adapting to Conditions*, 133.
33. Natalia Pushkareva, *Women in Russian History from the Tenth to the Twentieth Century*, ed and trans. Eve Levin (New York: M.E. Sharpe, 1997), 173–74.
34. Wirtschafter, 219.
35. Kopperman, "The British High Command and Soldiers' Wives," 32.
36. Stark, 110.
37. Miller, 262–63.
38. Wilson, 138.
39. Screen, 298.
40. Kopperman, "The British High Command and Soldiers' Wives," 32.
41. Screen, 298.
42. Kathleen Wilson, *The Sense of the People: Politics, Culture and Imperialism in England, 1715–1785* (Cambridge: Cambridge UP, 1995), 280–82, Emmet Kennedy, *A Cultural History of the French Revolution* (New Haven, CT: Yale UP, 1989), 281, and

Lynn Hunt, *Politics, Culture and Class in the French Revolution* (Berkeley: U of California P, 1984), 93.

43. Joan B. Landes, "Representing the Body Politic: The Paradox of Gender in the Graphic Politics of the French Revolution," in *Rebel Daughters: Women and the French Revolution*, ed. Sara E. Melzer and Leslie Rabine (New York: Oxford UP, 1992), 31.

44. Quoted in John T. Alexander, *Catherine the Great: Life and Legend* (New York: Oxford UP, 1989), 65.

45. Mary Lacy, *The History of the Female Shipwright . . . Written by Herself* (1773), quoted in Ian Cordingly, *Women Sailors and Sailors' Women: An Untold Maritime History* (New York: Random House, 2001), 58.

46. Rudolf M. Dekker and Lotte C. van de Pol, *The Tradition of Female Transvestism in Early Modern Europe*, trans. Judy Marcure and Lotte Van de Pol (London: Macmillan, 1989), 1–4.

47. Janet L. Polasky, "Women in Revolutionary Belgium: From Stone Throwers to Hearth Tenders," *History Workshop* 21 (1986), 92.

48. Quoted in David Hopkin, "Female Soldiers and the Battle of the Sexes in France: The Mobilization of a Folk Motif," *History Workshop Journal* 56 (2003), 82.

49. Hopkin, 86.

50. The Medal Committee, 1847, quoted in Commander Rowbotham, 46.

51. John Childs, *Armies and Warfare in Europe, 1648–1789* (Manchester: Manchester UP, 1982), 163.

52. Pruneau de Pommegorge, *Description de la Nigritie* (1789), quoted in Robin Law, "The 'Amazons' of Dahomey," *Paideuma* 39 (1993), 248.

53. Emmerich von Vattel, *Le droit des gens* (1758), quoted in Richard Shelly Hartigan, *The Forgotten Victim: A History of the Civilian* (Chicago: Precedent Publishing, 1982), 108.

54. Childs, 155–58.

55. Quoted in Rowe, 114.

56. Esdaile, 7.

57. Ulrick Bräker, quoted in Childs, 164–65.

58. J. Muller, *A Treatise Containing the Practical Part of Fortification* (1755), quoted in Anderson, 173.

59. Rebecca Gates-Coon, *The Landed Estates of the Esterházy Princes: Hungary during the Reforms of Maria Theresia and Joseph II* (Baltimore, MD: Johns Hopkins UP, 1994), 152.

60. Quoted in Dennis Showalter, "Matrices: Soldiers and Civilians in Early Modern Europe, 1648–1789," in *Daily Lives of Civilians*, 72–73.

61. Petition from the People of Herricks, Long Island, to General Carleton (July 1783), quoted in Mark Urban, *Fusiliers: The Saga of a British Redcoat Regiment in the American Revolution* (New York: Walker and Company, 2007), 290.

62. Screen, 282–83.

63. Esdaile, 25.

64. Angus Konstam, *Peter the Great's Army 2: Cavalry* (London: Osprey, 1993), 40.

65. Esdaile, 10–13.

66. Wilson, 130, 132, 158.

67. Quoted in Showalter, 62.

68. Alan Forrest, *Conscripts and Deserters: The Army and French Society during the Revolution and Empire* (New York: Oxford UP, 1989), 234.

69. Julius R. Ruff, *Violence in Early Modern Europe* (Cambridge: Cambridge UP, 2001), 57.
70. Quoted in Showalter, 72.
71. Stark, 108.
72. Anne-Marie Kilday, *Women and Violent Crime in Enlightenment Scotland* (Rochester, NY: The Boydell Press, 2007), 72–73.
73. Wilson, 146–47.

SUGGESTED READING

Anderson, M. S. *War and Society in Europe of the Old Regime, 1618–1789.* London: Fontana Paperbacks, 1988.

Dekker, Rudolf M., and Lotte C. van de Pol. *The Tradition of Female Transvestism in Early Modern Europe,* translated by Judy Marcure and Lotte Van de Pol. London: Macmillan, 1989.

Dugaw, Dianne. *Warrior Women and Popular Balladry, 1650–1850.* Chicago: U of Chicago P, 1989.

Esdaile, Charles J. *The Spanish Army in the Peninsular War.* Manchester: Manchester UP, 1988.

Forrest, Alan. *Conscripts and Deserters: The Army and French Society during the Revolution and Empire.* New York: Oxford UP, 1989.

Frey, Linda S., and Marsha L. Frey, eds. *Daily Lives of Civilians in Wartime Europe, 1618–1900.* Westport, CT: Greenwood Press, 2007.

Hartigan, Richard Shelly. *The Forgotten Victim: A History of the Civilian.* Chicago: Precedent Publishing, 1982.

Lynn, John A., II. *Women, Armies, and Warfare in Early Modern Europe.* Cambridge: Cambridge UP, 2008.

Screen, J. E. O. *The Army in Finland during the Last Decades of Swedish Rule (1770–1809).* Helsinki: Finnish Literature Society, 2007.

Stark, Suzanne J. *Female Tars: Women Aboard Ship in the Age of Sail.* Annapolis, MD: U.S. Naval Institute, 1996.

Ultee, Maarten, ed. *Adapting to Conditions: War and Society in the Eighteenth Century.* n.p.: U of Alabama P, 1986.

Selected Bibliography

Aaslestad, Katherine. "Republican Traditions: Patriotism, Gender, and War in Hamburg, 1770–1815." *European History Quarterly* 37 (2007): 582–602.
Ackerknect, E. H. "Midwives as Experts in Court." *Bulletin of the New York Academy of Medicine* 52, no. 10 (December 1976): 1224–28.
Adams, Christine. "A Choice Not to Wed? Unmarried Women in Eighteenth-Century France." *Journal of Social History* 29, no. 4 (1996): 883–94.
———. *A Taste for Comfort and Status: A Bourgeois Family in Eighteenth-Century France*. University Park: Pennsylvania State UP, 2000.
Anderson, James M. *Daily Life during the French Revolution*. Westport, CT: Greenwood Press, 2007.
Anderson, M. S. *War and Society in Europe of the Old Regime, 1618–1789*. London: Fontana Paperbacks, 1988.
Anisimov, Evgenii Viktorovich. *Five Empresses: Court Life in Eighteenth-Century Russia*. Kathleen Carroll, trans. Westport, CT: Praeger, 2004.
Aravamudan, Srinivas. "Lady Mary Wortley Montagu in the Hammam: Masquerade, Womanliness, and Levantinization." *English Literary History* 62, no. 1 (1995): 69–104.
Ariès, Philippe. *Centuries of Childhood: A Social History of Family Life*. Robert Baldick, trans. New York: Vintage Books, 1962.
Arkush, Allan. *Moses Mendelssohn and the Enlightenment*. Albany: State University of New York Press, 1994.
Arru, Angiolina. "The Distinguishing Features of Domestic Service in Italy." *Journal of Family History* 15, no. 4 (1990): 547–66.
Bailey, Joanne. " 'I Dye by Inches': Locating Wife Beating in the Concept of a Privatization of Marriage and Violence in Eighteenth-Century." *Social History* 31, no. 3 (2006): 273–94.
———. *Unquiet Lives: Marriage and Marriage Breakdown in England, 1660–1800*. Cambridge: Cambridge UP, 2003.

Barahona, Renato. *Sex Crimes, Honour, and the Law in Early Modern Spain: Vizcaya, 1528–1735*. Toronto: U of Toronto P, 2003.
Barker, Hanna, and Elaine Chalus, eds. *Gender in Eighteenth-Century England: Roles, Representations and Responsibilities*. New York: Longman, 1997.
Barnett, S. J. *The Enlightenment and Religion: The Myths of Modernity*. Manchester: Manchester UP, 2003.
Beattie, J. M. "The Criminality of Women in Eighteenth-Century England." *Journal of Social History* vii (1995): 80–116.
Beccaria, Cesare. *On Crimes and Punishments, Translated from the Italian in the Author's Original Order*. 1764, reprinted Indianapolis: Hackett Publishing, 1986.
Behrend-Martínez, Edward. "Female Sexual Potency in a Spanish Church Court, 1673–1735." *Law and History Review* 24, no. 2 (2006): 297–330.
Bengt, Ankarloo. "Agriculture and Women's Work: Directions of Change in the West, 1700–1900." *Journal of Family History* 4, no. 2 (1979): 111–21.
Benjamin, Marina. "Elbow Room: Women Writers on Science, 1790–1840." In *Science and Sensibility: Gender and Scientific Enquiry, 1780–1845*, edited by Marina Benjamin. Oxford: Basil Blackwell, 1991.
Berg, Maxine. *Luxury and Pleasure in Eighteenth-Century Britain*. Oxford: Oxford UP, 2005.
Billington, James H. *The Icon and the Axe: An Interpretive History of Russian Culture*. New York: Vintage Books, 1970.
Bogucka, Maria. *Women in Early Modern Polish Society, against the European Background*. Aldershot, Hampshire: Ashgate, 2004.
Bohstedt, John. "Gender, Household and Community Politics: Women in English Riots 1790–1810." *Past and Present* no. 120 (August 1988): 88–122.
Bradley, D. "Unmarried Cohabitation in Sweden: A Renewed Social Institution?" *Journal of Legal History* 11, no. 2 (1990): 300–308.
Brandon, Ruth. *Governess: The Lives and Times of the Real Jane Eyres*. New York: Walker & Company, 2008.
Brennan, James F. *Enlightened Despotism in Russia: The Reign of Elizabeth, 1741–1762*. New York: Peter Lang, 1987.
Bridenthal, Renate, Claudia Koonz, and Susan Stuard, eds. *Becoming Visible: Women in European History*. 2nd ed. Boston, MA: Houghton Mifflin, 1987.
Broomhall, Susan, ed. *Emotions in the Household, 1200–1900*. New York: Palgrave Macmillan, 2008.
Browne, Alice. *The Eighteenth-Century Feminist Mind*. Detroit: Wayne State UP, 1987.
Burford, E. J., and Sandra Shulman. *Of Bridles and Burnings: The Punishment of Women*. New York: St. Martin's Press, 1992.
Butterwick, Richard. "Between Anti-Enlightenment and Enlightened Catholicism: Provincial Preachers in Late-Eighteenth-Century Poland-Lithuania." *SVEC* (*Studies on Voltaire and the Eighteenth-Century*) (January 2008): 201–28.
Caldwell, Norman W. "Civilian Personnel at the Frontier Military Post (1790–1814)." *Mid-America* 38, no. 2 (1956): 101–19.
Calvi, Giulia. "'Cruel' and 'Nurturing' Mothers: The Construction of Motherhood in Tuscany (1500–1800)." *L'Homme Z. F. G* 17, no. 1 (2006): 75–92.
Campbell, Ruth. "Sentence of Death by Burning for Women." *Journal of Legal History* 5, no. 1 (1984): 44–59.

Cavallo, Sandra, and Simona Cerutti. "Female Honour and the Social Control of Reproduction in Piedmont between 1600 and 1800." *Sex and Gender in Historical Perspective*, edited by Edward Muir and Guido Ruggiero. Translated by Mary M. Gallucci. Baltimore, MD: Johns Hopkins UP, 1990.

Chilcote, Paul W. *She Offered Them Christ: The Legacy of Women Preachers in Early Methodism*. Nashville, TN: Abingdon Press, 1993.

Chuchiak, John F. IV. "The Sins of the Fathers: Franciscan Friars, Parish Priests, and the Sexual Conquest of the Yucatec Maya, 1545–1808." *Ethnohistory* 54, no. 1 (Winter 2007): 69–127.

Cizauskas, Albert C. "The Unusual Story of Thaddeus Kosciusko." *Lituanus* 32, no. 1 (Spring 1986): 47–66.

Cocalis, Susan L., and Ferrel Rose, eds. *Thalia's Daughters: German Women Dramatists from the Eighteenth Century to the Present*. Tübingen: Franke Verlag, 1996.

Cody, Lisa. "The Doctor's in Labour; or a New Whim Wham from Guildford." *Gender & History* 4, no. 2 (Summer 1992): 175–96.

Conn, Marie A. *Noble Daughters: Unheralded Women in Western Christianity, 13th to 18th Centuries*. Westport, CT: Greenwood Press, 2000.

Dacome, Lucia. "Women, Wax and Anatomy in the 'Century of Things,'" *Renaissance Studies* 21, no. 4 (2007): 322–50.

DaMolin, Giovanna. "Family Forms and Domestic Service in Southern Italy from the Seventeenth to the Nineteenth Centuries." *Journal of Family History* 15, no. 4 (1990): 503–27.

Darling, John, and Maaike van de Pijpekamp. "Rousseau on the Education, Domination and Violation of Women." *British Journal of Educational Studies* 42, no. 2 (1994): 115–32.

Darnton, Robert. *The Great Cat Massacre and Other Episodes in French Cultural History*. New York: Vintage Books, 1985.

Darrow, Margaret H. "French Noblewomen and the New Domesticity, 1750–1850." *Feminist Studies* 5, no. 1 (Spring 1979): 41–65.

Davidoff, Leonore, and Catherine Hall. *Family Fortunes: Men and Women of the English Middle Class, 1780–1850*. Chicago: U of Chicago P, 1987.

Dekker, R. M. "Women in Revolt: Popular Protest and Its Social Basis in Holland in the Seventeenth and Eighteenth Centuries." *Theory and Society* xvi (1987): 337–62.

Dekker, Rudolf M., and Lotte C. van de Pol. *The Tradition of Female Transvestism in Early Modern Europe*, translated by Judy Marcure and Lotte Van de Pol. London: Macmillan, 1989.

De Renzi, Silvia. "Medical Expertise, Bodies, and the Law in Early Modern Courts." *Isis: Journal of the History of Science in Society* 98, no. 2 (2007): 315–22.

———. "Witnesses of the Body: Medico-Legal Cases in Seventeenth-Century Rome." *Studies in History and Philosophy of Science* 33A, no. 2 (2002): 219–42.

Dervin, Dan. "Childrearing in Central and Eastern Europe." *Journal of Psychohistory* 35, no. 3 (Winter 2008): 218–229.

Desan, Suzanne. *The Family on Trial in Revolutionary France*. Berkeley: U of California P, 2004.

———. *Reclaiming the Sacred: Lay Religion and Popular Politics in Revolutionary France*. Ithaca: Cornell UP, 1990.

Diederiks, Herman. "Punishment during the *Ancien Régime*; the Case of the Eighteenth-Century Dutch Republic." *Crime and Criminal Justice in Europe and Canada*, edited by Louis Knafla. Waterloo, Ont: Published for Calgary Institute for the Humanities by Wilfred Laurier UP, 1981.

Duden, Barbara. *The Woman beneath the Skin: A Doctor's Patients in Eighteenth-Century Germany*. Translated by Thomas Dunlap. Cambridge, MA: Harvard UP, 1991.

Dugaw, Dianne. *Warrior Women and Popular Balladry, 1650–1850*. Chicago: U of Chicago P, 1989.

Durova, Nadezhda. *The Cavalry Maiden: Journals of a Female Russian Officer in the Napoleonic Wars*. First published 1836. Reprint: Translated by Mary Fleming Zirin. London: Angel Books, 1988.

Eccles, A. *Obstetrics and Gynaecology in Tudor and Stuart England*. Kent, OH: Kent State UP, 1982.

Elias, Norbert. *The Civilizing Process: Sociogenetic and Psychogenetic Investigations* [1939]. Rev. ed. Translated by E. Jephcott. Oxford: Blackwell Publishing, 2000.

Elmsley, Clive. *Crime, Police, and Penal Policy: European Experiences 1750–1940*. Oxford: Oxford UP, 2007.

Emch-Dériaz, Antoinette. "Health and Gender Oriented Education: An Eighteenth-Century Case-Study." *Women's Studies* 24, no. 6 (1995): 521–30.

Engel, Barbara Alpern. *Women in Russia 1700–2000*. Cambridge: Cambridge UP, 2004.

Ericsson, Tom. "Women, Family and Small Businesses in Late Nineteenth-Century Sweden." *History of the Family* 6 (2001): 225–39.

Esdaile, Charles J. *The Spanish Army in the Peninsular War*. Manchester: Manchester UP, 1988.

Evans, Jean Silvan. "Howell Harris: A Welsh Icon and the Two Women Closest to Him." *Journal of the United Reformed Church History Society* 7, no. 10 (2007): 593–604.

Faedo, María José Álvarez. *A Bio-bibliography of Eighteenth-Century Religious Women in England and Spain*. Lewiston, NY: Edwin Mellen Press, 2005.

Fairchilds, Cissie. *Domestic Enemies: Servants and Their Masters in Old Regime France*. Baltimore, MD: Johns Hopkins UP, 1984.

Faragó, Tamás. "The Seasonality of Marriages in Hungary from the Eighteenth to the Twentieth Century." *Journal of Family History* 19, no. 4 (1994): 333–50.

Fauve-Chamoux, Antoinette. "Continuity and Change among the Rhemish Proletariat: Preindustrial Textile Work in Family Perspective." *History of the Family* 6, no. 2 (2001): 112–29.

Findlen, Paula. "Science as a Career in Enlightenment Italy: The Strategies of Laura Bassi." *ISIS: Journal of the History of Science in Society* 84, no. 3 (1993): 440–69.

Findlen, Paula, Wendy Wassyng Roworth, and Catherine M. Sama, eds. *Italy's Eighteenth Century: Gender and Culture in the Age of the Grand Tour*. Stanford: Stanford UP, 2009.

Fine, Elsa Honig. *Women and Art: A History of Women Painters and Sculptors from the Renaissance to the 20th Century*. Montclair, NJ: Abner Shram, 1978.

Fischer-Yinon, Yochi. "The Original Bundlers: Boaz and Ruth, and Seventeenth-Century English Courtship Practices." *Journal of Social History* 35, no. 3 (2002): 685–706.

Foreman, Amanda. *Georgiana, Duchess of Devonshire*. New York: Random House, 1998.

Forrest, Alan. *Conscripts and Deserters: The Army and French Society during the Revolution and Empire*. New York: Oxford UP, 1989.

———. *The Soldiers of the French Revolution*. Durham: Duke UP, 1990.

Foyster, Elizabeth. *Marital Violence: An English Family History, 1660–1857.* Cambridge: Cambridge UP, 2005.

———. "Parenting Was for Life, Not Just for Childhood: The Role of Parents in the Married Lives of Their Children in Early Modern England." *History* 86, no. 283 (2001): 313–27.

Frey, Linda S., and Marsha L. Frey, eds. *Daily Lives of Civilians in Wartime Europe, 1618–1900.* Westport, CT: Greenwood Press, 2007.

Fronius, Helen. "Der Reiche Mann und die Arme Frau: German Women Writers and the Eighteenth-Century Literary Market-Place." *German Life and Letters* 56, no. 1 (2003): 1–19.

Gat, Azar. *The Origins of Military Thought: From the Enlightenment to Clausewitz.* Oxford: Clarendon Press, 1989.

Gates-Coon, Rebecca. *The Landed Estates of the Esterházy Princes: Hungary during the Reforms of Maria Theresia and Joseph II.* Baltimore, MD: Johns Hopkins UP, 1994.

Gerber, Matthew. "Illegitimacy, Natural Law, and Legal Culture on the Eve of the French Revolution." *Proceedings of the Western Society for French History* 33 (2005): 240–57.

Gleadle, Kathryn. "British Women and Radical Politics in the Late Nonconformist Enlightenment." *Women, Privilege, and Power: British Politics, 1750 to the Present*, edited by Amada Vickery. Stanford, CA: Stanford UP, 2001.

Glover, Jane. *Mozart's Women: His Family, His Friends, His Music.* London: Pan Macmillan, 2006.

Godineau, Dominique. *The Women of Paris and Their French Revolution.* Translated by Katherine Streip. Berkeley: U of California P, 1998.

Goldie, Mark, and Robert Wokler, eds. *The Cambridge History of Eighteenth-Century Political Thought.* Cambridge: Cambridge UP, 2006.

Gooch, G. P. *Maria Theresa and Other Studies.* n.p.: Archon Books, 1965.

Goodden, Angelica. *Miss Angel: The Art and World of Angelica Kauffmann.* London: Pimlico, 2005.

Göpfert, Frank. "Observations on the Life and Work of Elizaveta Kheraskova (1737–1809)." In *Women and Gender in 18th-Century Russia*, translated by Roger and Hannah Bartlett. Edited by Wendy Rosslyn. Aldershot, Hants: Ashgate, 2003.

Gray, Colleen. *The Congrégation de Notre-Dame, Superiors, and the Paradox of Power, 1693–1796.* Montreal: McGill-Queen's UP, 2007.

Green, David R., and Alastair Owens, eds. *Family Welfare: Gender, Property, and Inheritance since the Seventeenth Century.* Westport, CT: Praeger, 2004.

Greenleaf, Monika. "Performing Autobiography: The Multiple Memoirs of Catherine the Great (1756–96)." *Russian Review* 63, no. 3 (2004): 407–26.

Grieco, Sara F. Matthews. "The Body, Appearance, and Sexuality." In *A History of Women in the West, Vol. III, Renaissance and Enlightenment Paradoxes*, edited by N. Z. Davis and A. Farge. Cambridge, MA: Belknap Press of Harvard UP, 1993.

Grigg, David. *The Transformation of Agriculture in the West.* Cambridge, MA: Basil Blackwell, 1992.

Gruder, Vivian R. "The Question of Marie-Antoinette: The Queen and Public Opinion before the Revolution." *French History* 16, no. 3 (2002): 269–98.

Hargreaves, Reginald. "The Eternal Problem." *Marine Corps Gazette* (April 1973): 42–48.

Hartigan, Richard Shelly. *The Forgotten Victim: A History of the Civilian.* Chicago: Precedent Publishing, 1982.
Hay, Douglas. "Master and Servant in England: Using the Law in the Eighteenth and Nineteenth Centuries." In *Private Law and Social Inequality in the Industrial Age: Comparing Legal Cultures in Britain, France, Germany, and the United States*, edited by W. Steinmetz. Oxford: Oxford UP, 2000.
Hayhoe, Jeremy. "Illegitimacy, Inter-generational Conflict and Legal Practice in Eighteenth-Century Northern Burgundy." *Journal of Social History* 38, no. 3 (2005): 673–84.
Heijden, Manon van der. "Women as Victims of Sexual and Domestic Violence in Seventeenth-Century Holland: Criminal Cases of Rape, Incest, and Maltreatment in Rotterdam and Delft." *Journal of Social History* 33, no. 3 (2000): 623–44.
Henn, Marianne. "The Other Voice: The Reaction of German Women Writers to the French Revolution." *Occasional Papers in German Studies* 8 (February 1996): 1–22.
Hertz, Deborah. *Jewish High Society in Old Regime Berlin.* New Haven, CT: Yale UP, 1988.
Hill, Bridget. *Women Alone: Spinsters in England, 1660–1850.* New Haven, CT: Yale UP, 2001.
———. *Women, Work and Sexual Politics in Eighteenth-Century England.* Oxford: Basil Blackwell, 1989.
Hochedlinger, Michael. "Mars Ennobled: The Ascent of the Military and the Creation of a Military Nobility in Mid-Eighteenth-Century Austria." *German History* 17, no. 2 (1999): 141–76.
Hudson, Pat, and W. R. Lee, eds. *Women's Work and the Family Economy in Historical Perspective.* Manchester: Manchester UP, 1990.
Hufton, Olwen H. *The Prospect before Her: A History of Women in Western Europe, Volume One: 1500–1800.* New York: Alfred A. Knopf, 1996.
———. *Women and the Limits of Citizenship in the French Revolution.* Toronto: U of Toronto P, 1992.
Hunt, Lynn. "Pornography and the French Revolution." In *The Invention of Pornography: Obscenity and the Origins of Modernity, 1500–1800*, edited by Lynn Hunt. New York: Zone Books, 1996.
Hunt, Margaret. "Wife Beating, Domesticity and Women's Independence in Eighteenth-Century London." *Gender and History* 4, no. 1 (1992): 10–33.
Hurl-Eamon, Jennine. "Domestic Violence Prosecuted: Women Binding Over Their Husbands for Assault at Westminster Quarter Sessions, 1685–1720." *Journal of Family History* 26, no. 4 (October 2001): 435–55.
———. "Insights into Plebeian Marriage: Soldiers, Sailors, and Their Wives in the *Old Bailey Proceedings*." *London Journal* 30, no. 1 (2005): 22–38.
———. " 'I Will Forgive You if the World Will': Wife-Murder and Limits on Patriarchal Violence in London, 1690–1750." In *Violence, Politics, and Gender in Early Modern England*, edited by Joseph P. Ward. New York: Palgrave Macmillan, 2008.
———. "The Fiction of Female Dependence and the Makeshift Economy of Soldiers, Sailors and Their Wives in Eighteenth-Century London." *Labour History* 49, no. 4 (November 2008): 481–501.

Joeres, Ruth-Ellen B., and Mary Jo Maynes, eds. *German Women in the Eighteenth and Nineteenth Centuries: A Social and Literary History*. Bloomington: Indiana UP, 1986.
Johnson, Eric A., and Eric H. Monkkonen, eds. *The Civilization of Crime: Violence in Town and Country since the Middle Ages*. Urbana: U of Illinois P, 1996.
Jones, Vivien, ed. *Women in the Eighteenth Century: Constructions of Femininity*. London: Routledge, 1990.
Kaiser, Daniel H. "He Said She Said: Rape and Gender Discourse in Early Modern Russia." *Kritika: Explorations in Russian and Eurasian History* 3, no. 2 (2002): 197–216.
Kale, Steven. *French Salons: High Society and Political Sociability from the Old Regime to the Revolution of 1848*. Baltimore, MD: Johns Hopkins UP, 2004.
Keener, Frederick M., and Susan E. Lorsch, eds. *Eighteenth-Century Women and the Arts*. New York: Greenwood Press, 1988.
Kennedy, Emmet. *A Cultural History of the French Revolution*. New Haven, CT: Yale UP, 1989.
Kern, Edmund M. "An End to Witch Trials in Austria: Reconsidering the Enlightened State." *Austrian History Yearbook* 30 (1999): 159–85.
Kertzer, David I., and Marzio Barbagli, eds. *The History of the European Family, Volume One: Family Life in Early Modern Times 1500–1789*. New Haven, CT: Yale UP, 2001.
Kevorkian, Tanya. "The Rise of the Poor, Weak, and Wicked: Poor Care, Punishment, Religion, and Patriarchy in Leipzig, 1700–1730." *Journal of Social History* 34, no. 1 (2000): 163–82.
Kienzle, Beverly Mayne, and Pamela J. Walker, eds. *Women Preachers and Prophets through Two Millennia of Christianity*. Berkeley: U of California P, 1998.
Kingston, Rebecca E. "Criminal Justice in Eighteenth-Century Bordeaux, 1715–24." In *Crime, Punishment, and Reform in Europe*, edited by Louis A. Knafla. Westport, CT: Praeger, 2003.
Knott, Sarah, and Barbara Taylor, eds. *Women, Gender and Enlightenment*. New York: Palgrave Macmillan, 2005.
Kopperman, Paul E. "The British High Command and Soldiers' Wives in America, 1755–1783." *Journal of the Society for Army Historical Research* 60 (1982): 14–34.
———. "Medical Services in the British Army, 1742–1783." *Journal of the History of Medicine and Allied Sciences* 34, no. 4 (1979): 428–455.
Kostroun, Daniella, and Lisa Vollendorf, eds. *Women, Religion and the Atlantic World (1600–1800)*. Toronto: U of Toronto P, 2009.
Laqueur, Thomas. *Making Sex: The Body and Gender from the Greeks to Freud*. Cambridge: Cambridge UP, 1990.
Lemire, Beverly. "The Theft of Clothes and Popular Consumerism in Early Modern England." *Journal of Social History* 24, no. 2 (1990): 255–76.
Lemmings, David. "Marriage and the Law in the Eighteenth Century: Hardwicke's Marriage Act of 1753." *The Historical Journal* 39, no. 2 (1996): 339–61.
Leslie, Glenda. "Cheat and Impostor: Debate Following the Case of the Rabbit Breeder." *The Eighteenth Century* 27, no. 3 (1986): 269–86.
Levack, Brian, Marijke Gijswijt-Hofstra, and Roy Porter, eds. *Witchcraft and Magic in Europe: The Eighteenth and Nineteenth Centuries*. London: The Athlone Press, 1999.

Lewis, Judith. " 'Tis a Misfortune to be a Great Ladie': Maternal Mortality in the British Aristocracy, 1558–1959." *Journal of British Studies* 37, no. 1 (January 1998): 26–53.

Lindemann, Mary. "Love for Hire: The Regulation of the Wet-Nursing Business in Eighteenth-Century Hamburg." *Journal of Family History* 6 (1981): 379–95.

———. *Patriots and Paupers: Hamburg, 1712–1830*. New York: Oxford UP, 1990.

Lindgren, Jarl. *Towards Smaller Families in the Changing Society: Fertility Transition during the First Phase of Industrialization in Three Finnish Municipalities*. Helsinki: The Population Research Institute, 1984.

Linebaugh, Peter. *The London Hanged: Crime and Civil Society in the Eighteenth Century*. Cambridge: Cambridge UP, 1993.

Logan, Gabriella Berti. "The Desire to Contribute: An Eighteenth-Century Italian Woman of Science." *American Historical Review* 99, no. 3 (1994): 785–813.

———. "Women and the Practice and Teaching of Medicine in Bologna in the Eighteenth and Early Nineteenth Centuries." *Bulletin of the History of Medicine* 77 (2003): 506–35.

Longworth, Philip. *The Three Empresses: Catherine I, Anne and Elizabeth of Russia*. New York: Holt, Rinehart and Winston, 1972.

Lonza, Nella. " 'Two Souls Lost': Infanticide in the Republic of Dubrovnik (1667–1808)." Translated by Vesna Bace. *Dubrovnik Annals* 6 (2002): 67–107.

Lucas, Catherine. "Gifts of Clothing to the Troops in 1793–5." *Journal of the Society for Army Historical Research* 55 (1977): 2–7.

Lynn, John A., II. *Women, Armies, and Warfare in Early Modern Europe*. Cambridge: Cambridge UP, 2008.

MacCarthy, B. G. *The Female Pen: Women Writers and Novelists, 1621–1818*. New York: New York UP, 1994.

Madariaga, Isabel de. *Russia in the Age of Catherine the Great: A Short History*. New Haven: Yale UP, 1991.

Marland, Hilary, ed. *The Art of Midwifery: Early Modern Midwives in Europe*. London: Routledge, 1993.

Maroger, Dominique, ed. *The memoirs of Catherine the Great*. Translated by Moura Budberg. New York: Collier Books, 1961.

Martin, Laura, ed. *Harmony in Discord: German Women Writers in the Eighteenth and Nineteenth Centuries*. Bern: Peter Lang, 2001.

May, Gita. *Madame Roland and the Age of Revolution*. New York: Columbia UP, 1970.

Maynes, Mary Jo. "Gender, Labor and Globalization in Historical Perspective." *Journal of Women's History* 15, no. 4 (Winter 2004): 47–66.

Maza, Sarah C. *Private Lives and Public Affairs: The Causes Célèbres of Prerevolutionary France*. Berkeley: U of California P, 1993.

———. *Servants and Masters in Eighteenth-Century France: The Uses of Loyalty*. Princeton, NJ: Princeton UP, 1983.

Mazzotti, Massimo. "Maria Gaetana Agnesi: Mathematics and the Making of the Catholic Enlightenment." *Isis: Journal of the History of Science in Society* 92, no. 4 (2001): 656–83.

McConnell, Allen. "Catherine the Great and the Fine Arts." In *Imperial Russia 1700–1917: State, Society, Opposition*, edited by Ezra Mendelsohn and Marshall S. Shatz. DeKalb: Northern Illinois UP, 1988.

McMahon, Richard, ed. *Crime, Law and Popular Culture in Europe, 1500–1900*. Portland: Willan Publishing, 2008.
McManners, John. *The French Revolution and the Church*. New York: Harper & Row, 1969.
Meldrum, Tim. *Domestic Service and Gender, 1660–1750: Life and Work in the London Household*. London: Pearson Education, 2000.
———. "A Women's Court in London: Defamation at the Bishop of London's Consistory Court, 1700–1745." *London Journal* 19, no. 1 (1994): 1–20.
Mendelson, Sara Heller. " 'To Shift for a Cloak': Disorderly Women in the Church Courts." *Women and History: Voices in Early Modern England*, edited by Valerie Frith. Toronto: Coach House Press, 1995.
Mezelaar, Helen H. *From Private to Public Spheres: Exploring Women's Role in Dutch Musical Life from 1700 to c. 1880 and Three Case Studies*. Utrecht: Koninklijke Vereniging voor Nederlandse Muziekgeschiedenis, 1999.
Miller, Gary M. "Bourbon Social Engineering: Women and Conditions of Marriage in Eighteenth-Century Venezuela." *Americas* 46, no. 3 (1990): 261–90.
Montanari, Massimo. *The Culture of Food*. Translated by Carl Ipsen. Cambridge, MA: Blackwell Publishers, 1996.
Montfort, Catherine R. "Mme de Sévigné and the Jesuits in the *siècle des Lumières*." *SVEC (Studies on Voltaire and the Eighteenth-Century)* (December 2001): 167–77.
Moody, Margaret J. *The Royal Poorhouse in Eighteenth-Century Turin, Italy: The King and the Paupers*. Lewiston, NY: Edwin Mellen Press, 2001.
Morgan, Jennifer L. " 'Some Could Suckle over Their Shoulder': Male Travelers, Female Bodies, and the Gendering of Racial Ideology, 1500–1770." *The William and Mary Quarterly*, Third Series. 54, no. 1 (January 1997): 167–92.
Myers, Sylvia Harcstark. *The Bluestocking Circle: Women, Friendship, and the Life of the Mind in Eighteenth-Century England*. Oxford: Clarendon Press, 1990.
Naeshagen, Ferdinand Linthoe. "Private Law Enforcement in Norwegian History: The Husband's Right to Chastise His Wife." *Scandinavian Journal of History* 27, no. 1 (2002): 19–29.
Nussbaum, Felicity, ed. *The Global Eighteenth Century*. Baltimore, MD: Johns Hopkins UP, 2003.
Ogilvie, Sheilagh. *A Bitter Living: Women, Markets and Social Capital in Early Modern Germany*. Oxford: Oxford UP, 2003.
Oppenheim, Walter. *Habsburgs and Hohenzollerns 1713–1786*. London: Hodder & Stoughton, 1993.
Ozouf, Mona. *Festivals and the French Revolution*. Translated by Alan Sheridan. Cambridge, MA: Harvard UP, 1988.
Palazzi, Maura. "Female Solitude and Patrilineage: Unmarried Women and Widows during the Eighteenth and Nineteenth Centuries." *Journal of Family History* 15, no. 4 (1990): 443–59.
Palk, Dierdre. *Gender, Crime and Judicial Discretion, 1780–1830*. Woodbridge, Suffolk: The Boydell Press, 2006.
Parker, Rozsika, and Griselda Pollock. *Old Mistresses: Women, Art and Ideology*. New York: Pantheon, 1981.

Perry, Ruth. "Colonizing the Breast: Sexuality and Maternity in Eighteenth-Century England." In *Forbidden History: The State, Society, and the Regulation of Sexuality in Modern Europe,* edited by J. Fout. Chicago: U of Chicago P, 1992.

Petig, William E. *Literary Antipietism in German during the First Half of the Eighteenth Century.* New York: Peter Lang, 1984.

Petrovich, Vesna. "Women and the Paris Academy of Sciences." *Eighteenth-Century Studies* 32, no. 3 (1999): 383–91.

Pfister, Ulrich. "Women's Bread—Men's Capital: The Domestic Economy of Small Textile Entrepreneurs in Rural Zurich in the 17th and 18th Centuries." *History of the Family* 6, no. 2 (2001): 147–66.

Phillips, Patricia. *The Scientific Lady: A Social History of Women's Scientific Interests, 1520–1918.* London: Weidenfeld and Nicolson, 1990.

Phillips, Roderick. *Untying the Knot: A Short History of Divorce.* Cambridge: Cambridge UP, 1991.

———. "Women's Emancipation, the Family, and Social Change in Eighteenth-Century France." *Journal of Social History* 12, no. 4 (Summer 1979): 553–67.

Phillips, Roderick. "Women, Neighbourhood, and Family in the Late Eighteenth Century." *French Historical Studies* 18, no. 1 (1993): 1–12.

Polasky, Janet L. "Women in Revolutionary Belgium: From Stone Throwers to Hearth Tenders." *History Workshop* 21 (1986): 87–104.

Pollock, Linda. *Forgotten Children: Parent-Child Relations from 1500–1900.* Cambridge: Cambridge UP, 1983.

Porter, Roy, and Lesley Hall. *The Facts of Life: The Creation of Sexual Knowledge in Britain, 1650–1950.* New Haven, CT: Yale UP, 1995.

Pushkareva, Natalia. *Women in Russian History from the Tenth to the Twentieth Century,* edited and translated by Eve Levin. New York: M.E. Sharpe, 1997.

Quataert, Jean H. "The Shaping of Women's Work in Manufacturing: Guilds, Households and State in Central Europe, 1648–1870." *American Historical Review* 90, no. 5 (December 1985): 1122–49.

Rahikainen, Marjatta. "Ageing Men and Women in the Labour Market: Continuity and Change." *Scandinavian Journal of History* 26, no. 4 (2001): 297–314.

Rauser, Amelia. "The Butcher-Kissing Duchess of Devonshire: Between Caricature and Allegory in 1784." *Eighteenth-Century Studies* 36, no. 1 (2002): 23–46.

Reher, David S. *Perspectives on the Family in Spain, Past and Present.* Oxford: Clarendon Press, 1997.

Riasnovsky, Nicholas V. *A History of Russia.* New York: Oxford UP, 1993.

Rice, John A. *Empress Marie Therese and Music at the Viennese Court, 1792–1807.* Cambridge: Cambridge UP, 2003.

Ritchie, Leslie. *Women Writing Music in Late Eighteenth-Century England: Social Harmony in Literature and Performance.* Aldershot, Hampshire: Ashgate, 2008.

Roberts, Michael. "Sickles and Scythes: Women's Work and Men's Work at Harvest Time." *History Workshop Journal* 7 (1979): 3–29.

Roe, F. Gordon. *The Georgian Child.* London: Phoenix House, 1961.

Roland, Jeanne-Marie. *The Private Memoirs of Madame Roland,* edited by Edward Gilpin Johnson. Chicago: A. C. McClurg & Co., 1901.

Rosslyn, Wendy, ed. *Women and Gender in 18th-Century Russia.* Aldershot, Hants: Ashgate, 2003.

Roudinesco, Elizabeth. *Madness and Revolution: The Lives and Legends of Théroigne de Méricourt*, translated by Martin Thom. London: Verso, 1991.
Rowbotham, W. B., Commander R. N. "Soldiers' and Seamen's Wives and Children in H.M. Ships." *The Mariner's Mirror* 47, no. 1 (1961): 42–48.
Rublack, Ulinka. "The Public Body: Policing Abortion in Early Modern Germany." In *Gender Relations in German History: Power, Agency and Experience from the Sixteenth to the Twentieth Century*, edited by Lynn Abrams and Elizabeth Harvy. London: UCL Press, 1996.
Schiebinger, Londa. "Maria Winkelmann at the Berlin Academy." *ISIS: Journal of the History of Science in Society* 78, no. 2 (1987): 174–200.
———. *The Mind Has No Sex? Women in the Origins of Modern Science*. Cambridge, MA: Harvard UP, 1989.
Schmidt, Leigh Eric. "From Demon Possession to Magic Show: Ventriloquism, Religion, and the Enlightenment." *Church History* 67, no. 2 (June 1998): 274–304.
Screen, J. E. O. *The Army in Finland during the Last Decades of Swedish Rule (1770–1809)*. Helsinki: Finnish Literature Society, 2007.
Sensbach, Jon F. *Rebecca's Revival: Creating Black Christianity in the Atlantic World*. Cambridge, MA: Harvard UP, 2005.
Sharpe, J. A. *Instruments of Darkness, Witchcraft in England, 1551–1750*. Philadelphia: U of Pennsylvania P, 1997.
Sherwood, Joan. *Poverty in Eighteenth-Century Spain: The Women and Children of the Inclusa*. Toronto: U of Toronto P, 1988.
Shoemaker, Robert B. *Gender in English Society, 1650–1850: The Emergence of Separate Spheres?* London: Addison Wesley Longman, 1998.
———. *The London Mob: Violence and Disorder in Eighteenth-Century England*. London: Hambledon and London, 2004.
Shorter, Edward. *The Making of the Modern Family*. New York: Basic Books, 1975.
Siena, Kevin. "Searchers of the Dead in Long Eighteenth-Century London." In *Marginality and Gender in Pre-Modern Europe*, edited by Kim Kippen and Lori Woods. Toronto: Centre for Reformation and Renaissance Studies, forthcoming.
Simões, Ana, Ana Carneiro, and Maria Paula Diogo. "Constructing Knowledge: Eighteenth-Century Portugal and the New Sciences." In *The Sciences in the European Periphery during the Enlightenment*, edited by Kostas Gavroglu. Dordrecht: Kluwer Academic Publishers, 1999.
Simonton, Deborah. *A History of European Women's Work: 1740 to the Present*. New York: Routledge, 1998.
———, ed. *The Routledge History of Women in Europe since 1700*. London: Routledge, 2006.
Singer, Barnett. "A Remnant: The Jews of Vaucluse in the Nineteenth Century." *Jewish Social Studies* 40, no. 2 (1978): 159–76.
Smaby, Beverly Prior. "Female Piety among Eighteenth-Century Moravians." *Pennsylvania History* 64 (1997): 151–67.
Smith, Theresa Ann. *The Emerging Female Citizen: Gender and Enlightenment in Spain*. Berkeley: U of California P, 2006.
Spalding, Almut. *Elise Reimarus (1735–1805): The Muse of Hamburg*. Würzburg: Königshausen & Neumann, 2005.
Stark, Suzanne J. *Female Tars: Women Aboard Ship in the Age of Sail*. Annapolis, MD: U.S. Naval Institute, 1996.

———. "Women at Sea in the Royal Navy in the Age of Sail." *The American Neptune* 57, no. 2 (1997): 101–20.

Stone, Lawrence. *The Family, Sex and Marriage in England, 1500–1800*. Abridged ed. London: Penguin, 1990.

Sunstein, Emily. *A Different Face: The Life of Mary Wollstonecraft*. New York: Harper & Row, 1975.

Taylor, Charles. *A Secular Age*. Cambridge, MA: The Belknap Press of Harvard UP, 2007.

Thompson, E. P. "The Moral Economy of the English Crowd in the Eighteenth Century." *Past and Present*, no. 50 (1971): 76–136.

Todd, Dennis. "Three Characters in Hogarth's *Cunicularii*—and Some Implications." *Eighteenth-Century Studies* 16, no. 1 (Autumn 1982): 26–46.

Tone, John Lawrence. "A Dangerous Amazon: Augustina Zaragoza and the Spanish Revolutionary War, 1808–1814." *European History Quarterly* 37, no. 4 (2007): 548–61.

Ulbrich, Claudia. *Shulamit and Margarete: Power, Gender, and Religion in a Rural Society in Eighteenth-Century Europe*, translated by Thomas Dunlap. Boston, MA: Brill, 2004.

Ultee, Maarten, ed. *Adapting to Conditions: War and Society in the Eighteenth Century*. Tuscaloosa: U of Alabama P, 1986.

Valiant, Sharon. "Maria Sibylla Merian: Recovering an Eighteenth-Century Legend." *Eighteenth-Century Studies* 26, no. 3 (1993): 467–79.

Vickery, Amanda. "Golden Age to Separate Spheres? A Review of the Categories and Chronology of English Women's History." *The Historical Journal* 36, no. 2 (1993): 383–414.

Vigarello, Georges. *A History of Rape: Sexual Violence in France from the 16th to the 20th Century*, translated by Jean Birrell. Cambridge: Polity Press, 2001.

Walker, Garthine. "Rereading Rape and Sexual Violence in Early Modern England." *Gender and History* 10, no. 1 (April 1998): 1–25.

Walker, Timothy. "Physicians and Surgeons in the Service of the Inquisition: The Nexus of Religion and Conventional Medical Training in Enlightenment-Era Portugal." In *Medicine and Religion in Enlightenment Europe*, edited by Ole Peter Grell and Andrew Cunningham. Aldershot: Ashgate, 2007.

Ward, W. R. "'An Awakened Christianity': The Austrian Protestants and Their Neighbours in the Eighteenth Century." *Journal of Ecclesiastical History* 40, no. 1 (1989): 53–73.

Watkins, Susan Cotts. "Spinsters." *Journal of Family History* 9, no. 4 (1984): 310–25.

Watt, Jeffrey R. "The Family, Love and Suicide in Early Modern Geneva." *Journal of Family History* 21, no. 1 (1996): 63–86.

Weisser, Michael R. *Crime and Punishment in Early Modern Europe*. Bristol: The Harvester Press, 1979.

Williams, Helen Maria. *Letters Written in France, in the Summer 1790, to a Friend in England; Containing Various Anecdotes Relative to the French Revolution*, edited by Neil Fraistat and Susan S. Lanser. Peterborough, Ont: Broadview Press, 2001.

Wilson, Kathleen. *The Sense of the People: Politics, Culture and Imperialism in England, 1715–1785*. Cambridge: Cambridge UP, 1995.

Wilson, Peter H. "German Women and War, 1500–1800." *War in History* 3, no. 2 (1996): 127–60.

Wirtschafter, Elise Kimerling. "Social Misfits: Veterans and Soldiers' Families in Servile Russia." *Journal of Military History* 59, no. 2 (1995): 215–35.
Yonan, Michael E. "Modesty and Monarchy: Rethinking Empress Maria Theresa at Schönbrunn." *Austrian History Yearbook* 35 (2004): 25–47.
Zantop, Susanne. *Colonial Fantasies: Conquest, Family, and Nation in Precolonial Germany, 1770–1870*. Durham: Duke UP, 1997.
Zinsser, Judith P. "A Prologue for *La Dame D'esprit*: The Biography of the Marquise Du Châtelet." *Rethinking History* 7, no. 1 (2003): 13–22.

Index

Academies of arts and sciences, 56–57, 91, 96, 101, 103, 105–6
Adultery, 16, 60
Africa, xiv, 141
Agaja of Dahomey, King, 141
Agnesi, Maria Gaetana, xxi, xxiii, 102, 106, 118
Agricultural reforms, 28–29
Agricultural work, xi, 29–32, 33, 135
Aix, 32, 33
Alameda de Osuna, 90
Albany, 121
Algarotti, Francesco, xx, 101
Amazon. *See* Women: soldiers
America. *See* North America
American Revolution, 137
Analytical Institutions (*Instituzioni Analitiche*), xxiii, 102
Anatomy. *See* Medicine
Anglicanism, 12, 114–16
Anna, Empress, xxii, 55, 137
Ant, Jan van, xxiii, 140
Antwerpen, Maria/Machiel van, xxiii, 140
Aphra Behn, 92
Aristocracy, 2, 6, 12, 32, 35–36, 51, 68, 89, 93, 114, 119, 126
Army. *See* Soldiers
Artisanal work. *See* Guild system

Asia, 121
Astell, Mary, xiii, xxi
Astrakhan, 120
Astronomy, 101, 118
Astro-Turkish War, xv
Aufklärers, xii
Austria, xiv, xv, 36, 48, 51–54, 58, 60, 71, 79, 98, 115, 119, 124, 135, 140
Authors. *See* Women: writers
Avallon, 113
Azzoguidi, Germano, 103

Bamburg, 135
Barracks, 142–43
Bassi, Laura, xx, xxii, 103–4, 106, 118
Bastille, 48
Bavaria, 135
Beccaria, Cesare, xxvii, 57, 69
Becker, Antoinette Elisabeth, 34
Belgium, 48, 140
Belgrade, xiv
Benavente, Maria Josefa Alonso-Pimentel Tellez-Giron, Count-Duchess of, 90, 106
Benedict XIV, Pope. *See* Pope Benedict XIV
Berlin, 92, 93, 106, 123
Bertache, Élisabeth de la, 121

Besançon, 112
Bethlehem, 122
Bihéron, Marie Marguerite, xxi, 103
Billington, Elizabeth Weichsel, xxvi, 99
Bishop, Eliza, 35
Bloody code, 68
Bluestockings, 91
Bocage, Anne-Marie du, 106
Bohemia, 53
Bologna University, 103, 106
Bonaparte, Napoleon, xv, xxix, 49
Bony, Catherine, 121
Boom, Rijntje, 78
Bordeaux, 6, 26, 67, 75
Borromeo, Clelia, xxvii, 90
Botany, 97, 102
Boucher, François, 2–3
Bourgeoys, Marguerite, 121
Bovier, Bernard le, 101
Breastfeeding. *See* Wet-nursing
Britain, xv, 7, 37, 54, 70, 133, 136, 138, 139, 141, 145. *See also* England; Ireland; Scotland
Britannia, 138–39
Buenos Aires, 121
Burney, Fanny, xxiv, xxvii, 94

Calculus. *See* Mathematics
Camilla, 94
Camp followers, 132–34
Capuchin, 121
Carlisle House, 98
Carranque, María Luisa, xxvi, 96
Carriera, Rosalba, xxiv, 97
Catherine I, Empress, xxi, 55
Catherine II, the Great, Empress, xxi, xxv, 55–59, 94, 105, 115, 138–40
Catholicism, xii, 49, 51, 53, 106, 113, 116–22, 126
Cauiche, Francisca, 122
Cecelia, 94
Champagne, 32
Chapone, Hester, 100
Charles III, King, xxv, 134
Charles VI, King, 51–52, 55
Charles XII, King, 115
Charrière, Isabelle de, xxvii, 93–94
Chastenay, Victorine de, 2

Châtelet, Emilie du, xix, 16, 103, 106
Chetmno Law, 67
Childhood, 1–3, 75
China, xv, 58
Christian Amazon, The, 139–40
Christian V, King, 74
Christina, Queen, 106
Cleaning, 33, 113
Cohabitation, 18–19, 131, 134–35
Colchester, 92
Colonial expansion, xiv–xv, 1, 7, 56, 58–59; and Christianity, 120–23
Committee of public safety, 49, 142
Compte, Marguerite le, 106
Condorcet, Marquis de, 50
Congrégation de Notre-Dame, 121
Conner, Lydia, 133
Conscription, 144–45
Consumerism, xi, 1, 2, 26–27, 38
Contat, Nicolas, xvi
Corday, Charlotte, xxvi, xxviii, 48, 51, 80–81
Cornaglia, Isabella, 40
Corne de Chaptes, Marie-Madeleine de la, 121
Cornelys, Teresa (Anna Maria Teresa Imer), xxi, 98
Cottage industry, 7, 30–32, 37–38, 40
Cotton industry. *See* Textile industry
Counter-Reformation, 117
Courts: civil, 66–67; ecclesiastical: 67–68. *See also* legislation
Croatia, 71, 76, 78
Crosby, Sarah, xxii, xxv, 115
Cross-dressing. *See* Transvestism
Cuccovilla, Maria Pizzelli, xxii, 91
Cuenca, 7
Cult of the Supreme Being. *See* Festival of the Supreme Being
Czapska, Magdalena, 15–16

Dagoe, Hannah, 68
Danzig, 37
Davies, Christian, 141
Defamation, 68, 74
Deism, 112, 122
Demographic change, xv, 14, 18, 25, 28, 71

Denmark, xiv, 74, 79, 80
Deptford, 140
Derby, 115
Deutschkreutz, 143
Diderot, Denis, xx, 57, 105
Dijon, 121
Divorce, 16–17, 67
Doctors in Labour; or a new Whim Wham from Guildford, The, 10
Domestic service, 15, 32–34, 41, 124, 143. *See also* Cleaning
Domestic sphere and domesticity, issues of, xi, 25–28, 54, 60–61, 89, 93, 100
Domestic violence, 15–16, 72–74
Donne, Maria Dalle, xxix, 100
Dowry, 144
Drama. *See* Women: writers
Dresden, 106
Durand, Claude, 121
Durova, Nadezhda, 132
Düsseldorf, 97

Ebhausen, 30, 40
Echazarreta, Bachiller Luis Antonio de, Father, 122
Edgeworth, Maria, 35–36, 100
Edgeworth, Richard, 35–36
Education, xv, 1, 2, 6, 7, 34–36, 40, 57, 89, 93, 118–19, 121, 123
Ekaterina Sergeevna Urusova, Princess, xxiii, 92
Elizabeth, Empress, xxiii, 55–59, 68
Empire. *See* Colonial expansion; Women: and race
Encyclopédie, xiii, xxiv, 57, 105
England, 5, 7, 8, 10, 12, 16, 29, 31, 32, 33, 36, 49, 58, 59, 61, 66, 68, 69, 72, 78, 79, 91, 96, 99, 106, 112, 118, 121, 123, 137, 138–41. *See also* Britain
Enlightenment, 3–6, 111. *See also Aufklärers*; Catholicism; Education; *Ilustrados*; *Philosophes*; *Salonnières*; Secularism; *Tertulias*
Ericksen, Peter, 138
Esquilache, Rising of the, 28
Esterházys, 34, 70, 120
Être Suprême. See Festival of the Supreme Being

Evelina, xxvii, 94
Execution. 49, 55, 57, 60, 62 n26, 65, 68–71, 79, 80–81, 83

Family tribunals, 67
Farming. *See* agricultural work
Fashion, 11, 54, 55
Female Rights Vindicated, or the Equality of the Sexes Morally and Physically Proved, xxv, 101
Feme couvert, 66
Feme sole, 66
Femininity, new views of, xii, 3–6, 7, 11–12, 114
Feminization of piety, 114
Fernando, King, 34
Festival of the Supreme Being, xxix, 49, 112–13
Finland, xv, 15, 33, 34, 78, 137, 143
Foundlings, foundling hospitals, 8, 71
Fragonard, Jean-Honoré, xxii, 3–4, 11
France, xv, xii, 2, 6, 8, 11, 12, 18, 31, 36, 48–51, 52, 58, 60, 66, 69, 70, 76, 78, 93, 96, 97, 99, 103, 105, 111–14, 118–20, 123–24, 132, 135, 136, 138, 141, 144
Francis I, 54
Franklin, Benjamin, 103
Frederick II, the Great, King, xv, xxiii, 52, 56, 57, 66, 97, 135, 142
French Amazons, The, 141
French Republic. *See* French Revolution
French Revolution, xiii, 2, 16, 48–51, 60–61, 67, 71, 82–83, 111–14, 119, 124, 136, 138, 142
French Revolutionary tribunal, xxviii, 49, 66, 80–83. *See also* Family tribunals
Friezland, 30

Gay, John, 26
Geneva, 14, 16, 18
Genlis, Stéphanie Félicité, Mme de, xxiii, 36
Geoffrin, Marie Thérèse Rodet, Mme, xxiv, xxvi, 90
Geometry. *See* Mathematics
George I, King, 10
George III, King, 59
Georgiana, Duchess, xxvii, 60

German territories, 9, 10, 29, 30, 31, 33, 34, 37, 38, 40, 48, 56, 66, 67, 70, 92, 94, 95, 97, 101, 116, 118, 124, 132, 133, 135, 137, 140, 141, 144, 145
Geschlechtsvormundschaft, 66
Ghettos, 123
Gillray, James, 72–73, 80–81
Glarus, 78
Glässlin, Magdalena, 40
Goddess of Reason, 112
Goettingen, 143
Göldi, Anna, xxvii, 78
Gottsched, Luise Adelgunde, xx, 93, 116
Gouges, Olympe de, xxviii, 51
Governesses, 35–37
Goynes, Mary, 77
Gozzi, Luisa Bergalli, xix, 95
Graffigny, Françoise d'Issembourg d'Happencourt, Mme de, xxiii, xxiv, 93–94
Great Northern War, xiv
Greece, xiv, 145
Greenland, 122
Griffith, Sidney, xxiv, 116
Guatemala, 122
Guild system, xv–xvi, 17–18, 37–39
Gynecocracy, 55–59

Halifax, 144
Hamburg, 26, 40, 48, 92, 93, 123–24
Hand-to-mouth trades. *See* Poverty
Hanway, Jonas, 7
Haratschon, 71
Harris, Howell, xxiv, 116
Harvestehude, 48
Haywood, Eliza, xxiv, 94
Heroine of Breda, The (*De Bredasche Heldinne*), 140
Herz, Henriette, xxv, 92, 123
Hessen-Kassel, 135, 144
Hippocrates, 4
History of Jamaica, xiv
History of Lady Sophia Sternheim (*Geschichte des Fräuleins von Sternheim*), xxvi, 94
Holland. *See* Netherlands
Hosiery industry. *See* Textile industry

Hungary, 15, 16, 28, 29, 34, 35, 40, 53, 70, 72, 79, 120, 124, 126, 143

Iconoclasm, 112
Iconography, 138
Illegitimacy, 7–8, 33, 71, 76–77, 145
Ilustrados, xii, 90
Imperialism. *See* Colonial expansion; Women: and race
Imprisonment, 69, 71, 74, 79
India, xv
Industrialization, xv
Infanticide, 67, 71, 76–78, 145
Inn-keeping, 27–28, 143
Inquisition, 122
Introduction to Botany, An, 100
Ireland, 29, 32, 91, 116
Islam. *See* Women: Muslim
Italy, 11, 18, 29, 32, 39, 40, 70, 77, 79, 90, 97, 100–107, 119, 132
Ivan VI, Emperor, xxii, xxiii, 55

Jansenists, 118–20
Jesuits, 117–18
Joret, Catherine, 16
Joseph II, Emperor, xxiii, xxvii, 15, 53–54, 58, 71, 124, 140
Judaism, xxviii, 53, 92, 111, 120, 123–26
Judge Thumb, 72–73
Jury of Matrons, 76

Kant, Immanuel, xiii, xxi
Kauffmann, Angelica, xxiii, 97
Kaunitz, Anton von, Count, 52
Keller, Rose, 75
Keralio, Louise de, 51
Keraskova, Elizaveta, xxv, 92–93
Kirch, Gottfried, 101
Königsberg, 93
Kosciuszko, Thaddeus, xxix, 48

La Chapelle, Johannes Baptista, de 114
La Roche, Sophie von, xxii, xxvi, 6
Lacombe, Claire, 50
Lacy, Mary, xxvi, 139
Lambert, Anne-Thérèse de Marguenat de Courcelles, Mme de, xx, xxii, 90

Lambertini, Prospero. *See* Pope Benedict XIV
Lamothe, Daniel, 26
Lamothe, Marianne, 6, 17
Lamothe, Marie, 6, 17, 26
Lane, Harriet Fox, 106
Laundry work, 41, 132
Law: civil, 66–67; ecclesiastical: 67–68
Le Ventriloque, ou l'engastrimythe, 114
Lee, Ann, Mother, xxii, xxvi, 121
Legislation: counterrevolutionary suspects, xxix; domestic service, 32; domestic violence, 74, 75; fashion, 11; marriage, 7–8, 12–13, 16, 134–35; midwifery, 77; new legislative codes, 57, 66; poor relief, 39; pregnancy, 8, 71; religious, 53, 56, 112, 115, 118, 124; serfdom, 53; trade, 27–28; war 141; widowhood, 18; witchcraft, 78
Leibniz, Gottfried Wilhelm, 101
Leipzig, 69, 72
Léon, Pauline, 50
Leopold, Grand Duke, 68
Leopold, II, Emperor, 59
Letters of a Peruvian (*Letters d'une Péruvienne*), xxiii, 94
Letters of Mistress Fanny Butler (*Lettres de Mistress Fanny Butler*), xxiv, 93
Letters of Mistress Henley published by her friend (*Lettres de Mistriss Henley publiées par son amie*), xxvii, 93
Letters on the Improvement of the Mind addressed to a Young Lady, 6, 100
Levin, Rahel, 126
Liberty, figure of, 138
Lima, 121
Lincolnshire, 30
Linen trade. *See* Textile industry
Lisbon, 99
Lisiewska-Therbusch, Anna Dorothea, xxi, 97
Literacy. *See* Education
Locke, John, 6
Lombardini-Sirmen, Maddalena, xxiii, 100
Lomonosov, Mikhail, xx, 56
London, 27, 38, 67–68, 70, 72, 91, 94, 98, 100, 106, 135, 137
Long, Edward, xiv

Louis XIV, King, 57, 78, 119
Louis XV, King, xxi, 105
Louis XVI, King, xxvi, xxviii, 50, 59, 80
Louise, Princess, 54
Louvres, 28
Lubomirska, Princess (Ludvika Sosnowska), xxix, 48

Madrid, 28, 96, 121
Magdeburg Law, 66
Marat, Jean-Paul, xxvi, xxviii, 48, 51
marchande publique, 66
Maria, 19
Maria I, Queen, xxii, xxvii, 105
Maria Theresa, Empress, xxi, xxiii, xxiv, xxvi, 15, 34, 51–54, 56, 57, 58, 60, 79, 104–5
Marianne, 138
Marie Antoinette, Queen, xxiv, xxvi, xxviii, 51, 59–61, 80, 97
Marriage, 5, 10–17, 18, 34, 36, 54, 76, 103, 120, 124–26, 134–38, 144–45. *See also* Cohabitation
Mathematics, 92, 102
Maya, 122
Mechanization, 32
Medicine, 3–4, 7, 33, 92, 96, 100–103, 139. *See also* Midwifery; Nursing; Physicians; Women: healers
Mendelssohn, Dorothea, xxv, 124, 126
Mendelssohn, Moses, 124
Merian, Maria Sybylla, xix, xxi, 102
Méricourt, Théroigne de, xxv, 81–82
Metamorphosis of the Insects of Surinam (*Metamorphosis Insectorum Surinamensium*), xix, 102
Methodism, 115–17
Microscopes, 101
Middle class, xi–xii, 2, 6, 10–11, 15, 18, 19, 26, 34, 35–36, 70, 72, 89, 93, 98, 123
Midwifery, xiv, 34–35, 76–77
Milan, 90, 97, 102
Missionaries, 119, 122–23
Monstrous births, 9–10, 122
Montagu, Elizabeth, xxi, 91
Montagu, Mary Wortley, Lady, xxv, 121
Montesquieu, Charles-Louis de Secondat, Baron de, 57

Montreal, 121
Moral economy, 28
Morandi, Anna, xx, 103–4, 106–7
Moravian Pietists. *See* Pietism
Moscow, 100, 120
Mothers, motherhood, xii, 1, 2, 5, 6, 7–10, 53–54, 58, 71, 104, 122, 132, 143, 145
Mozart, Leopold, xxi, 54
Mozart, Nannerl, xxi, xxiv, 6, 18, 98
Mozart, Wolfgang Amadeus, xxi, xxiv, 14, 99
Muller, Anna Elizabeth, 69
Music. *See* Women: musicians
Mystics, 114, 116, 118

Nantes, 28, 33
Naples, 104
Napoleonic wars, 48
Narva, 120
Nationalism, 136, 138–39
Navy, 132, 135–37, 139–40, 144–45
Necker, Suzanne Curchod, Mme, xxii, xxvi, xxvii, 90
Netherlands, xv, 1, 35, 58, 66, 71, 72, 74, 75, 79, 93, 96, 99, 123, 140, 141, 144
New Lebanon Society, 121
New Spain, 122
New York, 121, 143
Newton, Isaac, Sir, 16, 103
Newtonianism for Ladies (*Il Newtonianismo per le dame*), xx, 101
Newtonianism, xii
Nitschmann, Anna, 122
Noble savage, xiv
Nonconformism, 114
North America, xv, 70, 115, 121, 122, 133
Norway, 68–69, 74
Novels. *See* Women: writers
Nuns, 18, 82, 113, 119, 121
Nursing, 133. *See also* Wet-nursing

October march, 50
Ödenburg, 120
Officers, xv, 36, 53, 131, 135, 137–38, 141–42
Oldenburg, 30

Opera, 99, 104–6
Ottomans, xiv, 56, 57–58, 121–22

Painting. *See* Women: visual artists
Paisiello, Giovanni, 104
Palermo, 78
Palm d'Aelders, Etta, xxviii, 50
Paris, 48–51, 76, 90, 97, 118, 121
Patronesses. *See* Women: patrons
Pauw, Cornelius de, xiv
Peddling. *See* Poverty
Pennsylvania, 122
Peraud, Marie, 75
Peru, 121
Peter I, the Great, Emperor, xxi, 7, 11, 55, 137, 144
Peter III, Emperor, xxv, 55, 58
Petty treason, 68
Philanthropy, 17
Philosophes, xii–xiv, 35, 57, 75, 90, 124, 135
Physicians, 2, 7, 34, 65, 76–77, 118
Pietà, Anna Maria della, xxiii, 98
Pietism, xx, xix, 93, 115–17, 120, 122–23
Pietism in a Whale-Bone Corset (*Die Pietisterey im Fischbein-Rocke*), xxii, 93, 116
Pignatelli, Faustina, 106
Playwrights. *See* Women: writers
Poetry. *See* Women: writers
Poissardes (fishwives), 76
Poland, Old, xiv, xv, xxvi, xxviii, 12, 14, 16, 17, 26, 37, 48, 56, 66, 67, 78, 106, 118
Pommegorge, Pruneau de, 141
Pompadour, Jeanne-Antoinette Poisson, Mme de, xxi, 57, 105
Pope Benedict XIV, xxiii, 106–7, 118
Porter, Agnes, 36
Port-Royal, 119
Portugal, xii, 78, 79, 99, 105, 118, 120
Potsdam, 144
Poverty, xv, 17–19, 38–41, 124, 131, 135–36
Practical Education, 35
Pragmatic Sanction, 52
Prague, 124

Prairial rebellion, 50
Pregnancy, xi, 9–10, 39, 76. *See also* Monstrous births
Priesterinnen (female ministers). *See* Women: spiritual leaders
Prostitution, 18, 41, 71–72, 133–35
Protestantism, 53, 113–17, 119, 121
Proto-industrialization. *See* Cottage industry
Protten, Rebecca, xxii, 122
Prussia, xiii, xv, 52, 59, 66, 78, 79, 97, 105, 115, 123, 131, 135, 142, 142
Pugachev, Yemelyan Ivanovich, 57
Pugachev's uprising, xxvi, 57
Putting-out system. *See* cottage industry

Quartering of troops, 131, 142–43

Race. *See* Women: and race
Rape, 33, 65, 72, 75–77, 122, 144
Razumovski, Cyril, 56
Recruitment of troops, 144–45
Reimarus, Elise, xxii, 92, 93, 124
Reimarus, Hermann Samuel, 124
Religious persecution, 53, 56, 113, 116, 118–20, 122, 124–26
Religious toleration, 56, 124
Rémy, Thérèse, 121
Republic of France. *See* French Revolution
Resistance movements: Belgian, 48; Hungarian, 53; Polish, 53; Pugachev's uprising, 57
Revolution. *See* American Revolution; French Revolution; Resistance movements
Revolutionary Republican Women, Society of, xxviii, 50
Rheims, 14, 32
Riccoboni, Marie-Jeanne, xx, xxiv, 93–94
Riga, 105
Rino, xxvi, 93
Riots. *See* Women: rioters
Rivaz, Etienne de, 39
Riviera, Tarsizio, 100
Robespierre, Maximilien de, xxv, xxix, 49, 112
Roccati, Christina, 106

Roland, Jeanne-Marie, xxiv, xxviii, 81
Romania, 9
Rome, 77, 90, 96
Rosa, María, Mother, xx, 121
Rotterdam, 75
Rouen, 121
Rousseau, Jean-Jacques, xiii, xx, 2–3, 6
Russia, xii, xiv, xv, 7, 11, 12, 13, 16, 30, 36, 48, 52, 55–59, 66, 68, 75, 76, 79, 92–93, 98, 115, 118, 120, 136, 137, 144
Russian gynecocracy, 55–59
Russian Orthodox Church, 13–14, 56
Ruysch, Rachel, xxiv, 96

Šabadinka, Anica, 78
Sade, Marquis de (Donatien Alphonse François), 76
Salgues, Marie, 75
Salonnières, 90–92, 104, 123–26
Saltykova, Dar'ia Nikolaevna, 57
Salzburg, 18, 116, 120
Savina, María, 122
Saxony, xiv, xv, 99, 106, 142
Schaitberger, Joseph, xxii, 116, 120
Schauth, Christina, 10
Schönbrunn Palace, 54
Schupp, Johann Balthasar, 40
Science. *See* Women: scientists
Scotland, 31, 49, 78, 145
Seamstress work. *See* Textile industry
Secularism, 13, 56, 111–14, 124
Selim III, Sultan, 59, 140
Serfdom, 15, 30, 53, 57, 136
Seven Years' War, xv, 52, 56, 139
Sévigné, Marie de Rabutin-Chantal, Mme de, 119
Sewing. *See* Textile industry
Sexual assault. *See* Rape
Sexuality. *See* Women: sexuality
Shakers, 121
Shop-keeping, 27. *See also* Sutlers
Sieveking, Georg Heinrich, 48
Silesean wars, 52
Silesia, 52, 115
Silk trade. *See* Textile industry
Single women, 1, 17–19, 80
Slander, 68, 74
Slavery, xii–xiv, 57, 70, 122

Snell, Hannah, 141
Soldiers, 72, 131–38, 142–45. *See also* Officers; Women: soldiers
Sophie Charlotte, Queen, xix, 106
South America, xiv, xv, 102, 121, 122
Southcott, Joanna, xxiv, xxviii, 115–16
Spain, xii, xiv, 7, 14, 18, 30, 33, 34, 40, 48, 67, 69, 70, 71, 76, 78, 79, 90, 96, 106, 120–22, 132, 134, 137, 142, 143, 144
Spinning. *See* Textile industry
Spinsters. *See* Single women
St. Petersburg, 97, 120
St. Thomas, 122
Stein, Charlotte von, xxiii, 93
Stiernvall, Erik Johan, 137–38
Stockholm, 27, 78, 137
Storch, Johann, 9
Supreme Being. *See* Festival of the Supreme Being
Surinam, 102
Sutlers, 133. *See also* Shop-keeping
Swabia, 123
Sweden, xiv, xv, 12, 30, 33, 69, 70, 71, 74, 115
Swing, The, 11
Switzerland, 1, 7, 14, 31, 32, 39, 78, 93, 141, 142
Symphorosa, Maria Antonia Walpurgis, Electress 99, 106
Syphilis, 132

Taming of the Shrew, The, 58
Tartini, Giuseppe, 100
Tencin, Claudine Alexandrine Guérin, Mme de, xxii, xxiii, 90
Terror, the, xiii, xxviii, 49, 80, 82
Tertulias, 90
Textile industry, xi, 31–32, 37–39, 40, 132–33, 135–36
Theatre. *See* Opera; Women: musicians
Theft, 11, 68–70, 124, 135
Theory or System of Several New Inhabited Worlds, The (*Entretiens sur la pluralité des Mondes*), 101
Tipper, John, 101
Tobol'sk, 120
Todi, Luisa Rosa, xxiv, 99
Toft, Mary, xxii, 10

Total war, 141–42
Translators, women as, 94–95
Transportation, 70
Transvestism, 138–41
Tribunaux de famille, 67
Tricoteuses (knitters), 51
Triumph of Fidelity, The (*Il Trionfo della fedeltà*) 99. *See also* Opera
Troyes, 32, 121
Turin, 38, 40, 97
Turkey, 121
Tuscany, 68
Tussaud, Marie, Mme, 102–3

Urbanization, 14, 17, 28, 33, 74
Ursuline, 120
Useful Entertainment (*Poleznoe Uveselenie*), xxv, 93

Vattel, Emmerich von, 141
Vendée, 142
Venel, Jean-André, 7, 9
Venice, xiv, xv, 27, 95, 97, 98, 100
Ventriloquism, 114
Versailles, 50
Vesey, Elizabeth, 91
Victoria, Queen, 54
Vienna, 40, 104–5
Vigée-Lebrun, Elisabeth-Louise, xxiv, 97
Violence, decline in 33, 72. *See also* Domestic violence
Vivaldi, Antonio, xxiii, 98
Voltaire (François-Marie Arouet), xiii, xxvii, 16, 57, 75, 104–5, 112, 135
Von La Roche, Sophie, 94

Wages. *See* Women: wages
Wales, 116
Wanderer, The, 94
War of the Austrian Succession, 52
War of Spanish Succession, 121
War, victims of. *See* Women: victims of war
Wars. *See* American Revolution; Astro-Turkish War; French Revolution; Great Northern War; Napoleonic wars; Resistance movements; Seven Years' War; Silesean wars; Total war; War of

the Austrian Succession; War of Spanish Succession
Weaving. *See* Textile industry
Weber, Aloysia, xxv, 99
Wenham, Jane, 78
Wesley, John, xix, 115
Westminster, 60
Westphalen, Christine, 48
Wet-nursing, 8–9
Whipping, 69
Whitfield, George, xx, 115–16
Widows, widowhood, 1, 17–19, 54, 72, 79–80, 101, 106–7, 136–38
Wieland, Christopher Martin, 94
Wife. *See* Marriage
Wildberg, 32, 35
Wilkes, John, 138–39
Williams, Helen, xxv, 49, 80
Winkelmann, Maria, xix, xxi, 101
Winning Ways (*El don de gentes*), 106
Witchcraft, 64, 78–80, 114
Wollstonecraft, Mary, xxv, xxvii, xxviii, 19, 36–37, 48–49
Women: citizenship, 50–51; criminals, 68–72; electoral canvassing, 60–61; healers, 35, 118; house-builder, 140; musicians, 98–100; Muslim, xiv, 121–22; patrons, 56, 91, 104–7; prosecutors, 72–76; and race, xiv, 122–23; rioters, xi, 28, 47–48, 50–51, 144; scientists, 89, 100–104, 106–7, 118; sexuality 5–6, 11–12, 57–61, 67, 75, 80; soldiers, 48, 138–41; spiritual leaders, 115–17, 119–23; victims of war, 28, 141–45; visual artists 89, 95–98; wages 30, 32–35, 38, 44 n. 54, 107; writers 48–51, 57, 81, 92–95
Work. *See* Agricultural work; Cleaning; Cottage industry; Domestic service; Governesses; Inn-keeping; Laundry work; Midwifery; Nursing; Poverty; Prostitution; Shop-keeping; Sutlers; Textile industry; Wet-nursing; Women: house-builder, healers, visual artists
Workhouse. *See* Poverty
Württemberg, 10, 31, 38, 78, 97, 132, 135
Würzburg, 135, 137

Young, Ann, xxviii, 99

Zaragoza, Agustina, xxvii, 48
Zurich, 31

About the Author

JENNINE HURL-EAMON is Associate Professor of History at Trent University in Peterborough, Ontario, Canada. A specialist in eighteenth-century Europe, she is the author of *Gender and Petty Violence in London, 1680–1720* (2005).